Yorkists and Tudors

Sarah Newman

Basil Blackwell

First published 1989
© Sarah Newman 1989

Published by Basil Blackwell Ltd
108 Cowley Road
Oxford OX4 1JF
England

All rights reserved. No part of this publication may be reproduced, stored in a retrieval system, or transmitted in any form or by any means, electronic, mechanical, photocopying, recording or otherwise, without the prior permission of the publisher.

British Library Cataloguing in Publication Data
Newman, Sarah, *1933–*
  Reading historical documents: Yorkists and
  Tudors 1450–1603.
  1. England, 1461–1603. Historical sources.
  Documents
  I. Title
  942.05

ISBN 0–631–90258–9

To my 'A' level History students.
  I should like to thank the Girls' Public Day School Trust and particularly Blackheath High School for letting me take up a Schoolteacher Fellowship for a term at New Hall, Cambridge. It was during this term that I was able to complete the work on this book, and I am grateful to New Hall and the Clothworkers for arranging my stay there.
  I would also like to thank the libraries of Oxford and Cambridge Universities, New Hall, and the Guildhall, as well as Woodlands Library, Greenwich, the Public Records Office, and the Education Department of the Tower of London.

Typeset in 10/11½pt Goudy by Joshua Associates Ltd, Oxford
Printed in Great Britain by Butler & Tanner Ltd, Frome

Cover illustration: Elizabeth of York (daughter of Edward IV and wife of Henry VII), reproduced by permission of The National Portrait Gallery, London.

Introduction

The period 1450–1603 saw the coming of the printing press. It was a great time for propaganda. There is a great deal of material to choose from and this collection is a very personal one. Shortage of space has meant that some of the better known sources have had to be omitted. But I have tried to cover many crucial aspects of the period: political, religious, social and economic, artistic. I have tried, also, to include material on some geographical areas which are often under-represented, as well as topics which too often have had short shift. But it is still obviously an idiosyncratic selection. Its bias needs watching!

S. E. Winbolt and Kenneth Bell, in their introduction to *York and Lancaster 1399–1485*, state: '... we have no wish to prescribe for the teacher the manner in which he shall exercise his craft, but simply to provide him and his pupils with materials.' This seems to me admirable, and nicely encapsulates my own aims in compiling this selection. The documents in *Yorkist and Tudors* can be used as sources for varying themes. The questions that accompany each section are by no means exhaustive – students and teachers alike will find many other issues and problems arising from the materials. The questions I have included only hint at ways of looking at the documents; they are general rather than precise and in many cases make references across themes and periods to encourage students to familiarise themselves with a wide range of texts.

Students are aware that if they get into trouble at school, their account of the incident may differ from the teacher's; it may also vary according to the audience. The spectator watching a football match from one side of the ground gets a different view of the match from someone observing from the other side – and both their impressions of events on the pitch may differ from the pictures seen by TV viewers. If someone tells a story, which is repeated and then passed on yet again, the end version may be very different from the original. It may well be embroidered, exaggerated and sensationalised. These are all points that the student must bear in mind when looking at documents from any period of history. Someone writing in the fifteenth and sixteenth century may be ignorant of many aspects of her theme, have her own axe to grind or be blinded by ignorance, fear or malice. You need to keep your wits about you when reading contemporary documents. Does the writer really know the facts she is narrating? Does she have a reason for perhaps being selective in what she recounts, or for slanting the facts? Why is she writing? Who is she writing for? Is it the truth you are reading – or one person's version of the truth?

To take two examples, preambles to Statutes were often vehicles for propaganda, and ambassadors' reports may reflect no more than the gossip of courtiers – or the version of the facts that an astute statesman wanted to be reported abroad.

Robert Fabyan – whose *Chronicle of London* is quoted in this book – had marked Lancastrian sympathies. His theme was the glory of Britain in general, and of London in particular. The 1542 and 1559 editions of his work cut out references to miracles, relics and pilgrimages, and the Pope was renamed the Bishop of Rome.

Other Lancastrian writers tried to persuade the Pope to canonise Henry VI. These attempts continued well into the reign of Henry VII. Clearly the account they produced of that inept monarch was slanted in a direction likely to achieve their aim. (A Henry VI Society exists today for the same purpose. Does this paragraph give you an impression that the writer is a member of it?)

Hall, an MP in 1529, supports the government,

glorifies the Tudors and, like earlier chroniclers, points to a moral. Some of his work was lifted from Polydore Vergil, and both were hostile to Wolsey. Hall's work was incorporated by Grafton, Holinshed and Stow. From Holinshed it fed into Shakespeare, and so we get our view of fifteenth century history – deriving from Richard II's deposition – possibly a Yorkist version of politics, coloured in the Tudor interest.

In most cases the documents are in modernised spelling, but a few are in the original. These may give an inkling of the problems of working from original sources – something I have not attempted to do. This volume is a 'garner of other men's flowers'. I have, however, enjoyed picking them, and I am very grateful to those who have enabled me to do so.

Contents

Introduction	iii
1 The Wars of the Roses	1
A Causes	1
B Eliminating the Opposition	3
C Establishing the Tudors	6
D Tudor Propaganda	9
2 The New Monarchy?	14
A The Monarch	14
B Royal Marriages	22
C Three of Henry VIII's 'Confusion of Wives'	25
D Tudor Children and the Succession	27
3 Rivals	29
A Richard, Duke of York	29
B The Pretenders	30
C Lady Jane Grey	34
D Mary Stuart	36
4 Rebellion	42
A 1450 and 1497	42
B The Pilgrimage of Grace	44
C The Mid-Tudor Crisis	45
D The Rising of the Northern Earls	49
5 The Court	51
A Royal Beasts	51
B The Aristocracy	53
C Upstarts	56
D Access to Elizabeth	60
6 Government	63
A Theory	63
B Institutions	65
C Law and Order	67
D Finance	70
7 Religion	74
A Henry VII	74
B Henry VIII	75
C Edward VI and Mary I	82
D The Elizabethan Settlement?	83

8 Social and Economic Issues 93
   A Mortality 93
   B Sex and Status 95
   C London and the Land 99
   D Poverty and the Price Rise 104

9 Learning and the Arts 107
   A Education 107
   B Buildings 110
   C The Arts 117
   D History 119

10 The Wider World 121
   A France and Scotland 'The Auld Alliance' 121
   B Ships and Seamen, Discovery and Exploration 123
   C Spain 127
   D Ireland 'England's Broken Arm' 129

Acknowledgements

The author and publishers are grateful to the following for permission to reproduce illustrations:

Ashmolean Museum, Oxford for page 96
Fotomas Archives for pages 21 and 80
Captain A. Fowler, Skegness, Lincolnshire, for page 128
Jesus College, Oxford for page 116
King's College, Cambridge for pages 52 and 113
The London Brass Rubbing Centre for page 95
The Mansell Collection for pages 115 and 117
The National Portrait Gallery for pages 12, 18, 20, 21, 81
The Norfolk Museum Service for page 96
The Duke of Northumberland for page 52
St John's College, Cambridge for pages 11 and 51
St Mary's Church, Ewelme for page 111
Sherborne Abbey, Dorset for page 112
The Society of Antiquaries of London for page 11
The University Library, Cambridge for page 16
Westminster Cathedral for page 114

The author and publishers also wish to thank the following for permission to reproduce copyright material:

The Bodley Head for extracts from:
   The Fugger Newsletters, ed. V. von Klarwill
   Landlord or Tenant?, by Magnus Magnusson
Cambridge University Press for extracts from:
   English Books and Readers 1475–1557, by H. S. Bennett
   English Books and Readers 1558–1603, by H. S. Bennett
   The Pastons and their England, by H. S. Bennett
   Tudor Constitution, by G. R. Elton
   Tudor Constitutional Documents, by J. R. Tanner
Methuen London for extracts from:
   English Historical Documents to 1485, ed. Myers
   English Historical Documents 1485–1558, ed. C. H. Williams
   Henry VII, by S. B. Chrimes
   Historical Writing in England c1307–early 16th century, by Antonia Gransden
   Mary Tudor, by H. F. M. Prescott
George Weidenfeld and Nicolson Limited for extracts from:
   Henry VIII and his Court, by N. Williams

The publishers have made every effort to trace copyright holders, but if any have been overlooked, Basil Blackwell will be happy to make the necessary arrangements at the earliest opportunity.

1 The Wars of the Roses

Without the Wars of the Roses there would have been no Tudor Monarchy. The deaths of so many of royal blood in the 30 years leading up to the battle of Bosworth Field left Henry Tudor as the Lancastrian claimant to the throne.

1A Causes

1 FAMILY TREE SHOWING THE YORKIST CLAIM TO THE THRONE THROUGH LIONEL, DUKE OF CLARENCE, AS WELL AS EDMUND, DUKE OF YORK.

Those parts of the family tree which show the descent of Richard Duke of York from Edward III are shown. Lionel was older than John, but could the claim be passed on by a woman?

2 ON HENRY VI, 1453

The author, or owner, of this account, John Whethamstede (d. 1465), was Abbot of St. Albans 1420–40 and 1451–65. The writer admired Henry VI as a person, but felt him to be an unsuitable ruler. He was sympathetic to Richard of York and welcomed Edward as King. The two battles of St. Albans brought home the horrors of civil war.

A disease and disorder of such a sort overcame the king that he lost his wits and memory for a time, and nearly all his body was so unco-ordinated and out of control that he could neither walk, nor hold his head upright, nor easily move from where he sat.

3 ON 1457

This extract comes from Hardynge's 'Chronicle of the Earliest Period of English History to 1461'. It is in

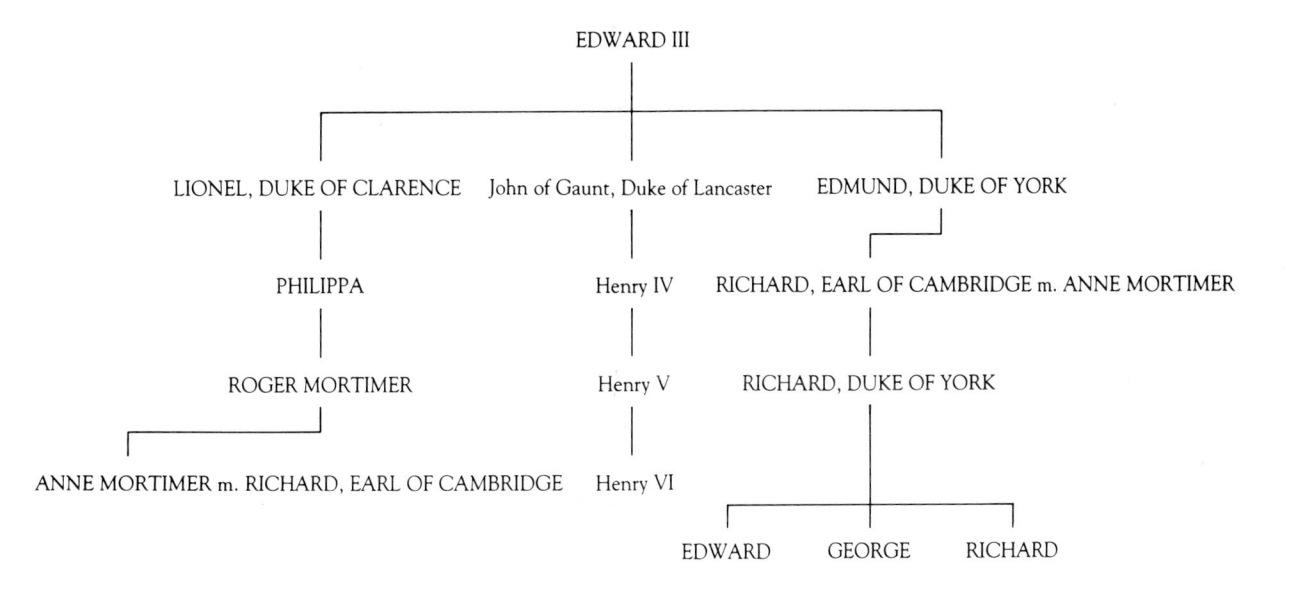

```
                              EDWARD III
          ┌───────────────────────┼───────────────────────┐
  LIONEL, DUKE OF CLARENCE   John of Gaunt,          EDMUND, DUKE OF YORK
          │                  Duke of Lancaster              │
       PHILIPPA                   │            RICHARD, EARL OF CAMBRIDGE m. ANNE MORTIMER
          │                    Henry IV                     │
    ROGER MORTIMER                │               RICHARD, DUKE OF YORK
          │                    Henry V                      │
  ANNE MORTIMER m. RICHARD, EARL OF CAMBRIDGE    ┌──────────┼──────────┐
                              Henry VI         EDWARD    GEORGE    RICHARD
```

English verse and was completed in about 1465. John Hardynge (d. 1465?) had no respect for Henry VI's intelligence, though he pitied his 'benign innocence'. He hoped Edward IV would keep law and order, which Henry had failed to do.

In every shire with Jacks and salets clean (1)
Misrule doth rise, and maketh neighbours war;
The weaker goes beneath, as oft is seen,
The mightiest his quarrel will prefer.

They kill your men always by one and one
And who says ought, he shall be beaten doubtless
For is your realm Justices of Peace are none
That dare ought now the quarrelers oppress.

The law is like unto a Welshman's hose,
To each man's leg that shapen is and mete,
So maintainers subvert it and transpose,
Though might it is full laid low under feet.

1 armed with coat of mail and light helmets.

4 ON 1459

This extract is from an English Chronicle compiled by a Yorkist between 1461 and 1471.

... the realm of England was out of all good governance, as it had been many days before, for the King was simple and led by covetous counsel, and owed more than he was worth. His debts increased daily, but payment there was none; all the possessions and lordships that pertained to the Crown the King had given away, some to lords and some to other simple persons, so that he had almost nought to live on. And such impositions as were put to the people, as taxes ... all that came from them were spent in vain, for he held no household nor maintained no wars. For these misgovernances, and for many other, the hearts of the people were turned away from them that had the land in governance, and their blessing was turned into cursing. The queen with such as were of her affinity ruled the realm as they liked, gathering riches innumerable. The officers of the realm ... peeled the poor people and disinherited rightful heirs and did many wrongs. The queen was defamed and slandered ...

5 EDWARD IV'S FIRST PARLIAMENT

This extract is taken from the Parliamentary roll of Edward IV's first parliament.

(Henry IV) with temerity and against righteousness and justice, by force and arms, against his faith and allegiance, waged war at Flint in Wales against Richard II, whom he took and imprisoned in the Tower of London with great violence; and the same King Richard being thus in prison and yet living nevertheless, Henry usurped and intruded himself into the royal power, estate, dignity, pre-eminence, possessions and lordship; and not satisfied or content with that, but attempting worse, he wickedly, unnaturally, unmanly and cruelly murdered and destroyed the same King Richard, who was the anointed king, crowned and consecrated, and Henry's own liege and most high lord on earth, against God's law, man's allegiance and his oath of fidelity; and Richard was done to the most vile, heinous and lamentable death; as a result of which the heavy exclamation in the doom of every Christian man sounds even in God's hearing in heaven, and not forgotten on earth, especially in this realm of England, which therefore has suffered intolerable persecution, punishment and tribulation since, whereof the like has not been seen or heard in any other Christian realm, by any memory or record ...

(Edward IV removed Henry VI) from the occupation, usurpation, intrusion, reign and government of the same realm of England and lordship, to the universal comfort and consolation of all his subjects and liegemen, who plenteously enjoyed their removal and departure from the obedience and government of the wrongful usurper, in whose time was no plenty, peace, justice and good government, policy and virtuous conversation but unrest, civil war and trouble, wrongfulness, shedding and spilling of innocent blood, abuse of the laws, partiality, riot, extortion, murder, rape and vicious living.

Questions

1 Do the documents presented lead you to believe the Wars of the Roses were caused by
  a the usurpation of Henry IV?
  b the misrule of Henry VI?
  c the ambitions of Richard, Duke of York?
  d the escalation of private feuds?
  Which material seems to support any one cause?

2 Does Whethamstede's description give you any idea what Henry VI's illness may have been (1A2)? Do you have any idea what might have caused it?

3 Would you have supported the Yorkist or Lancastrian claim to the throne? What in the family tree would convince you whom to support? Would you have thought about the issue at all before the 1450s? The 1400s were the first great period of propaganda. What propaganda might you have produced to bolster the side you favoured?

4 In the Parliamentary Roll of Edward IV's first Parliament (1A5), what is being stressed and what tricky issue skirted around?

1B Eliminating the Opposition

The following documents describe the deaths of some of those who stood between Henry Tudor and the Crown. As you read them try to decide how likely they are to be accurate and if any are impartial.

1 THE BATTLE OF WAKEFIELD, 1460

This extract is taken from Hall's Chronicle, 'The Union of the Families of Lancaster and York', first published 1542. It gives the only account of the Battle of Wakefield in 1460. It is not contemporary, but one of Hall's (d. 1547) ancestors had been killed in the fighting. (See ID6.)

The duke of York with his people descended down the hill in good order and array and was suffered to pass forward toward the main battle: but when he was in the plain ground between his castle and the town of Wakefield, he was environed on every side, like a fish in a net or a deer in a buckstall: so that he manfully fighting, was within half an hour slain and dead, and his whole army discomfited... While this battle was in fighting a priest ... chaplain and schoolmaster to the young earl of Rutland, second son to the abovenamed duke of York, of the age of 12 years ... secretly conveyed the earl out of the field ... but the lord Clifford espied, followed and taken, and by reason of his apparell demanded what he was. The young gentleman, dismayed, had not a word to speak, but kneeled on his knees imploring mercy ... 'Save him,' said the Chaplain, 'for he is a prince's son and peradventure may do you good hereafter.' With that word the Lord Clifford marked him and said, 'By God's blood, thy father slew mine, and so will I do to thee and all thy kin,' and with that word stuck the earl to the heart with his dagger, and bade the chaplain bear the earl's mother and brother word what he had done ... This cruel Clifford and deadly blood-supper, not content with this homicide or child-killing, came to the place where the dead corpse of the duke of York lay, and caused his head to be stricken off, and set on it a crown of paper and so fixed it on a pole and presented it to the Queen, not lying far from the field, in great despite and much derision, saying, 'Madame, your war is done; here is your King's ransom.'

2 TEWKESBURY ABBEY CHRONICLE, 1471

... on may 3rd, that is, on the feast of the finding of the holy Cross, there came to Tewkesbury Prince Edward, son of King Henry VI, with a great army, and on the morrow entered the great field which is called Gastons. When King Edward IV arrived with his army, he slew Prince Edward in the field, when also John Somerset, brother of the Duke of Somerset, the Earl of Devon, and Lord Wenlock with many others were killed.

3 THE DEATH OF HENRY VI, 1471

Warkworth was Master of St. Peter's (Peterhouse), Cambridge, where the manuscript of his 'Chronicle of the First Thirteen Years of the Reign of Edward IV' is still preserved, from 1473–1498 or 1500. He died in 1500. This extract is taken from his chronicle.

And the same night that King Edward came to London, King Henry, being in ward, in prison in the Tower of London, was put to death, the 21 day of May, on a Tuesday night, betwixt 11 and 12 of the clock; being then at the Tower the Duke of Gloucester, brother to king Edward, and many others; and on the morrow he was coffined and brought to St. Paul's, and his face was open that every man might see him ... and in his lying, he bled on the pavement there; and afterward at the Black Friars was brought, and there he bled anew and afresh; and from thence he was carried to Chertsey Abbey in a boat, and buried there in our Lady Chapel.

4 ARRIVAL OF KING EDWARD IV

No medieval copy of Fleetwood's 'The Arrival of Edward IV', from which this extract is taken, survives. Fleetwood, recorder of London in the sixteenth century, owned one which John Stow copied. The author, an ardent Yorkist, describes himself as 'a servant of the king that presently saw in effect a great part of his exploits.'

Here it is to be remembered, that from the time of Tewkesbury-field, where Edward, called Prince, was slain, then, and soon after, were taken and slain at the King's will, all the noblemen that came from beyond the sea with the said Edward, called Prince, and others also their partakers as many as were of any might or puissance. Queen Margaret herself was taken and brought to the King, and in every part of England, where any commotion was begun for King Henry's party, anon they were rebuked, so that it appeared to every man at once, the said party was extinct and repressed for ever, without any manner of hope or relief. The certainty of all which came to the knowledge of the said Henry, late called King, being in the Tower of London. Not having before knowledge of the said matters, he took it to so great displeasure and melancholy, he died the 23rd day of the month of May. Whom the king did order to be brought to the friars preachers at London, and there his funeral service done, to be carried by water to an Abbey upon Thames' Side, 16 miles from London, called Chertsey, and there honourably interred.

5 ROUS'S HISTORIA REGNUM ANGLIE

During the reigns of Edward IV, Richard III and Henry VII, John Rous was chantry priest of Guy's Cliff, near Warwick. Between 1483 and 1485 he wrote a 'History of the Earls of Warwick' in both English and Latin. After the battle of Bosworth Field he managed to cut comments favourable to Richard III out of the former, but not the latter! He dedicated his 'History of the Kings of England' – from which both of the following documents are taken – to Henry VII.

(a) And what was most detestable to God, to the English, and to all nations that had news of it, was that he killed that most saintly man king Henry VI, either by means of others, or, as many believe, with his own hands.

(b) To King Edward succeeded but for a lamentably short time, his son King Edward V Richard duke of Gloucester ... came upon him with a strong force at Stony Stratford and took the new king, his nephew into his governance by right of his protectorship. The rest, namely Anthony Earl Rivers ... were unjustly put to death. And so the new king was removed from his loyal servants and received with kisses and embraces, like an innocent lamb falling into the hands of the wolves...

... at once the duke of Gloucester, the protector, found a title to the crown to disinherit his lord the king, Edward V: that is not found but feigned it for his own advancement. And shortly he imprisoned his lord King Edward V, king in deed but not crowned, together with his brother Richard who had been taken away from Westminster on promise of safety. In this way it was known to very few by what manner of death they had suffered. The usurper King Richard III then ascended the throne of the slaughtered children whose protector he was himself.

6 SPEECH OF THE CHANCELLOR OF FRANCE TO THE STATES GENERAL OF TOURS, 15 JANUARY 1484

If I were determined to recall special proofs of your loyalty to your prince and the treachery of others, a whole day would not suffice me. It would be enough to cite as an example our neighbours, the English. Look, I pray you, at the events which have happened in that land since the death of King Edward. Reflect how his children, already big and courageous, have been killed with impunity, and the crown has been transferred to their murderer by the favour of the people.

7 KING RICHARD III

Sir Thomas More's 'History of Richard III', written 1513, was unfinished and not published in More's own lifetime (1478–1535). It is not clear whether More wrote it as a balance to 'Utopia', to show the evils of tyranny, nor how seriously he took it as history. He made up a lot of long speeches for it, as well as a lot of circumstantial detail.

... through all the time of his reign never ceased there cruel death and slaughter ... began he with the most piteous and wicked; I mean the lamentable murder of his innocent nephews, the young king and his tender brother ... his mind gave him that, his nephews living, men would not reckon that he could have right to the realm, he thought therefore without delay to rid them.

8 USURPATION OF RICHARD III, 1483

Dominic Mancini, an Italian, visited England in the autumn of 1482 and stayed until July 1483. He was a priest with humanist friends. One of these was friendly with Robert Brackenbury, Lieutenant of the Tower. On his return to France he told Angelo Cato of the usurpation. Cato, physician to Louis XI, who was also to get Comines (2A4) writing, asked him to write the account down. He did so by December 1483. His 'Usurpation of Richard III' is the first account to suggest that the murder of the Princes was already rumoured in 1483. He puts down gossip and racy stories, trying to be balanced, but his English was possibly weak and his informants probably biased. He gives interesting details, such as that until the death of Hastings official documents were issued in Edward's name, and that Buckingham hated Elizabeth Woodville as he had been forced to marry her sister, his social inferior, whereas Richard hated her as he believed her responsible for Clarence's death.

He ... resolved to get into his power the Duke of York ... for Gloucester foresaw that the Duke of York would by legal right come to the throne if his brother were removed ... At about this time Gloucester gave orders that the son of the Duke of Clarence ... should come to the city; and commanded that the lad should be kept in confinement in the household of his wife, the child's maternal aunt. For he feared that if the entire progeny of King Edward became extinct, yet this child who was also of royal blood, would still embarrass him.

Having got into his power all the blood royal of the land, yet he considered his prospects were not sufficiently secure, without the removal or imprisonment of those who had been the closest friends of his brother, and were expected to be loyal to his brother's offspring ... Therefore the protector rushed headlong into crime.

9 POLYDORE VERGIL'S 'HISTORIE OF ENGLAND'

Polydore Vergil, an Italian humanist from Urbino, came to England in about 1501 as a collector of papal taxes for Alexander VII. He stayed 50 years. In 1505 Henry VII asked him to write a history of England. He took great pains to obtain information and did not automatically accept all he was told. He knew the 'Croyland Chronicle'. He debunked many myths, rejecting many popular stories. More may have consulted him. His 'Anglica Historia' was completed in 1513. A second edition, taking the story from 1506, where the first stopped, to 1509, was published in 1534. His writing still has elements of Tudor propaganda. It was much read by the Elizabethans. Much of the early part of Hall's chronicle is translated from Vergil. He died in 1555. (See 5C10.)

... he sent warrant to Robert Brackenbury, lyvetenant of the towr of London, to procure ther death with all diligence ... King Richard carried with him Edward earle of Warwick, the soone of his brother George duke of Clarence, by reason of whom least any danger to himself might be derived, he sent him to be kept in ward at a castle cauld Shyriff Huton. But the Lyvetenant of the towr at London after he had receaved the kinges horryble commyssion was astonyed with the crewletie of the fact ... when King Richard understooded the lyvetenant to make delay ... he anon commyted the charge of hastening the slaughter unto another, that is to say James Tyrrell, who being forcyd to do the kings commandment, rode sorrowfully to London, and to the worst example that hath been almost ever herd of murderyd those babes of thyssew royall.

Questions

1 In 1B1 what implies the blood feud is already part of the conflict? How accurate is that source likely to be?
2 **a** Explain the variations in the accounts of Henry's death in 1B3, 4 and 5. Do you give one account more or less credit than the others? If so, why?
  b If Henry VI was murdered why was the deed not ordered before May 1471? (There is a clue in 1B2!)
  c If he was murdered, whose was the ultimate responsibility?
3 Explain the position in the line of succession of the son of the Duke of Clarence (1B8 and see 1B9). What was his name? and his title? For

6 The Wars of the Roses

what reasons might Mancini be either more or less reliable than English chroniclers?
4 Look at 1B6–9. Would you accept any of the accounts of the end of the princes in the Tower? Explain your answer. What motives are credited to Richard? Whom else is he accused of murdering?
5 Why do you think Richard has been so condemned for the deaths of the princes when Edward IV is less censured for the deaths of Henry VI, the Lancastrian Prince Edward and George, Duke of Clarence, and Henry VII less criticised for those of the Earl of Warwick and of Richard III's illegitimate son?

1C Establishing the Tudors

As you read the documents, see if you can work out who still had to die – following the deaths of Henry VI and son, and of Edward IV – before Henry Tudor could ascend the throne. See, too, if you can find any inaccurate reports of deaths in battle.

1 THE BEAUFORT FAMILY TREE

This family tree shows Henry Tudor's claim to the throne. Kathryn Swynford's children were born out of wedlock but legitimated by Act of Parliament in 1397. A later Act debarred them and their descendants from succession to the throne.

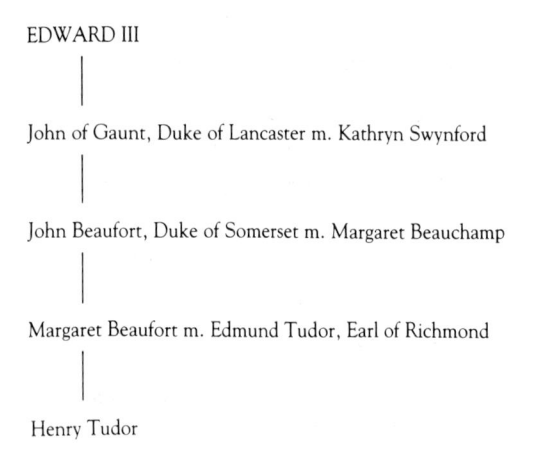

EDWARD III
|
John of Gaunt, Duke of Lancaster m. Kathryn Swynford
|
John Beaufort, Duke of Somerset m. Margaret Beauchamp
|
Margaret Beaufort m. Edmund Tudor, Earl of Richmond
|
Henry Tudor

2 A LETTER FROM RICHARD III SUMMONING VERNONS OF DERBYSHIRE, AUGUST 11 1485

. . . our rebels and traitors accompanied with our ancient enemies of France and other strange nations departed out of the water of Seine the first day of this present month, making their course westwards been landed at Angle beside Milford Haven in Wales on Sunday last passed, as we be credibly informed, intending our utter destruction, the extreme subversion of this our realm and disinheriting our true subjects of the same, towards whose recountering, God being our guide, we be utterly determined in our own person to remove in all haste goodly that we can or may.

3 THE GREAT CHRONICLE OF LONDON

The Great Chronicle of London is in two parts. The second part, which deals with the period 1439–1512, is probably by Robert Fabyan, a clothier, who was Sheriff of London in 1493. He died in 1513.

. . . word sprang quickly of a gentleman being in the parts of Brittany named Henry, and son to the earl of Richmond that made speedy provision for to come into England to claim the Crown as his right, considering the death of King Edward's children, of whom as then men feared not openly to say that they were rid out of this world, but of their death's manner was many opinions . . . But howsoever they were put to death, certain it was that before that day they were departed from this world. Of which cruel deed Sir James Tyrell was reputed to be the doer . . . When these tidings were blown about the world, the gentleman and men of honour were in such a doubt that they wist not which party to lend unto, howbeit the more in number grudged so sore against the King for the death of the innocents that as gladly would they have been French, as to be under his subjection, and for that, some fled unto that other party . . . And . . . true knowledge came to the King, in the beginning of August, of the landing of the forenamed prince Henry, the which so soon as he was landed at Milford Haven in Wales kneeled down upon the bare ground, and holding his hands towards heaven meekly and devoutly said these words: '*Judica me deus et discerne causam meam*', and after proceeded upon his journey. Then King Richard in all haste arrayed his people, and made quick provision for to meet his enemies, which at the beginning were but of small strength, but anon as his landing was known to many of the knights and esquires of this land, they gathered much people in the King's name, and straight sped them unto that other party, by means whereof his power hugely increased ... In this while the earl of Derby and the earl of Northumberland, which had everyone of them great companies, made slow speed toward King Richard, so that he with the duke of Norfolk and the earl of Surrey, the lord Lovell and others departed from Leicester with great triumph and pomp upon the morn being the xxij day of August, and after continued his journey till he came unto a village called Bosworth where, in the fields adjoining, both hosts met, and fought there a sharp and long fight ... In this battle was slain King Richard, the duke of Norfolk, the lord Lovell, with Brackenbury and many others, and incontinently, as it was said, Sir William Stanley, which won the possession of King Richard's helmet with the Crown being upon it, came straight to King Henry, and set it upon his head saying, Sir here I make you King of England. In this field was taken the earl of Surrey with others ... and Richard late King as gloriously as he by the morning departed from that town, so as irreverently was he that afternoon brought into that town, for his body despoiled to the skin, and nought being left about him, so much that would cover his privy member, he was trussed ... as a hog or another vile beast, and so all to bespiring with mire and filth was brought to a church in Leicester for all men to wonder upon, and there lastly irreverently buried ...

4 INGULPH'S CHRONICLE

Ingulph's Chronicle is from Croyland Abbey.

At length a glorious victory was granted by heaven to the said earl of Richmond, now sole King, together with the crown, of exceeding value, which King Richard had previously worn on his head. For while fighting and not in the act of flight, the said King Richard was pierced with numerous deadly wounds, and fell in the field like a brave and most valiant prince ...

Through this battle peace was obtained for the entire kingdom, the body of the said King Richard being found among the dead. Many insults were heaped upon it, and, not exactly in accordance with the laws of humanity, a halter being thrown round the neck, it was carried to Leicester; while the new King also proceeded to that place, graced with the crown which he had so gloriously won.

5 THE ROSE OF ENGLAND

Richard III used the white boar as his symbol. Ebor was the Latin name for York. Heraldry is full of puns.

In the midst of a garden there sprang a tree
Which tree was of mickle price,
And therupon sprang the rose soe redd
The goodlyest that ever sprang on hie.

This rose was ffaire, ffresh to behold,
Springing from many a royall lance;
a crowned king, with a crowne of gold,
over England, Ireland and of ffrance.

then came a beast men call a bore,
and he rooted this garden upp and downe,
by the seede of the rose he sette noe store,
but afterwards itt wore the crowne.

hee tooke the branches of this rose away
and all in sunder did them teare,
and he buryed them under a clod of clay,
Swore they shold neuer bloome nor beare.

then came in an Egle gleaming gay,
of all ffaire birds well worth the best;
he tooke the branche of the rose away,
and bore itt to Latham to his nest (1)

but now is this rose out of England exiled,
this certaine truth I will not faine;
but if itt please you to sit a while
Ile tell you how the rose came in againe.

Att Milford haven he entered in;
to claime his right, was his delight,
he brought the blew bore in with him, (2)
to encounter with the bore soe white.

then a messenger the rose did send
to the Egle's nest, and bidd him hye;
'to my father the old egle I doe me commend,
his aide and help I crave speedyle'.

saies, 'I desire my father att my cominge
of men and money att my need,
and alsoe my mother of her dear blessing,
the better then I hope to speede'

then Sir Rice ap Thomas drawes Wales with him
a worthy sight itt was to see,

how the Welchmen rose wholly with him,
and shogged him to Shrewsbury.

but at Attherson these Lordes did meete;
a worthy sight itt were to see,
how Erle Richmond tooke his hatt in his hand,
and said 'Cheshire and Lancashire, welcome to me.'

but now is a bird of the Egle taken;
from the white bore he cannot fflee.
therfore the old egle makes great moane,
and prayes to god most certainly:

then the blew bore the vanward had;
he was bith warry and wise of wit;
the right hand of them he tooke,
the sunne and the wind of them to gett.

then the egle followed fast upon his pray;
with some dints he did them smyte
the Talbot he bitt wondrous sore,
soe well the unicorn did him quitt

and then came in the harts head;
a worthy sight itt was to see,
they jackets that were of white and redd,
how they laid about them lustilye.

but now is the fierce ffeld foughten and ended,
and the white bore ther lyeth slaine;
and the young Egle is preserved,
and come to his nest againe.

but now this garden fflouruishe ffreshly and gay,
with ffragrant fflowers comely of hew;
and gardners itt doth maintain
I hope they will proue just and true.

Our king, he is the rose soe redd,
that now does fflourish ffresh and gay.
Confound his ffoes, Lord wee beseeche,
and loue his grace both night and day.

ffinis.

1 The family crest of Thomas Stanley (Henry Tudor's stepfather), later 1st Earl of Derby, was an eagle and child. His chief seat was at Latham.
2 The crest of the Earl of Oxford was a 'boar statant azure'.

6 BILL IN PARLIAMENT, NOVEMBER 1485

To the pleasure of All mighty God, the Wealth, Prosperite, and Suretie of this Roialme of England, to the singular comfort of all the Kings Subjects of the same, and in avoiding of all Ambiguities and Questions, be it ordained, stablished, and enacted, by the auctorite thys present Parliament, that the Inheritance of the Crownes of the Roialmes of England and of France, with all the preheminence and dignitie Royall to the same pertaineing, and all other Seignories to the king belonging beyond the see, with th' appurtenaunces thereto in any wise due or perteineing, be rest, remaine and abide in the most Royall persone of our now Soveraigne Lord King Harry the VIIth, and in the heirs of hys body lawfully comen, perpetually with the grace of God so to indure, and in non other.

7 A LETTER FROM JOHN DE GIGLIS, PAPAL COLLECTOR, TO POPE INNOCENT VIII, 6 DECEMBER 1485

Most blessed Father, after most humble commendation and kisses of thy most blessed feet. Since the last letters which I wrote to you, most Holy Father, little or nothing new has occurred in the state of these affairs. Certainly a public assembly of the kingdom, which they call Parliament, is being held for the information of the kingdom, and in this some acts have been passed, the chief of which is a general pardon of all offence committed against the king. The earl of Northumberland, who has been captured and imprisoned, has been set at liberty, but on security from all the prelates, temporal lords, and also the commons. The earl of Surrey is still kept in prison: but I hear that he will be released. The eldest daughter of King Edward has been declared Duchess of York. There are persistent rumours that the king is about to marry her, a thing which all consider will be most beneficial for the kingdom. The king himself is considered most prudent and also very merciful: all things seem disposed towards peace if only men's minds remain constant. For there is nothing more harmful to this kingdom than ambition and insatiable greed, the mother of all faithlessness and inconstancy: and if God will preserve us from this, the condition of this kingdom will be peaceful . . .

PS Ambassadors are here from the king of France and the dukes of Austria and Britanny. It is believed there will be peace with them.

Questions

1 Using the family tree (1C1), write a sentence explaining Henry Tudor's claim to the throne.

2 a What 'strange nations' is Richard III referring to in 1C2?
   b Why does he comment on the French? (See 1C3.)
3 What is the attitude of the Chronicler in 1C4 towards each of the monarchs? Is there anything surprising in this?
4 a In 1C6 explain 'the garden' line 1. Where else in literature do you find this metaphor?
   b Explain 'the bore' line 9, and 'the rose out of England exiled', line 21.
   c Explain the relationships referred to in the verses.
   d What kind of audience might the ballad be meant for?
5 What is the point of 1C7?
6 Explain the sentences 'The earl of Surrey is still kept in prison: but I hear that he will be released. The eldest daughter of King Edward has been declared Duchess of York'.

1D Tudor Propaganda

The Tudors used propaganda to great effect both before and after Bosworth. This was not only to vilify Richard III, but more importantly, to show they had rescued England from the ravages of a long and bloody civil war, and to make clear the horrors that could reoccur were war to be resumed.

1 HENRY TUDOR AND THE WELSH, 1485

1a *and* **b** *are translated extracts from Welsh prophetic poems – 'bruts' – of the period. These were written and circulated to stir the Welsh chieftains to support Henry Tudor. Henry was to adopt the dragon of Cadwaladr to stress his alleged descent from ancient British Kings. This symbol was also used on his banner at Bosworth.*

a The knell of the Saxon shall be our satisfaction; a prince shall we have of our own race ... Cadwaladr (1) will come to his own again ... Jasper will breed for us a Dragon; of the fortunate blood of Brutus (2) is he. The Bull of Anglesey (3) is our joy; he is the hope of our race.

A great grace was the birth of Jasper from the stock of Cadwaladr of the beautiful (spear) shaft.

b We are waiting for him (Henry) to show, when he comes, the Red Rose in high pomp. The Thames will run with blood on that day, and there shall we be satisfied ... There is longing for Harry, there is hope for our race. His name comes down from the mountains as a two-edged sword; and his descent from the high places; and his sword wins the day. He will win, ere his life be done, the unbelieving to the creed of the cross.

1 *Cadwaladr* The last king of Britain. The Tudors claimed descent from Cadwaladr.
2 *Brutus* The mythical founder of the British race.
3 *The Bull of Anglesey* Henry Tudor. The home of the Tudors was at Penmynydd, Anglesey.

2 A LETTER FROM HENRY TUDOR AT ROUEN TO HIS FRIENDS AT HOME, 1485

Right trusty, worshipful and honourable good friends, and our allies, I greet you well. Being given to understand your good devoir and entreaty to advance me to the furtherance of my rightful claim, due and lineal inheritance of that crown, and for the just depriving of that homicide and unnatural tyrant which now unjustly bears dominion over you, I give you to understand that no Christian heart can be more full of joy and gladness than the heart of me, your poor exiled friend, who will, upon the instant of your sure advertising what power you will make ready and what captains and leaders you get to conduct, be prepared to pass over the sea with such good force as my friends here are preparing for me. And if I have such good speed and success as I wish, according to your desire, I shall ever be most forward to remember and wholly to requite this your great and moving loving kindness in my just quarrel. Given under our signet
                                H
I pray you give credence to the messenger of that he shall impart to you.

3 LETTER FROM HENRY TUDOR, 1485

This letter was sent from Henry Tudor to John Ap Maredudd in August 1485, after Henry's landing at Mill Bay, Pembrokeshire. John Ap Maredudd (Meredith), who was related to Henry Tudor, was an important local figure in Eifionydd, Gwynedd.

10 The Wars of the Roses

Right trusty and well beloved, we greet you well. And where it is so that through the help of almighty God, the assistance of our loving friends and true subjects, and the great confidence that we have to the nobles and commons of this our principality of Wales, we be entered into the same, purposing by the help of the above rehearsed in all haste possible to descend into our realm of England not only for the adeption (recovery) of the crown unto us of right appertaining, but also for the oppression of that odious tyrant Richard late duke of Gloucester, usurper of our said right, and moreover to reduce as well our said realm of England into his ancient estate, honour and prosperity, as this our said principality of Wales, and people of the same to their erst liberties, delivering them of such miserable servitudes as they have piteously long stand in. We desire and pray you and upon your allegiance straitly command you that immediately upon the sight hereof, with all such power as ye may make defensibly arrayed for the war, ye address you towards us without any tarrying upon the way ... wherein ye shall cause us in time to come to be your singular good lord and that ye fail not hereof as ye will avoid our grievous displeasure and answer unto at your peril.

Given under our signet ...

4 FROM POLYDORE VERGIL, 1537

See 1B9.

It is legitimate to attribute this (marriage) to divine intervention, for plainly by it all things which nourished the two most ruinous factions were utterly removed, by it the two houses of Lancaster and York were united, and from this union the true and established royal line emerged which now reigns.

5 HALL'S INTRODUCTORY EPISTLE TO EDWARD VI

Edward Hall's Chronicle is a Tudor panegyric. The part dealing with Henry VII is based on Polydore Vergil. Hall was responsible for the material on the reign of Henry VIII up to 1532, the remainder was put together by Grafton from Hall's notes. Holinshed and Stowe both made great use of his account, as did Shakespeare. The first edition came out in 1542, the second in 1548, just after Hall's death. Hall was a lawyer, undersheriff of the city of London, and MP. He believed in the need for order and good government.

What mischiefe hath insurged in realmes by intestine devision, what depopulacion hath ensued in countries by civill discention, what detestable murder hath been committed in cities by separate faccyons, and what calamitte hath ensued in famous regions by domesticall discorde and unnaturall controversie: Rome hath felt, Italie can testifie, Fraunce can bere witnes ... and especially thys noble realme of Englande can appaurantly declare and make demonstracion.

6 TABLE OF CONTENTS OF HALL'S CHRONICLE, 1548

An introduction into the division of the two houses of Lancaster and York:
  I   The unquiet time of King Henry the Fourth
  II The victorious acts of King Henry the Fifth
  III The troublesome season of King Henry the Sixth
  IV The prosperous reign of King Edward the Fourth
  V   The pitiful life of King Edward the Fifth
  VI The tragical doings of King Richard the Third
  VII The politic governance of King Henry the Seventh
  VIII The triumphant reign of King Henry the Eighth

7 THE BISHOP OF CARLISLE'S SPEECH FROM SHAKESPEARE'S 'RICHARD II' ACT 4, SCENE 1

And shall the figure of God's majesty,
His captain, steward, deputy-elect,
Anointed, crowned, planted many years,
Be judged by subject and inferior breath
And he himself not present? O, forfend it, God,
That in a Christian climate souls refined
Should show so heinous, black, obscene a deed!
I speak to subjects, and a subject speaks,
Stirr'd up by God, thus boldly for his king.
My lord of Hereford here, whom you call king,
Is a proud traitor to proud Hereford's king:
And if you crown him let me prophesy:
The blood of English shall manure the ground,
And future ages groan for this foul act;
Peace shall go sleep with Turks and infidels,
And in this seat of peace tumultuous wars
Shall kin with kin and kind with kind confound;
Disorder, horror, fear and mutiny
Shall here inhabit, and this land be call'd
The field of Gollgotha and dead men's skulls.
O, if you raise this house against this house,
It will the woefullest division prove

That ever fell upon this cursed earth,
Prevent it, resist it, let it not be so,
Lest child, child's children, cry against you 'woe'.

8–11

In figures 8–11 the white rose is the Yorkist symbol (Edward IV was known as the 'Rose of Rouen', his birthplace). The red rose was not a contemporary term and was rarely used to represent the Lancastrians during the later named 'Wars of the Roses'. The symbol of the Tudor rose was made much of by Henry VII and his successors.

8 HENRY VII BY AN UNKNOWN ENGLISH ARTIST

9 MARGARET BEAUFORT

12 *The Wars of the Roses*

10 ELIZABETH OF YORK, HENRY VII'S QUEEN

The white rose is the Yorkist symbol.

The Wars of the Roses 13

11 HENRY VII, PAINTED IN 1505 BY MICHAEL SITIUM

Questions

1 **a** What different emotions is Henry appealing to in 1D2 and 3?
  b How could Richard have replied?
2 **a** What besides 'divine intervention' accounts for the marriage referred to in 1D4?
  b Why did Henry VII not marry Elizabeth of York as soon as he became king?
3 In what respects is 1D6 Tudor propaganda?
4 When the Tudors were established did they place much emphasis on their Welsh origins? How did Henry VII stress his before and after 1485?
5 **a** How far does the quotation from Shakespeare (1D7) exemplify the idea that came to be known as 'the divine right of kings'?
  b What document in Section 1A of this chapter is it reminiscent of?
  c How does it relate to 1D5?
6 Compare the two portraits of Henry VII (1D8 and 11). What have they in common with that of Elizabeth of York? (1D10) Why do you think this might be?
7 What points are being made in the portrait of Margaret Beaufort? (1D9) What is shown about her, her personality and her position? What symbol of royalty is shown in 1D9?

2 The 'New' Monarchy?

There is some dispute whether 'the new monarchy' in England – a line of innovating, centralising 'modern' rulers – began with Edward IV or Henry VII. The personality of the monarch was certainly of prime importance. The monarch was assumed to be an adult male, ready to marry a wife who would bear sons.

2A The Monarch

Later monarchs took care to avoid the mistakes of Henry VI.

The break with Rome was an act of nationalism. It was partly justified by the historical assertion that England was an empire, and led to a unique stress on royal ecclesiastical supremacy, exalting the monarch above the merely human. This model was very congenial to Henry VIII.

In part to compensate for the loss of the virgin Mary as an object of adoration Elizabeth came to be depicted as a virtual goddess. See if you feel this image is effectively conveyed in any of the portraits of Henry VIII or Elizabeth.

As you look at the following material, see, too, if you can trace any family characteristics; is there a resemblance between Edward IV and Henry VIII, or between Henry VII and Elizabeth I? Consider, too, if there is any discrepancy between foreign and English comments.

1 ON HENRY VI

This is taken from Chastillon (d. 1475?), historiographer to Charles the Bold, Duke of Burgundy.

No more than a shadow on a wall.

2 JOHN BLAKMAN, 1504

Henry VII was trying to get Henry VI canonised. Polydore Vergil set to work on this, using Blakman's 'Compilation of the Madness and Good Life of King Henry VI', from which the following extract is taken. It is not clear when Blakman wrote this, nor indeed whether he wrote or merely owned it. Blakman had been Fellow and precentor of Eton, and then at King's Hall, Cambridge, before becoming a monk at Witham Charterhouse, Somerset. It was Rous who popularised the idea of Henry VI as a holy man, through a series of rather suspect anecdotes.

Concerning his humility in his gait, raiment, and demeanour, he was wont from a youth to wear square shoes and boots, like a farmer. Also his cloak was long, with a round hood such as a burgess wears, and his tunic reached below his knees, all dove-coloured, he avoided anything fanciful.

3 LONDONERS ON EDWARD IV'S ENTRY, 1461

William Gregory (d. 1467) was Mayor of London from 1451. This extract is taken from his chronicle, which is of particular value for 1461–71.

Let us walk in a new wine-yard and let us make a gay garden in the month of March with this fair white rose and herb, the Earl of March.

4 COMMYNES'S MEMOIRES (1464–1498)

Philippe de Commynes (1447?–1510?) served Charles the Bold, Count of Charolais. In 1468 he was knighted in jousts celebrating Charles' marriage to Margaret, sister of Edward IV. In 1472 he left the Count of Burgundy and entered the service of

Louis XI of France. He helped negotiate the Treaty of Picquiny in 1475. He was exiled by Charles VIII in 1489 and then began his 'Mémoires', from which the following piece is taken.

King Edward was not a man of very high intelligence, but a very handsome prince – more so than any I have seen – and very brave ... He was accustomed to take his ease and pleasure ... more than any prince of his day, for he thought of nothing but women (more than was right), of hunting, and of the care of his person. When he went out a-hunting, he had always tents brought for the ladies.

5 MORE'S 'HISTORY OF RICHARD III'

See 1B7.

In King Edward's later days this realm was in quiet and prosperous estate; no fear of outward enemies, no war in hand, nor none toward, but such as no man looked for: the people toward the prince, not in constrained fear, but in willing and loving obedience: among themselves, the commons in good peace.

6 EDWARD IV, CHRISTMAS 1482

This piece is taken from the second continuator of the Crowland (formerly spelt Croyland) Chronicle which is an important source on 1471–85. It was probably compiled by two writers, one a former councillor of Edward IV and doctor of canon law who knew the court of Chancery.

He was usually dressed in a variety of costly clothes, in quite another fashion than we had seen before in our time. The sleeves of his cloak hung in ample folds like those of a monk's frock, lined inside with the richest furs and rolled on the shoulders. Thus the prince, who was of imposing build, taller than others, presented a novel and remarkable spectacle.

7 WARWICK ROLL OF RICHARD III'S REIGN, FROM ROUS, 1483

See 1B5.

The most mighty prince, Richard by the grace of God king of England and of France and lord of Ireland by very matrimony without discontinuance or any defiling in the law by heir male lineally descending from King Harry the Second, all avarice set aside, ruled his subjects in his realm fully commendably, punishing offenders of his laws, especially extortioners and oppressors of his commons, and cherishing tho[se] that were virtuous; by the which discreet guiding he got great thank of God and love of all his subjects rich and poor and great laud of the people of all other lands about him.

8 LETTER FROM THOMAS LANGTON

Thomas Langton was Bishop of St. David's. This letter was sent from him to William Sellyng, Prior of Christchurch in Canterbury, in September 1483.

He contents the poor where he goes best that ever did prince, for many a poor man that hath suffered wrong many days have been relieved and helped by him and his commands in his progress. And in many great cities and towns were great sums of money given him which he hath refused. On my truth, I never liked the condition of any prince so well as his. God hath sent him to us for the weal of us all.

9 CIRCULAR LETTER SENT TO THE BISHOPS BY RICHARD III, 10 MARCH 1484

Our principal intent and fervent desire is to see virtue and cleanness of living to be advanced, increased and multiplied, and vices and all other things repugnant to virtue, provoking the high indignation and fearful displeasure of God, to be repressed and annulled.

10 BOSWORTH FIELD

'Bosworth Field' was composed after 1495. It was popular with the Stanleys and their circle. Thomas, Lord Stanley was Margaret Beaufort's husband at the time of Bosworth. (See 1C5.) His younger brother, William, was executed by Henry for intrigue with Perkin Warbeck, although the support of the Stanleys for Henry had been crucial at Bosworth.

Then to King Richard there came a knight,
    And said, 'I hold it time to flee;
For yonder Stanley's dints they be so might,
    Against them no man may dree.

16 The 'New' Monarchy?

Here is horse at thy hand ready;
   Another day thou may worship win,
And for to reign with royalty,
   To wear the crown and be our king.'
'Nay! give me my battle-axe in my hand,
Set the crown of England on my head so high.
For by him that made both sea and land,
   King of England this day will I die.
One foot will I never flee
   Whilst the breath is my brest within,'
As he said, so did it be;
If he lost his life, he died a King.

11 ON RICHARD III

This is from Polydore Vergil's 'Anglica Historia'. (See 1B9.)

... Truly he had a sharp wit, provident and subtle, his courage also hault and fierce, which failed him not in the very death, which, when his men forsook him, he rather yielded to take with the sword than by foul flight to prolong his end.

12 ON HENRY VII

This extract comes from Polydore Vergil's 'Anglica Historia'. (See 1B9.)

Henry reigned 23 years and seven months. He lived 52 years. By his wife Elizabeth he had eight children, four boys and the same number of girls. Three survived him, an only son, Henry, prince of Wales, and two daughters, Margaret married to James King of Scotland, and Mary betrothed to Charles, prince of Castile. His figure was slim, but well-built and strong; in height he was above the average. Extremely attractive in appearance, his face was cheerful, especially when he was speaking. He had small, blue eyes, a few poor black-stained teeth. His hair was thin and white: his complexion sallow. He was distinguished, wise, prudent in character; and his spirit was so brave and resolute that never even in moments of greatest danger, did it desert him. He had a most tenacious memory and was in addition, not devoid of scholarship. Further, in government he was shrewd and farseeing.

13 THE CORONATION OF HENRY AND CATHERINE

A woodcut of the Coronation of Henry and Catherine from 1509 which shows the pomegranate (grenade) of Granada as well as the Tudor Rose.

14 LETTER FROM LORD MOUNTJOY TO ERASMUS, 1509

If you could see how everyone here rejoices in having so great a prince, how his life is all their desire, you would not contain yourself for sheer joy. Extortion is put down, liberality scatters riches with a bountiful hand, yet our King does not set his heart on gold or jewels, but on virtue, glory and immortality. The other day he told me 'I wish I were more learned'. 'But learning is not what we expect of a King', I answered, 'merely that he should encourage scholars'. 'Most certainly', he rejoined, 'as without them we should scarcely live at all'. Now what more splendid remark could a prince make?

15 ON HENRY VIII

This extract is taken from the chronicle of Edward Hall and describes the Field of the Cloth of Gold.

Then the King of England showed himself some deal forward in beauty and personage, the most goodliest Prince that ever reigned over the realm of England; his grace was apparelled in a garment of cloth of silver, of damask ribbed with gold, so thick as might be . . . The courser which his grace rode on, was trapped in a marvellous vesture of a new devised fashion, the trapper was of fine gold in bullion, curiously wrought, pounced and set with antique work of Roman figures.

16 MARIO SAVORGANO ON HENRY VIII, 1531

Mario Savorgano was a Venetian scholar and military engineer.

He is tall of stature, very well formed, and of very handsome presence, beyond measure affable, and I never saw a prince better disposed than this one.

17 LUTHER ON HENRY VIII

Squire Henry means to be God and do as he pleases.

18 CARL CAPELLO ON HENRY VIII, 1535

Capello and Michiel (2A25) were Venetian representatives in England.

Henry has rare endowments both of mind and body, such as personal beauty, genius, learning etc., and it is marvellous how he has fallen into so many errors and false tenets.

19 ANTHONY GILBY ON HENRY VIII, 1558

Antony Gilby (d. 1585), a puritan divine, was found a job and protected by the Earl of Huntingdon – 'the puritan earl'.

Thus there was no Reformation, but a deformation, in the time of that tyrant and lecherous monster.

20 JOHN AYLMER ON HENRY VIII, 1559

John Aylmer (1521–1594) was tutor to Lady Jane Grey and Bishop of London, 1577.

How did King Henry scourge them (the French)? In his youth, won Therouanne and Tournai, and in his age Boulogne, Blackness, Newhaven. (Blanc Nez and Ambleteuse.)

21 RALEIGH ON HENRY VIII

Raleigh's 'History of the World' was much admired by Oliver Cromwell. This is his account of Henry VIII.

Now, for King Henry VIII, if all the pictures and patterns of a merciless Prince were lost in the world, they might all be painted to the life out of the story of this King.

18 *The 'New' Monarchy?*

22 HOLBEIN'S CARTOON FOR A PAINTING OF HENRY VIII, 1531

23 EDWARD VI BY AN UNKNOWN ARTIST, 1547

24 ELIZABETH I AT THE TIME OF HER CORONATION

This account is taken from Sir John Hayward's Annals, possibly written in 1612 when he was 52. In 1636 it was printed, unfinished, as an appendix to his history of Edward VI.

Now, if ever any person had either the gift or the style to win the hearts of people, it was this queen; and if ever she did express the same, it was at that present, in coupling mildness with majesty as she did, and in stately stooping to the meanest sort. All her faculties were in motion, and every motion seemed a well-guided action; her eye was set upon one, her ear listened to another, her judgement ran upon a third, to a fourth she addressed her speech; her spirit seemed to be everywhere, and yet so entire in herself, as it seemed to be nowhere else. Some she pitied, some she commended, some she thanked, at others she pleasantly and wittily jested, contemning no person, neglecting no office; and distributing her smiles, looks, and graces . . . that thereupon the people again redoubled the testimonies of their joys.

She was a Lady upon whom nature had bestowed, and well placed, many of her fairest favours; of stature mean, slender, straight, and amiably composed; of such state in her carriage, as every motion of her seemed to bear majesty: her hair was inclined to pale yellow, her forehead large and fair, a seeming seat for princely grace; her eyes lively and sweet, but short-sighted; her nose somewhat rising in the middest; the whole compass of her countenance somewhat long, but yet of admirable beauty, not so much in that which is termed the flower of youth, as in a most delightful composition of majesty and modesty in equal mixture.

25 MICHIEL ON ELIZABETH I, 1557

Giovanni Michiel was a Venetian representative in England. This is from a report to the Venetian Doge and Senate.

She is a young woman, whose mind is considered no less excellent than her person, although her face is comely rather than handsome, but she is tall and well formed, with a good skin, although swarthy; she has fine eyes and above all a beautiful hand of which she makes a display and her intellect and understanding are wonderful . . .

26 DE FERIA ON ELIZABETH I

In these comments, Count de Feria, Spanish ambassador in England, describes Elizabeth to Philip II.

a 21 November 1558
. . . very much wedded to the people and thinks as they do.
b 7 December 1559
. . . incomparably more feared than her sister and gives her orders and has her way as absolutely as her father did.

20 The 'New' Monarchy?

27 THE 'DITCHLEY' PORTRAIT OF QUEEN ELIZABETH I

Storms vanish and sunshine appears before Elizabeth. Marcus Gheeraerts the Younger painted this for his patron, Sir Henry Lee, to commemorate his entertaining the Queen at Ditchley, September 1592. She is standing on the globe. In the centre of the globe is England. In the centre of England is Oxfordshire. Ditchley is there, beneath the Queen's feet. Elizabeth's earring is an armillary sphere – this represents the world, and is the device repeated on Sir Henry's sleeve in an earlier portrait of him. Her visit showed she had forgiven Lee for resigning his post as her Master of Ceremonies and leaving her court to live with his mistress. Some of the Latin on the picture refers to her generosity in forgiving him.

28 ELIZABETH I BY NICHOLAS HILLIARD, c. 1575

In this portrait Elizabeth holds a rose in one hand and at her breast is a pendant phoenix symbolising both her virginity and her uniqueness.

29 THE RAINBOW PORTRAIT, c. 1600, BY AN UNKNOWN ARTIST

The rainbow is a symbol of peace after storms.

30 DE MAISSE ON ELIZABETH I, 1597

This description of Elizabeth is by Monsieur de Maisse, the French ambassador.

As for her face, it is and appears to be very aged. It is long and thin, and her teeth are very yellow and unequal compared with what they were formerly, so they say, and on the left side less than on the right. Many of them are missing so that one cannot understand her when she speaks quickly. Her figure is fair and tall and graceful in whatever she does; so far as may be she keeps her dignity, yet humbly and graciously withal.

22   The 'New' Monarchy?

31 THE FAIR MAID OF THE WEST

Thomas Heywood's play, 'The Fair Maid of the West' was first acted in 1617 and printed in 1631. It is testimony to Elizabeth's reputation in James I's reign.

Mullisheg: The virgin queen, so famous through the world,
The mighty empress of the maiden isle,
Whose predecessors have o'errun great France,
Whose powerful hand does still support the Dutch,
And keeps the potent king of Spain in awe

Bess: Why, England's queen
She is the only phoenix of her age,
The pride and glory of the Western Isles.
Had I a thousand tongues, then all would tire,
And fail me in her true description.

Questions

1 Contrast the statements in 2A2 and 4.
2 Compare 2A7 with documents 1B5 and 6. Can you account for the difference? Can you use 1B5–9 and 2A7–11 to construct any coherent picture of Richard III?
3 a Do 2A14–18 give any idea of the image Henry VIII was trying to project or any idea of the personality behind the mask of royalty?
   b How far is the image of him in 2A21 supported by other material?
4 In 2A22 see if you can find the initials H I (Henricus Imperator). Is there another echo of a Roman emperor?
5 a How is Edward VI presenting himself in 2A23 and Elizabeth in 2A27–9?
   b How do the paintings of Elizabeth in 2A27 and 29 compare to the description of her in 2A30?

2B Royal Marriages

The prime purpose of the monarch's marriage was to produce a male heir to the throne. However, royal marriages were expected to serve diplomatic as well as dynastic purposes. Romance often had to be found elsewhere.

1 EDWARD'S COUNSELLORS REACT TO HIS MARRIAGE PLANS

Jehan (Jean) de Waurin (d. 1474) visited England while in the service of the Dukes of Burgundy. His 'Recueil des croniques et anciennes histories de la Grande Bretagne' is up to 1444 a collection of existing material on English history; from 1444 to 1471 it is Waurin's original work. Waurin collected oral information on the Wars of the Roses, visiting people like the Earl of Warwick to get his story. The extract below describes Edward's counsellors reacting to his marriage plans.

They told him that she was not his match; however good and fair she might be, he must know well that she was no wife for so high a prince as himself; she was not the daughter of a duke or an earl, but her mother, the duchess of Bedford, had married a knight by whom she had two children before her marriage. Therefore, although she was the daughter of the duchess of Bedford and the niece of the count of St. Pol, she was not, all things considered, a suitable wife for him, nor a woman of the kind who ought to belong to such a prince.

2 GREGORY'S 'CHRONICLE'

See 2A3.

... the first day of May, our sovereign lord the King Edward IV, was wedded to the Lord Rivers' daughter: her name is Dame Elizabeth that was wife unto Sir John Grey ... And this marriage was kept full secretly long and many a day, that no man knew it; but men marvelled that our sovereign lord was so long without any wife, and were ever feared that he had been not chaste of his living. But on All Hallows' day at Reading there it was known, for there the King kept his common council, and the lords moved him and exhorted him in God's name to be wedded and to live under the law of God and Church ... and then our sovereign no might no longer hide his marriage, and told them how he had done, and made that the marriage should be opened unto his lords.

3 WARKWORTH'S CHRONICLE

See 1B3.

Also the fourth year of king Edward the Earl of Warwick was sent into France for a marriage for the king, for one fair lady, sister daughter to the king of France, which was concluded by the Earl of Warwick. And while the said Earl of Warwick was in France, the King was wedded to Elizabeth Gray, widow, the which Sir John Gray that was her husband was slain at York field (Towton) in King Harry's Party; and the same Elizabeth was daughter to Lord Rivers, and the wedding was privily in a secret place, the first day of May, the year above said. And when the Earl of Warwick came home and heard this, then was he greatly displeased with the king; and after that great dissension rose ever more and more between the king and him, for that and other causes. And then the king put out of the Chancellorship the Bishop of Exeter, brother to the Earl of Warwick, and made the Bishop of Bath Chancellor of England. After that the Earl of Warwick took to him in fee as many knights, squires and gentlemen as he might, to be strong; and King Edward did what he could to enfeeble the Earl's power. And yet they were reconciled several times; but they never loved each other afterwards.

4 FABYAN CHRONICLE

See 1C3.

In secret manner, upon the first of May, 1464, king Edward espoused Elizabeth, late being wife of Sir John Gray, which espousailles was solemnized early in the morning at the town called Grafton near to Stoney Stratford. At which marriage was none present but the spouse, the spousesse, the duchesse of Bedford, her mother, the priest and two gentlemen and a young man who helped the priest to sing.

5 'OF HIS LOVE, CALLED ANNA'

The author of these poems, Thomas Wyatt (d. 1542), was a childhood neighbour of Anne Boleyn. Once she came to court he pursued her until warned off by Henry. He and the Earl of Surrey introduced the sonnet form into English, copying Petrarch.

What word is that, that changeth not
  Though it be turn'd and made in twain?
It is mine Anna, God it wot,
  And eke the causes of my pain,
  Who love rewardeth with disdain;
Yet is it loved; what would ye more?
It is my health, and eke my sore ...

... 'The Lover despairing to attain unto his Lady's grace, relinquisheth the pursuit'
  Who list her hunt, I put him out of doubt
    As well as I, may spend his time in vain!
    And graven with diamonds in letters plain,
  There is written her fair neck round about:
    'Noli me tangere; for Caesar's I am,
    And wild for to hold, though I seem tame.

6 HENRY VIII TO ANNE BOLEYN, 1527

... you will expressly certify me of your whole mind concerning the love between us two. For of necessity I must ensure me of this answer, having been now above one whole year struck with the dart of love, not being assurefd either of failure, or of finding place in your heart and grounded affection. Which last point has kept me for some time from calling you my mistress, since if you love me in none other sort save that of common affection, that name in no wise belongs to you, for it denotes a singular love, far removed from the common. But if it shall please you to do me the office of a true loyal mistress and friend, and to give yourself up, body and soul, to me ... I will take you for my only mistress, rejecting from thought and affection all others save yourself, to serve you only.

7 ANTHONY DENNY, 1540

Anthony Denny (1501–49), chief gentleman of the bedchamber to Henry VIII, was the only one who dared tell the King he was dying.

The state of princes in matters of marriage is far of worse sort than the conditions of poor men. For princes take as is brought them by others, and poor men be commonly at their own choice and liberty.

8 DANIEL BARBARO TO THE VENETIAN SENATE, 1551

In this confusion of wives, so many noblemen and great personages were beheaded, so much church plunder committed and so many acts of disobedience perpetrated that it may be said that all that ensued and is still going on, is the penalty of that first sin.

9 ELIZABETH I TO THOMAS SEYMOUR, 1547

My Lord Admiral,

The letter you have written me is the most obliging, and at the same time the most eloquent in the world. And as I do not feel myself competent to reply to so many courteous expressions, I shall content myself merely with unfolding to you, in a few words, my real comments. I confess to you that your letter, all elegant as it is, has very much surprised me; for, besides that neither my age nor my inclination allows me to think of marriage, I never could have believed that any one would have spoken to me of nuptials, at a time when I ought to think of nothing but sorrow for the death of my father. And to him I owe so much, that I must have two years at least to mourn for his loss. And how can I become a wife before I shall have enjoyed for some years my virgin state, and arrived at years of discretion?

Permit me, then, my Lord Admiral, to tell you frankly that, as there is no one in the world who more esteems your merit than myself, or who sees you with more pleasure as a disinterested person, so would I preserve to myself the privilege of recognizing you as such, without entering into the strict bond of matrimony, which often causes one to forget the possession of true merit. Let Your Highness be well persuaded that, though I decline the happiness of becoming your wife, I shall never cease to interest myself in all that can crown your merit with glory, and shall ever feel the greatest pleasure in being your servant, and good friend,

Elizabeth.
27th February

10 ELIZABETH I TO PRINCESS MARY, 1547

Princess, and very dear sister,

You are very right in saying, in your most acceptable letters, which you have done me the honour of writing to me, that, our interests being common, the just grief we feel in seeing the ashes, or rather the scarcely cold body of the King, our father, so shamefully dishonoured by the Queen, our step-mother, ought to be common to us also. I cannot express to you, my dear Princess, how much affliction I suffered when I was first informed of this marriage, and no other comfort can I find than that the necessity of submitting ourselves to the decree of Heaven; since neither you nor I, dearest sister, are in such condition as to offer any obstacle thereto, without running any risk of making our own lot much worse than it is; at least, so I think.

... We may rest assured that the memory of the King, our father, being so glorious in itself, cannot be subject to those stains which can only defile the persons who have wrought them. Let us console ourselves by making the best of what we cannot remedy. If our silence do us no honour, at least it will not draw down upon us such disasters as our lamentations may induce.

... With regard to the returning of visits, I do not see that you, who are the elder, are obliged to do this; but the position in which I stand obliges me to take other measures; the Queen having shown me so great affection, and done me so many kind offices, that I must use much tact in manooeuvring with her, for fear of appearing ungrateful for her benefits. I shall not, however, be in any hurry to visit her, lest I should be charged with approving what I ought to censure.

However, I shall always pay much deference to your instructions and commands, in all which you shall think convenient or serviceable to you, as being Your Highness's etc, etc.

11 CAMDEN ON ELIZABETH I

The 1615 edition of William Camden's 'Annals' covered the period to 1588; the 1625 edition took the history to the end of Elizabeth's reign. The idea was Burghley's, who, in 1596, persuaded Camden to write a history of Elizabeth's reign. Until 1608 he was collecting material for this. Camden used some extracts from Stowe. A part of his account of Elizabeth is reproduced below.

... some were of the opinion that she was fully resolved in her mind, that she might better provide both for the Commonwealth and her own glory by an unmarried life than by marriage; as forseeing that if she married a subject, she should disparage herself by the inequality of the match, and give occasion to domestical heartburnings, private grudges and commotions; if a stranger, she should then subject both herself and her people to a foreign yoke and endanger religion; having not forgotten how unhappy the marriage of her sister Queen Mary with King Philip, a foreigner, had been ... Her glory also, which whilst she continued unmarried she retained entire to herself and uneclipsed, she feared would by marriage be transferred to her husband. And besides, the perils by conception and child-bearing, objected by the physicians and her gentlewomen for some private reasons, did many times run in her mind, and very much deter her from thoughts of marrying.

12 WILLIAM CECIL TO THOMAS SMITH, AUGUST 1565

Lady Jane Grey had two younger sisters, Catherine (see 3D4 and 5) and Mary. They were possible Protestant successors, but no one took Mary seriously because she was virtually a dwarf (see 2B13). Thomas Smith was English ambassador to France, 1562–6.

Here is an unhappy chance and monstrous. The sergeant-porter, being the largest gentleman in the court, hath married secretly the lady Mary Grey the least of all the court. They are committed to several prisons. The offence is very great.

13 GUZMAN DE SILVA, SPANISH AMBASSADOR, TO PHILIP II, 20 AUGUST 1565

De Silva's letter includes the following description of Lady Mary Grey.

She is little, crook-backed and very ugly, and it came out yesterday that she had married a gentleman named Keys. They say the Queen is very much annoyed and grieved thereat.

Questions

1 How unsuitable a match does Edward IV's mariage to Elizabeth Woodville seem to be from the information in 2B1–4?
2 How accurate do you find Denny's comment (2B7) to be in view of the preceding documents?
3 Do sources 2B9–10 give any indication of Elizabeth's character? What is she writing about in these (unrelated) letters?
4 Do you agree with the points Camden makes in 2B11? Which reasons seem most weighty?
5 Why might Elizabeth feel 'annoyed and grieved' (2B12–13)?

2C Three of Henry VIII's 'Confusion of Wives'

As you read these documents, ask yourself if they modify the picture of Henry VIII created by the material in 2A and B.

1 LETTER FROM CATHERINE OF ARAGON TO HENRY THE EIGHTH, 1535

My Lord and Dear Husband,
 I commend me unto you. The hour of my death draweth fast on, and my case being such, the tender love I owe you forceth me, with a few words to put you in remembrance of the health and safeguard of your soul, which you ought to prefer before all worldly matters, and before the care and tendering of your own body, for the which you have cast me into many miseries and yourself into many cares.
 For my part I do pardon you all, yea, I do wish and devoutly pray God that He will also pardon you.
 For the rest I commend unto you Mary, our daughter, beseeching you to be a good father unto her, as I heretofore desired. I entreat you also, on behalf of my maids, to give them marriage-portions, which is not much, they being but three. For all my other servants, I solicit a year's pay more than their due, lest they should be unprovided for.
 Lastly, I do vow, that mine eyes desire you above all things.

2 LETTER FROM ANNE BOLEYN TO HENRY VIII, 1536

Your Grace's displeasure and my imprisonment are things so strange unto me, that what to write, or what to excuse, I am altogether ignorant . . . But let not Your Grace ever imagine that your poor wife will ever be brought to acknowledge a fault, where not so much as a thought ever proceeded, and to speak a truth, never a prince had a wife more loyal in all duty, and in all true affection, than you have found in Anne Bulen, with which name and place I could willingly have contented myself, if God and Your Grace's pleasure had been so pleased. Neither did I at any time so far forget myself in my exaltation or received queenship, but that I always looked for such alteration as I now find; for the ground of my preferment being on no surer foundation than

Your Grace's fancy, the least alteration was fit and sufficient to draw that fancy to some other subject.

You have chosen me from a low estate to be your queen and companion, far beyond my desert or desire; if, then, you found me worthy of such honour, Good your Grace, let not any light fancy or bad counsel of my enemies withdraw your princely favour from me; neither let that stain – that unworthy stain – of a disloyal heart towards your good grace ever cast so foul a blot on me, and on the infant Princess your daughter.

Try me, good King, but let me have a lawful trial, and let not my sworn enemies sit as my accusers and as my judges; Yea, let me receive an open trial, for my truth shall fear no open shames. Then shall you see either my innocency cleared, your suspicions and conscience satisfied, the ignominy and slander of the world stopped, or my guilt openly declared. So that, whatever God may determine of, Your Grace may be freed from open censure; and mine offence being so lawfully proved, Your Grace may be at liberty, both before God and man, not only to execute worthy punishment on me as an unfaithful wife, but to follow your affection already settled . . . But if you have already determined of me, and that not only my death, but an infamous slander must bring you the joying of your desired happiness, then I desire of God that He will pardon your great sin thereof; and that He will not call you to a strait account for your unprincely and cruel usage of me at His general judgment-seat, where both you and myself must shortly appear; and in whose judgement I doubt not (whatever the world may think of me), mine innocency shall be openly known and sufficiently cleared.

My last and only request shall be, that myself may only bear the burden of Your Grace's displeasure, and that it may not touch the innocent souls of those poor gentlemen who, as I understand, are likewise in strait imprisonment for my sake.

If ever I have found favour in your sight – if ever the name of Anne Bulen have been pleasing in your ears – then let me obtain this request; and so I will leave to trouble Your Grace any further, with mine earnest prayer to the Trinity to have Your Grace in good keeping, and to direct you in all your actions.

From my doleful prison in the Tower, the 6th of May,
Anne Bulen.

3 BACON, 'APOTHEGMS NEW AND OLD', 1625

Queen Anne Bullen, at the time when she was led to be beheaded in the Tower, called one of the King's privy chamber to her, and said to him, 'Commend me to His Majesty, and tell him he hath been ever constant in his career of advancing me; from a private gentlewoman he hath made me a marchioness, from a marchioness a queen, and now he hath left no higher degree of honour, he gives my innocency the crown of martyrdom'.

4 CHARLES DE MARILLAC, FRENCH AMBASSADOR IN LONDON, TO ANNE DE MONTMORENCY, SEPTEMBER 1540

'The king is so amorous of Catherine Howard that he cannot treat her well enough and caresses her more than he did the others.'

5 KATHERINE HOWARD TO THOMAS CULPEPPER, 1541

'Master Culpepper, I heartily commend me unto you . . . I never longed so much for thing as I do to see you and speak with you . . . It makes my heart die to think what fortune I have that I cannot be always in your company . . . Come when my Lady Rochford is here, for that I shall be at best leisure to be at your commandment . . . Yours as long as life endures, Katherine.'

6 THE INDICTMENT OF KATHERINE HOWARD

'that Katherine, Queen of England, formerly called Katherine Howard, late of Lambeth, Surrey, led an abominable base, carnal, voluptuous and vicious life like a common harlot with divers persons . . . led the King by word and gesture to love her and (he believing her to be pure and chaste and free from other matrimonial yoke) arrogantly coupled herself with him in marriage . . . invited the said Culpepper to have carnal intercourse with her, and insinuated to him that she loved him above the King and all others, and similarly the said Culpepper incited the Queen.'

7 THE PRIVY COUNCIL TO SIR WILLIAM PAGET, HENRY'S AMBASSADOR TO FRANCE, NOVEMBER 1541

'The king . . . being solicited by his council to marry again took to wife Catherine, daughter of the late Lord

Edmund Howard, thinking now in his old age to have obtained a jewel for womanhood, but this joy is turned to extreme sorrow . . . having heard that she was not a woman of such purity as was esteemed.'

Question

Do the documents in this section give any idea of the characters of any of Henry's wives? (Look back at document 2B6 as well.)

2D Tudor Children and the Succession

A vexed question! Edward IV and Elizabeth Woodville had ten children. Most outlived their father. The Tudors were less prolific.

1 THE CHRONICLE OF EDWARD VI

The year of Our Lord 1537 was a prince born to King Harry the Eight by Jane Seymour, then Queen, who within few days after the birth of her son died and was buried at the castle of Windsor. This child was christened by the Duke of Norfolk, the Duke of Suffolk and the Archbishop of Canterbury. Afterward was brought up, til he came to six years old, among the women. At the sixth year of his age he was brought up in learning by Mr Dr Cox, who was after his Almoner, and John Cheke, Master of Arts, two well-learned men, who sought to bring him up in learning of tongues, of the scripture, of philosophy, and all liberal sciences. Also John Belmaine, Frenchman, did teach him the French language. The tenth year not yet ended, it was appointed he should be created Prince of Wales, Duke of Cornwall and Count Palatine of Chester. At which time, being the year of Our Lord 1547, the said King died of a dropsy, as it was thought. After whose death incontinent came Edward, Earl of Hertford, and Sir Anthony Browne, Master of the Horse, to convey this prince to Enfield, where the Earl of Hertford declared to him and his younger sister Elizabeth the death of their father. . . . the same day the death of his father was proclaimed in London, where was great lamentation and weeping; and suddenly he proclaimed King. The next day . . . he was brought to the Tower of London, where he tarried the space of three weeks; and in the mean season the Council sat every day for the performance of the will and at length thought it best that the Earl of Hertford should be made Duke of Somerset, Sir Thomas Seymour Lord Sudeley . . . Also they thought best to choose the Duke of Somerset to be Protector of the realm and Governor of the King's person during his minority, to which all the gentlemen and lords did agree, because he was the King's uncle on his mother's side. Also in this time the late King was buried at Windsor with much solemnity . . . The Lord Lisle was made Earl of Warwick, and the lord great chamberlainship was given to him; and the Lord Sudeley made Admiral of England.

. . . Afterward, all things being prepared for the coronation, the King, being then but nine years old, passed through the City of London . . . and came to the Palace of Westminster, and the next day came into Westminster Hall . . . Then he was crowned King of England, France, and Ireland by the Archbishop of Canterbury and all the rest of the clergy and nobles, and anointed with such ceremonies as were accustomed, and took his oath, and gave a general pardon, and so was brought to the hall to dinner . . . where he sat with the crown on his head, with the Archbishop of Canterbury and the Lord Protector, and all the Lords sat at boards in the hall beneath . . . At night the King returned to his palace at Westminster, where there were jousts.

2 ELIZABETH I, 1559

'Do not upbraid me with miserable lack of children; for every one of you, and as many as are Englishmen, are children and kinsmen to me.'

3 ELIZABETH I TO MAITLAND, SCOTTISH REPRESENTATIVE IN ENGLAND, 1561

'I know the inconstancy of the people of England how they ever mislike the present government and have their eyes on the person that is next to succeed, and naturally men be so disposed. I have good experience of myself in my sister's time, how desirous men were that I should be in place and earnest to set me up. And if I would have consented, I know what enterprises would have been attempted to bring it to pass . . . No princes' revenues be so great that they are able to satisfy the insatiable cupidity of men. And if we . . . should miscontent any our subjects, it is to be feared that if they knew a certain successor of our crown they would have recourse thither. I deal plainly with you, albeit my subjects I think love me as becomes them, yet is nowhere so great perfection that all are content.'

4 BISHOP ALVARO DE QUADRA TO HIS PREDECESSOR AS SPANISH AMBASSADOR, JANUARY 1560

'the Queen calls Lady Catherine her daughter, although the feeling between them can hardly be that of mother and child, but the queen has thought best to put her in her chamber and makes much of her in order to keep her quiet. She even talks of formally adopting her.'

5 DE SILVA, SPANISH AMBASSADOR IN ENGLAND, 26 OCTOBER 1566

'The discussion about the succession still goes on in Parliament and the Queen is extremely annoyed, as she fears that if the matter is carried further they will adopt Catherine ... I have always pointed out to the Queen the grave difficulties which might result from such a nomination, and the peril in which she and her affairs would be if Catherine were appointed her successor ... She quite understands it, and three days ago told me that on no account would she allow this nomination to be discussed.'

Questions

1 Edward began his journal (2D1) on his accession and kept it until 1552. What impression of the ten-year-old do you get from its opening?
2 What reasons does Elizabeth give for not naming her sucessor (2D3)?
3 Why might De Silva not want Catherine Grey as Elizabeth's successor (2D5)? (3D and 4D might also help you answer this.)

3 Rivals

Between 1461 and 1483 the crown changed hands five times. The Yorkist dynasty, the shortest in Europe in the fifteenth century, lasted twenty-four years. Bosworth restored the Yorkist establishment, which had split in 1483, with the addition of Henry Tudor. The Tudors were to rule for 118 years, but were never secure; at first the threat came from 'the white rose', later from religious dissent. The Tudors were always aware that the throne could be lost, but under Henry VII political instability was on the wane. Or was it? As you look at this chapter, try to consider the merits of the rival claimants, and how great a threat each posed.

3A Richard, Duke of York

Richard's father, the Earl of Cambridge, was executed for treason before Henry V went to France. He was doubly descended from Edward III, from both Edmund Duke of York, and through Lionel, Duke of Clarence, elder brother of John of Gaunt, Duke of Lancaster, through Lionel's daughter (see 1A1). He was the greatest landowner in England, after the King. He owned vast estates on the Welsh border, and the Earldom of Ulster, as well as those of Rutland, Cambridge and York. Margaret had not wanted him as Protector during Henry's illness and, once her son was born, became yet more hostile. In 1459 the Parliament at Coventry had attainted him. His wife was Cecily Neville, aunt of Richard, Earl of Warwick.

1 ON THE DUKE OF YORK

This extract is taken from Whethamstede's Chronicle for October 1450. See 1B3.

But while . . . the Lord King with his Bishops and Barons and Commons sat in Parliament at Westminster, there came, almost at the beginning of the Parliament, the said Lord Duke of York with great pomp . . . with trumpets and clarions, with armed men, and an exceeding great retinue of his household. On entering the palace he marched straight through the great hall until he came to the solemn chamber where the king is wont to hold his Parliament with his Commons. And when he had come there he walked up to the king's throne and putting his hand on the cushion, as a man taking possession of his own, and kept it there for a short space. At length withdrawing it he turned his face towards the people and, standing quietly under the royal cloth of state, awaited the applause of the onlookers. While he stood master Thomas Bourchier, Archbishop of Canterbury, approached him, and with due reverence asked him whether he wished to come and see the Lord King. To which he answered thus: 'I mind me of no one in this kingdom to whom it is not more fitting that he should come to me than I to him.' Then the duke withdrew to the principal chambers in the whole palace (as the king occupied the queen's apartment), and the bolts having been broken and the doors forcibly opened, he took up his abode there for some time in the manner of a king rather than of a duke. But when this presumptuous conduct was noised abroad, forthwith people of every estate and degree began to murmur against him.

2 JEHAN DE WAURIN'S 'RECUEIL DES CHRONIQUES'

See 2B1.

. . . the earl showed the duke how ill-pleased the people were with him for having wished to strip the king of his crown. While they were speaking thus, came the Earl of Rutland and said to the Earl of Warwick, 'Fair cousin, be not angry, for you know it is our right to have the crown, and that it belongs to my lord father and he must have it.' To which the Earl of March, who was present, replied, saying, 'Brother, do not anger any man, for all will be well.'

After these words the Earl of Warwick understood well the Duke of York's intent, and he departed very ill pleased.

3 FROM THE PARLIAMENTARY ROLLS

On Saturday it was shewed unto the lords by the mouth of the Chancellor that the said Duke of York called busily to have hasty and speedy answer of such matters as touched his title . . . it is thought by all that the title of the said duke cannot be defected, and in eschewing of the great inconveniences that may ensue, a mean was found to save the king's honour and estate and to appease the said duke if he would, which is this; that the king shall keep the Crown and his estate and dignity royal during his life; and the said duke and his heirs to succeed him in the same . . . Whereupon, after sad . . . communication, it was concluded to take the mean above rehearsed. All these premises thus shewed and opened to the king's highness, he, inspired with the grace of the Holy Ghost, and in eschewing the effusion of Christian blood, condescended to an account to be made between him and the said duke, and to be authorised by the authority of this present Parliament.

Questions

1 Explain the Duke of York's statement which begins 'I mind me of no one . . .' (3A1). Do you agree with it? Can you support your decision?
2 What, according to the documents, was the reaction to his claim?

3B The Pretenders

As you read this section see if you feel that the Wars of the Roses ended in 1485 at the Battle of Bosworth. Some historians argue that the battle of Stoke, in 1487, marked their ending. Do you think it likely that Henry VII could have lost his throne as a result of that battle? And how would his reign have been compared with that of Richard III if it had ended so soon?

1 THE BOOK OF HOUTH

The Book of Houth, an Irish history, boosted Nicholas, Lord of Houth.

After that King Richard the third was slain worthily by King Henry VII, there was a priest called Sir Richard Symone in the second year of Henry VII, that worthy Solomon. This priest had elected a scholar named Lambart Symenell, one of a gentle nature and pregnant wit, to be the organ of his feigned enterprise, and to be the rightful inheritor to the Crown of England, and so thereof to make him King of England, and to make himself to be some great bishop and potentate; for that craftily feigned King Edward IV's sons was away fled, and thought to feign this scholar to be one. This crafty and subtle priest brought up his scholar with princely behaviour and manners, literature, declaring to this child, what lineage he was of and progeny, in so learning him he might inform the people, that they should the rather conceive the tale to be true.

Soon after he caused to be blown abroad that Edward the young Earl of Warwick was broken abroad out of the Tower, which was both of one year and one stature; and then he changed the child's name and called him Edward, after the name of the young Earl of Warwick. And he with this child sailed into Ireland, and there he declared this same to certain of the nobility there, which did both credit the matter and favoured the cause; in so much that Lord Thomas Geraldinge, Chancellor of Ireland, much furthered this matter, and published this same throughout all the realm. And so they called him King . . . and for that the throng of people was such that he could not be seen, the child was borne in, and upon Great Darsey of Platan's neck, that every man might see him; and so sent their letters secretly into England, and also to Flanders to Lady Margaret, sister to the king Edward, late wife of Charles Duke of Burgoyne, to further his purpose with all her might and power . . . The contents of that letter she did observe with all diligence to the uttermost of her ability. Sir Nicholas, Lord of Houth, perceiving all this but a mad dance, sent over to the King, and advertised him of all these matters . . . who was the doers and maintainers of the whole matters of Ireland and Flanders.

. . . And after the young Earl of Warwick was brought to Paul's Church through London, where as ever many might see him that thought he was run away, and that they might perceive the fondness of those of Ireland to make war against the King without any just matter.

The Earl of Lincoln, son of John Delapoll . . . secretly conveyed him to Flanders; and the Lord Lovelde landed there certain days before him; so they there concluded to go into Ireland that the honour might be more to this young King supposed, with one Martin Swarde, a good captain, out of Germany, and two thousand soldiers expert in the wars. And there in Dublinge in Ireland they proclaimed this child King of England, being borne and sitting upon Darsey's chouldiers to be seen of all men, for that Darsey was then the highest. After they gathered so much Irishmen as would take their parts, with one Thomas Geraldine as their leader, and for the most part naked, they took shipping and landed . . . in England . . . which doings . . . was certified the King by Lord Houth in Ireland.

The King, hearing these men's landings, concluded to encounter with them incontinent, lest that in long tarrying might enlarge their power and to increase, being but a few in the beginning . . . both the armies came within a little to Stocke, and the morrow after joined and fought very valiant on both sides, for those Allmayns were very good and apt soldiers, so were their captain Martin Swarthe; his like was not met in both the armies to all purposes. The Irishmen did as well as any naked men could do, and at length they were slain, about four thousand and more. Their captains was the Earl of Lincoln, Lord Loveld, Broghton, Martin Swarthe and Lord Thomas Gerald; and many of the King's side was killed and hurt. This feigned King and crafty priest his master was taken alive. The priest was condemned to perpetual prison, and this innocent child became falconer to the King after. This field was fought the 16 of June 1487.

After the King sent for all his Lords of Ireland . . . the King said to the Lords, 'My masters of Ireland, you will crown apes at length.'

This same day at dinner, where as those Lords of Ireland was at Court, a gentleman came where they was at dinner, and told them that their new King Lambarte Symenell brought them wine to drink, and drank to them all. None would have taken the cup out of his hands, but bade the great Devil of Hell him take before that ever they saw him. 'Bring me the cup if the wine be good' said the Lord of Houth, being a merry gentleman, 'and I shall drink it for the wine's sake and mine own sake also; and for thee, as thou art, so I leave thee, a poor innocent.' . . . the King did give the Lord of Houth the apparel that he ware that day, and £300 in gold, with thanks; and so departed.

2 HOLINSHED'S CHRONICLE

The first edition of Raphael Holinshed's (d. 1580?) 'Cronycle' came out in 1571 (See 3B7). Later editions were not by him. The next was in 1587. It was based on Leland and in some ways was the work of a syndicate, including William Harrison, whose 'Description of England' was included in it, and John Stowe, who edited it. Elizabethan dramatists drew on the Chronicle. Shakespeare used phrases from it. The Chronicle was kept up to date and on occasion cuts in it were ordered by the Privy Council.

. . . there was one Sir Richard Simond, priest, a man of base birth and yet well learned . . . he had a scholar called Lambert Simnel, one of a gentle nature and pregnant wit . . . The devil . . . put in the venomous brain of this disloyal . . . priest to devise how he might make his scholar . . . to be reputed as right inheritor to the crown of this realm. Namely for that the fame went that King Edward's children were not dead, but fled secretly . . . and that Edward, Earl of Warwick, son and heir to the Duke of Clarence, either was, or shortly should be put to death.

These rumours . . . encouraged this peevish priest to think the time come that his scholar Lambert might take upon him the person and name of one of King Edward's children. And therefore at Oxford, where their abiding was, the said priest instructed his pupil both with princely behaviour, civil manners and good literature, declaring himself of what lineage he should affirm himself to be descended . . . Soon after, the rumour was blown abroad, that the Earl of Warwick was broken out of prison. And when the priest . . . heard of this, he straight away intended . . . to bring his invented purpose to pass, and changing the child's name of baptism, called him Edward, after the name of the young Earl of Warwick, the which were both of like years and of like stature.

Then he with his scholar sailed into Ireland, where he so set forth the matter unto the nobility of that country, that not only the Lord Thomas Geraldine, Chancellor of that land, deceived through his crafty tale, received the counterfeit earl into his castle with all honour and reverence, but also many other noble men determined to aid him . . . as one descended of the blood royal and lineage come of the house of York, which the Irish people evermore highly favoured, honoured and loved above all other. By this mean every man throughout all Ireland was willing and ready to take his part and submit themselves to him; already reputing and calling him . . . king. So that now they . . . sent into England certain privy messengers to get friends there.

Also they sent unto Flanders to the lady Margaret, sister to King Edward and late wife to Charles, Duke of Burgoyne, to purchase aid and help at her hands. This

Lady Margaret bore no small rule in the low countries, and in very deed sore grudged in her heart that King Henry (being descended of the house of Lancaster) should reign and govern of the realm of England, and ... though she well understood that this was but a coloured matter, yet to work her malicious intention against King Henry, she was glad to have so fit an occasion, and ... promised the messengers all the aid she should be able to make ... and also to procure all the friends she could ...

King Henry ... called together his council ... it was agreed ... that the Earl of Warwick should personally be shewn abroad in the city and other public places; whereby the untrue report ... might be ... known for a vain imagined lie.

... But ... the Earl of Lincoln, son to John de la Poole, Duke of Suffolk, and Elizabeth, sister to King Edward the Fourth thought it not meet to neglect ... so ready an occasion of new trouble.

... he fled secretly into Flanders unto the said Lady Margaret, where Francis, Lord Lovell, landed certain days before ... it was agreed, that the Earl of Lincoln and the Lord Lovell should go to Ireland, and there attend upon the Duchess her counterfeit nephew, and to honour him as king ...

Now they concluded that if their doings had success, then the aforesaid Lambert ... should ... be deposed, and Edward the true Earl of Warwick delivered out of prison and anointed king. King Henry ... learning that the Earl of Lincoln was fled into Flanders, he ... caused soldiers to be put in readiness out of every part of his realm, and to bring them into one place assigned, that when his adversaries should appear he might suddenly set upon them ...

... the Earl of Lincoln had gotten together by the aid of the Lady Margaret about two thousand Almains, with one Martin Sward, a valiant and noble captain to lead them.

With this power the Earl of Lincoln ... at the city of Dublin caused young Lambert to be proclaimed and named King of England, after the most solemn fashion, as though he were the very heir of the blood royal lineally born and descended. And so with a great multitude of beggarly Irishmen almost all naked and unarmed, saving skins and mantles, of whom the Lord Thomas Geraldine was captain ... they sailed into England ... The King had knowledge of the enemies' intent and having assembled a great army ... he went to Coventry ... Here he took advice of his counsellors ... it was thought best to delay no time but give them battle before they should increase their power, and thereupon he removed to Nottingham ...

Shorly after this came to him the Lord George Talbot, Earl of Shrewsbury, the Lord Strange, Sir John Cheyne, right valiant captains, with many other noble and expert men of war, namely of the counties near adjoining, so that the King's army was wonderfully increased. In this space the Earl of Lincoln being entered into Yorkshire passed softly on his journey without spoiling or hurting any man, trusting thereby to have some company of people resort unto him. But after he perceived few of none to follow him, and that it was too late now to return back, he determined to try the matter by dint of sword, and thereupon direct his way from York to Newark-upon-Trent.

3 THE GREAT CHRONICLE OF LONDON

See 1C3.

And upon the xvjth day of June was the Field of Stoke. The which was by the force of the earl of Lincoln, son and heir of the duke of Suffolk, that late days before was fled this land, and so passed to the duchess of Burgundy, sister unto King Edward the IVth. The which duchess, as the fame went, aided and excited the said earl to make war upon England ... and so being furnished with a small company of Burgundians, having to their captain a fierce and strong soldier named Martin Swart, they to their sorrow landed ... and so held on their journey till they came near unto ... Stoke, where they encountered with the King's host, and there fought a sore and sharp fight ... the victory whereof fell unto the King ... This field was the sorer fought by reason that forenamed Martin Swart was deceived. For when he took this voyage upon him he was comforted and promised, by the earl of Lincoln, that great strength of this land after their landing would have resorted unto the said earl. But when he was far entered and saw no such resort, then he knew he was deceived. Wherefore he said unto the earl, 'Sir, now I see well that ye have deceived yourself and also me, but that notwithstanding, all such promise as I made unto my lady the duchess, I shall perform' ... exhorting the earl to do the same. And upon this sped them toward the field ... and there held promise in such wise that he and the earl both were slain upon the field, with much of their people. And when the tidings of this victory were brought unto the mayor, anon he caused *Te Deum* to be sung in the more part of all the churches of London.

4 CHRONICLE OF CALAIS

Ther was slayne the erle of Lyncoln, syr Martyn Swarte, a Fleminge that came into England with the forsayde erle out of Flaunders from the dutches of Burgoyne kyng Edward the fourth's systar, for she was the earles aunte, and she would have made hym kynge of England, but the erle was slayne and many other that bare armes that day, and the lorde Lovell was never sene aftar.

5 LETTER FROM PERKIN WARBECK TO ISABELLA OF CASTILE, 25 AUGUST, 1493

Most serene and most excellent princess, most honoured Lady and cousin, I commend me entirely to your Majesty. When the prince of Wales, eldest son of Edward formerly King of England ... my dearest lord and father, was miserably put to death, and I myself, then nearly nine years old, was also delivered to a certain lord to be killed, it pleased the Divine Mercy that the lord ... should preserve me alive and unhurt. First, however, he caused me to swear on the holy sacrament that I would not disclose my name, origin or family to anyone until a certain number of years had elapsed. He sent me abroad, therefore, with two persons to watch over and take charge of me. Thus I, an orphan, bereaved of my royal father and brother, an exile from my kingdom, and deprived of my country, inheritance, and fortune, a fugitive in the midst of extreme perils, led my wretched life in fear and grief and weeping, and for nearly eight years lay hidden in various provinces. At length, when one of those who had charge of me was dead and the other had returned to his country ... I remained awhile, scarcely emerged from childhood, alone and without means in the kingdom of Portugal. From there I sailed to Ireland where I was recognised by the illustrious lords, the Earls of Desmond and Kildare ... and by other noblemen of the island, and was received with great joy and honour. When the King of France invited me with many ships and attendants and promised me aid against Henry of Richmond, the wicked usurper of the kingdom of England, I came here to the aforesaid King of France, who received me honourably as a kinsman and friend. Since the promised assistance was not forthcoming, I went to the illustrious Princess, the lady Duchess of Burgundy, my father's sister and my very dear aunt, who ... welcomed me ... I promise if the Divine Grace should restore to me my hereditary kingdom that I shall continue with both Your Majesties in closer alliance and friendship.

6 ON PERKIN'S PRETENCE

This extract is from 'Registrum Annalium Collegii Mertonensis', 1497. This is a college history which was kept from 1483.

Memorandum, in that year on 7th September, one Perkin, by nationality a Fleming, pretending that he was the second son of Edward IV, and calling himself Richard, Duke of York, landed at the port of St. Ives in Cornwall and proclaimed himself king of England. About 10,000 Cornishmen who hated Henry VII on account of their defeat at Blackheath on the previous 17th June, and who wished to avenge themselves on the king joined him, and they set out towards the east in battle array.

7 PERKIN'S CONFESSION

This extract is taken from Holinshed's chronicle. See 3B2.

The confession of Perkin as it was written with his own hand, which he read openly upon a scaffold by the Standard in Cheape:
'It is first to be known that I was born in the town of Turney in Flanders, and my father's name is John Osbeck, which ... was controller of the said town ... and my mother's name is Katharine de Faro ... Also I had an uncle called master John Stalin ... with whom I dwelt a certain season. And after I was led by my mother to Antwerp, for to learne Flemish in a house of a cousin of mine ... And then ... to board in a skinner's house that dwelled beside the house of the English nation ...
After this ... with a merchant of Middlesborough to service for to learn the language ... and then I went into Portugal in company of Sir Edward Brampton's wife ... and then I put myself in service with a Breton called Pregent Meno, who brought me with him into Ireland. Now when we were there arrived in the town of Cork, they of the town (because I was arrayed with some kinds of cloths of silk of my said master's) came unto me and threatened upon me that I should be the Duke of Clarence's son that was before time at Dublin.
... And after this came unto me an English man ... and laid to me ... that they knew well that I was King Richard's bastard son ... They advised me not to be afeared but that I should take it upon me boldly ... so that they might be revenged on the King of England, and so against my will made me learn English and taught me what I should do and say. And after this they called

34   Rivals

me the Duke of York, second son to King Edward the fourth, because King Richard's bastard son was in the hands of the King of England . . . The French King sent an ambassador into Ireland . . . to advertise me to come into France. And thence I went to France and from thence into Flanders, and from Flanders into Ireland, and from Ireland into Scotland, and so into England.'

Questions

1 What do 3B1 and 7 show to be common in the very early stages of the appearance of the two pretenders?
2 What points of agreement about Martin Schwarz emerge from 3B1, 2, and 3?
3 What impression do you get of the Lord of Houth from 3B1?
4 How important were foreign backing, Ireland and the Yorkists to each claimant?

3C   Lady Jane Grey

Most writers have assumed that the initiative for diverting the succession from Mary to Lady Jane Grey came from the Duke of Northumberland. There is now a suggestion that the idea was that of Edward VI himself.

1 LADY JANE GREY'S FAMILY TREE

This family tree shows the Grey sisters' claim to the throne. (There has been mention of Catherine and Mary Grey in 2B12 and 13 and in 2D4 and 5.) Mary Tudor was the younger sister of Henry VIII. She had no children by her first husband, the King of France, and had married Charles Brandon, a great friend of Henry's, against her brother's wishes. Her daughter, Frances, was still alive when Jane was proclaimed Queen.

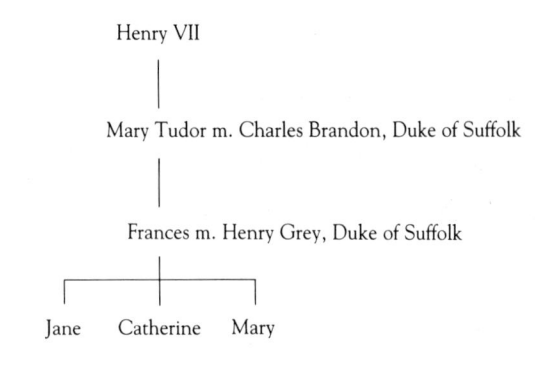

Henry VII
|
Mary Tudor m. Charles Brandon, Duke of Suffolk
|
Frances m. Henry Grey, Duke of Suffolk
|
Jane   Catherine   Mary

2 ELIZABETH TO THE DUKE OF NORTHUMBERLAND, 1553

My Lord Duke,

My sister and I were, some days ago, apprized of the plots . . . which your ambition for the advancement of your own house has led you to form, in order to exclude us both from the succession to the Crown. We were not, however, willing to give credit to these reports; because we could not conceive that a gentleman of your merit, of whom we hold so good an opinion and who evinced, when you took the reins of government of this kingdom, such ardour and zeal in the defence of laws and justice, was capable of doing one of the most scandalous acts of injustice – that of inducing . . . an innocent king, when in the langour of bodily infirmity, to exclude, under foolish suspicions and ill-founded pretexts, by a surreptitious and violent will, the lawful heirs of the Crown – those who have been so recognized by will and by a legitimate act of open Parliament.

Now, why do you do us this injustice? Is it to call to the inheritance of the Crown persons more remotely allied, of other blood, and other name, merely because they are your relations? Is this the fair renown that the King, our dear brother and sovereign lord, will, through your mad passion, leave behind? Is this the mighty honour your Lordship will gain – to make use of your present power, only to exclude from the succession the rightful daughters of King Henry our father, and the sisters on the father's side of King Edward, to bring in the daughter of the Duke of Suffolk, who has had no other claim than that of having married one of our aunts?

. . . we hope that . . . the Parliament and the judges, who are the defenders of the laws and of the Crown, will drag us out of the oppression into which your ambition has cast us. I remain, meanwhile, in that state in which you have placed me,

Elizabeth.

3 SPINOLA ON LADY JANE GREY, 1553

Baptisa Spinola was a Genoese merchant.

Today I saw Lady Jane Grey walking in a grand procession to the Tower. She is now called queen, but is not popular, for the hearts of the people are with Mary, the Spanish Queen's daughter. This Jane is very short and thin, but prettily shaped and graceful. She has small features and a well-made nose, the mouth flexible and the lips red. The eyebrows are arched and darker than her hair, which is nearly red. Her eyes are sparkling and reddish brown in colour. I stood so near her grace that I noticed her colour was good but freckled. When she smiled she showed her teeth, which are white and sharp. In all a gracious and animated figure. She wore a dress of green velvet stamped with gold, with large sleeves. Her headdress was a white coif with many jewels. She walked under a canopy, her mother carrying her long train, and her husband Guildford walking by her, dressed all in white and gold, a very tall strong boy with light hair, who paid her much attention. The new queen was mounted on very high chopines (1) to make her look much taller, which were concealed by her robes, as she is very small and short. Many ladies followed, with noblemen, but this lady is very heretical and has never heard Mass, and some great people did not come into the procession for that reason.

1 *Chopine* a kind of shoe raised above the ground by a *very* thick sole.

4 LADY JANE GREY TO MARY I, 1553

The Duke of Northumberland, as President of the Council, announced the death of King Edward, shewing afterward what cause we all had to rejoice for the virtuous and praiseworthy life that he had led, as also for his very good death . . . praising much his prudence and goodness, for the very great care that he had taken of his Kingdom at the very close of his life, having prayed God to defend it from the Popish Faith and to deliver it from the rule of his evil sisters.

He then said that His Majesty had well weighed an Act of Parliament, wherein it was already resolved that whoever should acknowledge the most serene Mary, that is Your most serene Majesty, or the Lady Elizabeth, and receive them as true heirs of the Crown of England, these should be held all for traitors, one of them having been formerly disobedient to her father, Henry the Eighth, and also to himself, concerning the truth of religion, and afterwards also capital enemies of the Word of God, and both bastards. Wherefore in no manner did he wish that they should be heirs of him and of that Crown, he being able in every way to disinherit them. And therefore, before his death, he gave order to the Council that, for the honour they owed to him, and for the love they bare to the realm, and for the affection that was due to their country, they should obey this his last will.

The Duke then added that I was the heir named by His Majesty to succeed to the Crown, and that my sisters should likewise succeed me in case of my default of issue. At which words all the Lords of the Council kneeled down before me, telling me that they rendered to me the honour that was due to my person, I being, of true and direct lineage heir to that Crown, and that it became them in the best manner to observe that which, with deliberate mind, they had promised to the King, even to shed their blood, exposing their own lives to death. Which things, as soon as I had heard . . . how I was beside myself stupified and troubled, I will leave it to those Lords who were present to testify, who saw me, overcome by sudden and unexpected grief, fall on the ground, weeping very bitterly; and then, declaring to them my insufficiency, I greatly bewailed myself for the death of so noble a prince, and at the same time turned myself to God, humbly praying and beseeching Him, that if what was given to me was rightfully and lawfully mine, His Divine Majesty would grant me such grace and spirit that I might govern it to His glory and service, and to the advantage of this realm.

On the day following . . . I was conducted to the Tower, and . . . afterwards were presented to me by the Marquis of Winchester, Lord High Treasurer, the jewels, with which he brought me also the Crown, although it had never been demanded from him by me . . . and he further wished me to put it on my head, to try whether it really became me well or no. The which, although with many excuses, I refused to do, he nevertheless added I might take it without fear, and that another also should be made to crown my husband with me. Which thing I . . . heard truly with a troubled mind, and with ill will, even with infinite grief and displeasure of heart . . . but afterwards I sent for the Earls of Arundel and Pembroke, and said to them that, if the Crown belonged to me, I should be content to make my husband a Duke, but would never consent to make him a King.

Questions

1 What motives does Elizabeth ascribe to the Duke of Northumberland for diverting the

36 *Rivals*

succession (3C2)? How do these differ from those stated in the second paragraph of 3C4?
2 Might there be a reason other than that which Spinola gives for 'great people' not joining Jane's procession (3C3)?
3 How good do you think Jane's claim to the throne was compared to that of Mary Tudor, or Elizabeth or Mary Stuart?
4 After Jane's death, how good was her sister Catherine's claim to the throne compared to Mary Stuart's?

3D Mary Stuart

At the time some thought that had Elizabeth died from her attack of smallpox in 1562 there would have been civil war between the supporters of Catherine Grey [2D] and those of Mary Stuart. Today, historians feel that Elizabeth favoured Mary as her successor, although she refused to name her. Can you find any evidence in the following documents to support or refute that idea?

1 ELIZABETH TO MARY, QUEEN OF SCOTS, 1567

Madam,
My ears have been so much shocked, my mind distressed, and my heart appalled, at hearing the horrible report of the abominable murder of your husband, my cousin, that I have scarcely as yet spirits to write about it; but although nature constrains me to lament his death, so near to me in blood as he was, I must tell you boldly that I am far more concerned for you than for him.
Oh Madam! I should neither perform in office as a faithful cousin nor that of an affectionate friend, if I studied rather to please your ears than to preserve your honour; therefore I will not conceal from you that people, for the most part, say 'That you will look through your fingers at this deed, instead of revenging it,' and that you have not cared to touch those who have done you this pleasure, as if the deed had not been without the murderers having that assurance ...
For the love of God, Madam, use such sincerity and prudence in this case, which touches you so nearly, that all the world may have reason to judge you innocent of so enormous a crime – a thing which unless you do, you will be worthily blotted out from the rank of princesses, and rendered, not undeservedly, the opprobrium of the vulgar; rather than which fate should befall you, I should wish you an honourable sepulchre instead of a stained life.

2 ELIZABETH TO MARY STUART, 1586

You have in various ways and manners attempted to take my life, and to bring my kingdom to destruction by bloodshed.
I have never proceeded so harshly against you, but have, on the contrary, protected and maintained you like myself. These treasons will be proved to you, and all made manifest.
Yet it is my will, that you answer the nobles and peers of the kingdom as if I were myself present. I therefore require, charge, and command that you make answer, for I have been well informed of your arrogance.
Act plainly, without reserve, and you wil sooner be able to obtain favour of me.
                                      Elizabeth

3 THE DEATH OF MARY STUART

This is one of the Fugger newsletters, and is labelled 'a Calvinist source'. The Fuggers of Augsburg were a family of merchant princes. As international businessmen they needed to know what was going on anywhere that might affect their trade and so set up reporting agencies in important cities. Emanuel Tomascon, who was present at the events, describes them below.

After there had been revealed to the Queen of England several plots, hatched at the instigation of the Pope and the heads of neighbouring states, enemies of the Crown of England, the said Queen found that she had not only to fear for her throne, but also for her life. She then realised that their aim was to release the Queen Mary of Scotland from her durance and to establish her as the next heir, although she was a Catholic and had been detained in prison ... for many years ... she was persecuted for a long time by the Parliament and States of the Scottish Kingdom, in order that she might be condemned to death, for she had murdered a king, and had set fire to a house with gunpowder, because she was in love with Bothwell, a Scottish baron. Thereupon she abdicated in favour of her son James, the present King of Scotland. But when she ... escaped from prison, she assembled troops, so as to rob the said son of his crown. However she was put to flight ... In spite of these charges Queen Elizabeth yet desired to spare her life, not wishing to be her judge, on account of her being such a near blood relation.

But as the Scottish Queen now presumed to covet the Crown of England, the English Queen could not let her go free ... because her life, her country and religion were imperilled. Also she did not wish to create any suspicion in the minds of the Scots. Although the Scottish Queen was kept in such ... pleasurable confinement that she could even go hunting and enjoy all the pleasures of the chase, she, nevertheless ... tried many ... devices to become free again, namely through encompassing the death of the Queen of England ... Also England was to have been attacked by foreign troops, the Scottish Queen set upon the thrones of Scotland and England, and the Romish faith established in both kingdoms. All of this the Queen of England gathered ... and the Queen of Scotland was proved guilty in the presence of the nobility, the knighthood and the officials.

It was discussed in Parliament ... how the person of the Queen and the religion of the country could be guarded in future against such dangers. As, however, the Scottish Queen was a close blood relation, her life was to be spared. Since also she was not in the free enjoyment of her liberty and rights, a sentence of death would make a rare and amazing departure.

Thereupon Parliament decided thus: the life of the Scottish Queen would mean the death of the English queen and the ruin and destruction of England and of her religion. Therefore it is admitted that she, the Scottish Queen, has to be put to death. Shortly thereafter, a conspiracy was discovered against the person of Her Majesty ... Thereupon, latterly, the Queen of England has resolved to abolish the cause of such evil and of the above-mentioned danger, although she agreed to the execution with but a heavy heart. She therefore dispatched several persons to carry out the sentence upon the Queen of Scotland. The officials who received this command hastened forward the execution, but this against the repeated injunction of the English Queen. Because of this, the secretary of Her Majesty, Davison was thrown into the Tower and several others fell into disgrace ...

At the command of the Queen of England ... the Earls of Shrewsbury and Kent, who were at the time in the neighbourhood of the castle of Fotheringay, together with other gentlemen, knights and noble persons, with Sir Amias Paulet and Sir Drury, who had order to guard the queen of Scotland, had on the previous day, namely the 17th day of February, made known to the imprisoned Queen the will of her Majesty of England. Thereupon she made reply that she was prepared and had long awaited this. She inquired when the execution would take place. Although this was left to her own choice, she asked that it might take place at once, on the very next day, namely on the 18th day of February of the new calendar, on a Wednesday. She besought God's help thereto ... Hence on the 18th day of February, at seven o'clock of the morning, the aforementioned earls, knights and noblemen forgathered in the castle of Fotheringay. Two followers were allocated to each knight, but only one to the others present, so that about eighty to a hundred persons entered the castle, beside the guard and the officials of the court.

There, in the great hall, in front of the fireplace, in which burnt a great fire, a daïs had been set up, which was twelve feet wide and eight feet high. It was completely covered with black cloth, and thereon stood a chair with a cushion. As all was now ready ... a message was sent to the imprisoned queen that the gentlemen had come on the errand of which she had been forewarned in the afternoon of yesterday, and wished to know whether she was ready.

The messenger, however, found the door of her chamber locked and bolted. All her people were with her in the chamber ... They sent a messenger to her once more ... he found the door unlocked. He sent one of the Queen's servants to her ... the servant brought answer that the Queen was not yet ready. After half an hour, the gentlemen sent to her once more, and thereto she made answer that she would be ready in half an hour.

After this time the chief official went to the Queen. He found her on her knees with her ladies-in-waiting, praying, and told her that her time was now come. Thereupon she stood up and said that she was ready. She was led between two men of her retinue into the antechamber. There she found all her people assembled. She exhorted them all to fear God and to live in humility of spirit. She took leave of them all, kissed the women and held out her hand to the men to kiss. She begged them not to grieve on her account but to be of good cheer and to pray for her. Then she was led to the stairway. There all the gentlemen advanced from the hall towards her, and the Earl of Shrewsbury said to the sorrowing Queen: 'Madame, we are here to carry out the behest of our most gracious Queen of England, which was communicated to you yesterday.' The warrant and sentence the Earl of Kent held in his hand.

The Great Seal of the Crown of England was thereon. Then the Queen replied that she would as lief die as live any longer. As she turned round she perceived her most distinguished servitor, Melville, and said to him: 'My faithful servant Melville, though thou art a Protestant and I am a Catholic, there is nevertheless but one Christendom and I am thy Queen, born and anointed, of the lineage of Henry VII. And so I adjure thee before God that thou give this command to my son: I beg him to serve God, and the Catholic Church, and to rule and keep his country in peace and to submit (as I have done) to no other Master, although I had the right good will to unite the kingdoms of this island. I renounce this, may he do likewise, and do not let him put overmuch trust in the presumption of the world. Let him trust God and then he will be blessed by Him. Let him speak no evil of the Queen of England, and thou, Melville, art my witness that I die like a true Scotswoman, Frenchwoman and Catholic, which belief has ever been mine.'

Thereupon Melville made answer: 'Most venerable and most august Princess, as I have been at all times your Majesty's faithful servant, so I will now with the help of God faithfully and honestly transmit to the King, your son, Your Majesty's words and message.'

Thereupon she turned to the above-mentioned gentlemen and desired to have her priest with her on the daïs, so that he might bear witness for her to the king of France and in other places, that she had died righteously and a good Catholic. To this the gentlemen made reply that it had been ordained otherwise.

She then demanded that her servants might remain with her. This was refused, in order to curb her impatience and to free her mind from certain superstitions. Nevertheless five of her servants and two tiring-women were permitted to come to her, because she complained that she was being poorly served. She promised that she would cause no hindrance, either by cries or by tears. Further she demanded for her servants and her maids liberty to depart, with good escort, and free of cost to their own countries without let or hindrance. This the gentlemen promised her. Also that they should be permitted to retain everything that the Queen of Scotland had presented to them . . . Thereupon she was led by two servants of the Governor to the daïs. There she seated herself upon a chair, for she could stand but with difficulty. The two earls seated themselves beside her. Then the Secretary Beale read the warrant and the sentence of execution in an over loud voice.

The gown in which the Queen was attired was of exquisite black velvet, which she had likewise worn when she appeared before the gentlemen. In her hand she held a small cross of wood or of ivory with the picture of Christ thereon, and a book. On her neck hung a golden crucifix, and from her girdle a rosary.

Near her stood a doctor of theology, Dean of Peterborough, who, at the command of the gentlemen, spoke words of Christian comfort to her, exhorting her to die as a Christian with a repentant heart. She at once interrupted him and begged him to keep his peace, for she was fully prepared for death. The Dean answered that he had been commanded to speak the truth to her. But she said for the second time: 'I will not listen to you, Mr Dean. You have naught to do with me. You disturb me.' Thereupon he was bidden to be silent by the gentlemen.

The Earl of Kent said to her: 'Madame, I am grieved on your account to hear of this superstition from you and to see that which is in your hand.' She said it was seemly that she should hold the figure of Christ in her hand thereby to think of Him. Thereupon he answered that she must have Christ in her heart, and further said that though she made demur in paying heed to the mercies vouchsafed to her by God All-Highest, they would nevertheless plead for her with God almighty, that He would forgive her sins and receive her into His Kingdom. Thereto the Queen made reply: 'Pray, then will I also pray.' Then the aforesaid Doctor fell on his knees on the steps of the daïs and read in an over loud voice a fervent and goodly prayer for her, most suitable to such an occasion, also for the Queen of England and the welfare of the Kingdom. All those standing around repeated the prayer. But as long as it lasted the Queen was praying in Latin and fairly audibly, holding the crucifix in her hand.

When this prayer was now ended . . . the executioner knelt in front of the Queen. Him she forgave his deed, as also all those who lusted after her blood, or desired her death. She further . . . craved from God that he might forgive her own trespasses. Thereafter she fell on her knees in ardent supplication and besought the remission of her sins. She said that she trusted to be saved through the death of Christ and His Blood and that she was ready to have her own blood spilt at His feet, wherefore she held his picture and the crucifix in her hands. Further she prayed for a happy, long and prosperous reign for the queen of England, for the prosperity of the British Isles, for the afflicted Christian Church and the end of all misery. She also prayed for her son . . . for his upright . . . Government and of his conversion to the Catholic Faith. At the last she prayed that all the saints in heaven might intercede for her on this day, and that God of His great goodness might avert great plagues from this Island, forgive her her sins and receive her soul into his Heavenly hand.

Thereupon she stood up and prepared herself for death. She doffed her jewels and her gown, with the help of two women. When the executioner wished to assist her, she said to him that it was not her wont to be disrobed in the presence of such a crowd, nor with the help of such hand-maidens. She herself took off her robe and pushed it down as far as the waist. The bodice of the underskirt was cut low and tied together at the back. She hastened to undo this.

Thereafter she kissed her ladies, commended them to God, and because one of them was weeping too loudly, she said to her: 'Have I not told you that you should not weep? Be comforted.' To her she gave her hand, and bade her leave the daïs. When she was thus prepared, she turned to her servitors, who were kneeling not far off, blessed them and made them all witnesses that she died a Catholic and begged them to pray for her. Afterwards she fell on her knees with great courage, did not change colour and likewise gave no sign of fear. One of her tirewomen bound a kerchief before her eyes. As she knelt down she repeated the 70th Psalm: '*In te, Domine, speravi* . . .' When she had said this to the end, she, full of courage, bent down . . . and laid her head on the block, exclaiming: '*In manuas tuas, Domine, commendo spiritum meum.*' Then one of the executioners held down her hands, and the other cut off her head with two strokes of the chopper. Thus ended her life.

The executioner took the head and showed it to the people, who cried: 'God spare our Queen of England!'

When the executioner held up the head, it fell in disarray so that it could be seen that her hair was quite grey and had been closely cropped.

Her raiment and other belongings were by command taken from the executioner, but he was promised their equivalent in money. Everything that had been sprinkled with her blood, also the garments of the executioner and other objects, were promptly taken away and washed. The planks of the daïs, the block cloth and all else were thrown into the fire, at once, so that no superstitious practices could be carried on therewith.

Her body was carried out, embalmed and made ready for burial . . . Her servants and courtiers were instructed to abide there until her remains had been honourably laid to rest. She was four-and-forty years of age, and was the most beautiful princess of her time.

She had as first spouse, France II, King of France, after him Henry Stuart, the son of the Earl of Lennox, her cousin, a truly handsome young man, by whom she had issue James VI, King of Scotland. But after she had caused Henry Stuart to be murdered, she took in marriage the Earl of Bothwell, who was imprisoned in Denmark, lost his senses and there died.

After this execution had taken place, the portals of the castle remained shut, until Henry Talbot, son of the Earl of Shrewsbury, had been dispatched to the English Court. When . . . he brought the tidings to London, the citizens of this town lit bonfires on all sides and rang the bells, because they were rid of the danger in which they had lived so long . . .

4 REPORT SENT TO WILLIAM CECIL, LORD BURGHLEY

Then she, lying very still upon the block, one of the executioners holding her slightly with one of his hands, she endured two strokes of the other executioner with an axe, she making very small noise or none at all, and not stirring any part of her from the place where she lay and so the executioner cut off her head, saving one little gristle, which being cut asunder, he lift up her head to the view of all the Assembly and bade 'God Save the Queen'. Then, her dress of lawn falling from her head, it appeared as grey as one of three score and ten years old, polled very short, her face in a moment being so altered from the form she had when she was alive, as few could remember her by her dead face. Her lips stirred up and down a quarter of an hour after her head was cut off.

Then one of the executioners, pulling off her gown, espied her little dog which was crept under her clothes, which could not be gotten forth but by force, and afterward would not depart from the dead corpse, but came and lay between her head and her shoulders, which being imbrued with her blood was carried away and washed . . .

5 THE FAERIE QUEEN

Spenser (1552?–1599) wrote 'The Faerie Queen' in 1596. In this romantic epic 'Duessa' is Mary Stuart and 'Mercilla' is Elizabeth. The following extract is from Canto IX, Book V.

First gan he tell, how this that seem'd so faire
   And royally arrayd, *Duessa* hight
   That false *Duessa*, which hath wrought great care,
   And mickle mischiefe unto many a knight,
   By her beguyled, and confounded quight:
   But not for those she now in question came,

>   Though also those mote question'd be aright,
>   But for vyld treasons, and outrageous shame,
> Which she against the dred *Mercilla* oft did frame.
>
>   For she whylome (as ye mote yet right well
>   Remember) had her counsel false conspyred,
>   With faithless *Blandamour* and *Paridell*,
>   . . . And with them practiz'd, how for to depryue
>   *Mercilla* of her crowne, by her aspyred,
>   That she might it vnto her selfe deryue,
> And triumph in their blood, whom she to death did dryue.
>
>   And then the law of *Nations* gainst her rose,
>   And reasons brought, that no man could refute;
>   Next gan *Religion* gainst her to impute
>   High Gods beheast, and powre of holy lawes;
>   Then gan the Peoples cry and Commons sute,
>   Importune care of their own publicke cause;
> And lastly *Justice* charged her with breach of lawes.
>
>   But then for her, on the contrarie part,
>   Rose many advocates for her to plead:
>   First there came *Pittie*, with full tender hart,
>   And with her ioyn'd *Regard* of womanhead;
>   And then came *Daunger* threatning hidden dread,
>   And high alliance unto forren powre;
>   Then came *Nobilitie* of birth, that bread
>   Great ruth through her misfortunes tragic stowre;
> And lastly *Griefe* did plead, and many teares forth powre.
>
>   Then brought he forth, with griesly grim aspect,
>   Abhorred *Murder*, who with bloudie knyfe
>   Yet dropping fresh in hand did her detect,
>   And there with guiltie bloudshed charge ryfe:
>   Then brought he forth *Sedition*, breeding stryfe
>   In troublous wits, and mutinous uprore:
>   Then brought he forth *Incontinence* of lyfe,
>   Euen foule *Adulterie* her face before,
> And lewd *Impietie*, that her accused sore.

6 MEMOIRS OF SIR JAMES MELVILLE

James Melville (1535?–1617) was Mary's envoy to Elizabeth and the brother of the Melville referred to in 3D3. He wrote from memory some time after the events. His memoirs were first published in 1683.

. . . after the decease of Walsingham, Secretary Cecil being advanced to be Lord Burleigh, and Great Treasurer of England, two Secretaries were chosen, one called Mr Smith, and this Davison, whose predecessor was a Scotsman . . .

The Council of England, a great part of the nobility and states, fell down upon their knees, humbly requesting her Majesty to have compassion upon their unsure estate, albeit she should slight her own; alleging, that her life was in hazard by the practices of the Queen of Scotland, and their lives and fortunes. She alleged, that her heart would not suffer her to let any sentence be given forth against the Queen, her dear sister and cousin, so near of her royal blood. Yet she was at last moved, for pity of their conditions, to let sentence of death pass against her, upon this express condition, that it should rather serve to be a terror to her, to oblige her to cease from making any more practices, than that she really intended to see the blood of so noble a princess shed. And in the meantime, the written sentence was given to be kept to Mr Davison, one of her Secretaries, not to be delivered without her Majesty's express command. Nevertheless the said Davison, being deceived by the Council, delivered unto them the said written sentence of death. Whereupon they gave the Queen warning a night before, to prepare her for God. Which short warning she took very patiently, and lay not down that night to sleep, but wrote some letters unto the King her son, the King of France, and some other princes, her friends . . . The rest of the night she employed in prayer. And being in the morning conveyed out of her chamber, to the great hall where the scaffold was prepared, she took her death patiently and constantly, courageously ending her life, being cruelly handled by the executioner, having received divers strokes of the axe, which execution was the boldlier performed, because that some Scotsmen assured them, that the King her son would soon forget it. Albeit his Majesty, when he understood this sorrowful news, took heavy displeasure, and convened a Parliament, wherein, lamenting the mishandling of his mother by his enemies who were in England, he desired the assistance of his subjects to be avenged. Where all the Estates in one voice cried out in a great rage, to set forward; promising that they should all hazard their lives, and spend their goods and estates largely to that effect, to revenge that unkindly and unlawful murder. Which put the Council of England in great fear for a while; but some of our countrymen comforted them, and so did some English that haunted our Court, alleging it would soon be forgot.

Questions

1. **a** In what ways could it be said Tomascon's report (3D3) favours Elizabeth rather than Mary?
   b In what ways does it show Mary to be enacting the role of a Catholic martyr?
   c How far would it support the accusations made against *Duessa* in the extracts from the *Faerie Queen*?
2. How far does the last paragraph of 3D6 explain Elizabeth's hesitation in dealing with Mary? What other reasons are given in the sources?

4 Rebellion

As you look at the following material consider which rebellion was the most dangerous to the Tudors. Were any of them inherently less likely to succeed than those between 1450 and 1485? What themes are common, if not to all, then to some of the rebellions?

4A 1450 and 1497

1 JACK CADE'S MANIFESTO

Cade's rebellion of 1450, against misgovernment and misuse of power, was a symptom of general unrest. It could possibly have been instigated by Richard of York to see how the land lay.

The King should take about his noble person men of true blood from his royal realm, that is to say, the high and mighty prince, the duke of York, exiled from our sovereign lord's person by the suggestions of those false traitors the duke of Suffolk and his affinity.

2 THE CORNISH UPRISING

This extract is taken from 'Registrum Annalium Collegii Mertonensis', 1497. (See 3B6.)

Memorandum in this year about the beginning of May, a great rising of the people occurred in the kingdom beginning in Cornwall where the ringleader was a smith named Michael Joseph. A great multitude of people supported him, but there was none of noble blood except lord Audley. Crossing the counties of Devon, Somerset, Wiltshire, Southampton, they came at length to Blackheath on June 16, where they pitched their camp for the night. On the morrow, 17 June, Henry VII met them with a great multitude of nobles. He gained the victory without great slaughter on either side and the said captain and lord Audley with others were captured and committed in chains to the Tower for their deeds. From there on the 27th of the month the said Michael and one Flammok, a lawyer, were drawn through the places of the city to Tyburn and there were hanged. Their bodies were taken down and quartered, and by the king's orders were hanged in various cities and places in the kingdom. On the next day, the 28th, the said lord Audley was drawn from Newgate through the places of the city to the place of punishment near the Tower, and there his head was struck off. His body was, by the King's grace, buried in the Preachers, but his head was fixed on London Bridge.

3 HOLINSHED'S CHRONICLE ON THE CORNISH UPRISING

See 3B2.

These unruly people, the Cornishmen, inhabiting in a barren country and unfruitful, at the first sore repined that they should be so grievously taxed and burdened by the king's council ... And thus being in a rave, two persons ... the one called Thomas Flammock, a gentleman learned in the laws of the realm, and the other Michael Joseph, a smith, men of stout stomachs and high courage, took upon themselves to be captains of this seditious company. They laid the fault and cause of this exaction unto John Morton, Archbishop of Canterbury, and to Sir Reginald Bray, because they were chief of the King's council ... Flammock and Joseph exhorted the common people to put on harness and not be afeared to follow them in that quarrel, promising not to hurt any creature, but only to see them punish that procured such exactions to be laid on the people, without any reasonable cause, as under the colour of a little trouble with the Scots, which (since they were withdrawn home) they took to be well quieted and appeased. So these captains, bent on mischief ...

persuaded a great number of people to assemble together and . . . do as their captains would . . . appoint. Then these captains . . . set forth with their army and came to Taunton, where they slew the Provost of Perin, which was one of the commissioners of the subsidy, and from thence came to Wells, so intending to go to London . . .

When the King was advertised of these doings, he was somewhat astonished . . . being thus troubled with the war against the Scots and this civil commotion of his subjects at one instant. But first meaning to subdue his rebellious subjects and after to proceed against the Scots, as occasion would serve, he revoked the Lord Daubeney which . . . was going against the Scots, and increased his army with many chosen and picked warriors. Also mistrusting that the Scots might now (having such opportunity) invade the realm again, he appointed the Lord Thomas Howard, Earl of Surrey (which after the death of the Lord Dinham was made high treasurer of England) to gather a band of men in the county of Palatine of Durham, that they, with the aid of the inhabitants adjoining and the borderers, might keep back the Scots if they chanced to make any invasion. The nobles of the realm, hearing of the rebellion of the Cornishmen, came to London every man with as many men of war as they could put in a readiness to aid the King if need should be . . .

In the meantime, James Twitchet, Lord Audley being confederate with the rebels of Cornwall . . . being come to Wells, and took it upon him as their chief captain to lead them against the natural lord and king . . . The captains of the rebels . . . brought their people to Blackheath, a four miles distant from London, and there in a plain on top of an hill they ordered their battles, either ready to fight with the King if he would assail them, or else assault the city of London; for they thought the King durst not have encountered with them . . .

The city was in a great fear . . . the rebels were encamped so near the city, every man getting himself to harness and placing themselves some at the gates some on the walls, so that no part was undefended. But the King delivered the city of that fear . . . There were slain of the rebels which fought and resisted, above two thousand men (as Edward Hall noteth), and taken prisoners an infinite number, and among them the blacksmith and the other chief captains, which were shortly after put to death . . .

. . . The prisoners as well as captains and others were pardoned, saving the chief captains and first beginners, to whom he shewed no mercy at all . . .

4 ANNALS OF ENGLAND, 1592

From about 1560 John Stowe (1525?–1605) was collecting manuscripts which dealt with English history. In 1573, on the death of Wolfe, the projector of Holinshed's Chronicle, Stow bought his collections. In 1565 he produced 'Summarie of Englishe Chronicles' and in 1580 he dedicated 'The Chronicles of England' to Leicester. In 1592 his 'Annales' were published, and they were reissued in 1605. He revised Holinshed's Chronicle 1585–7. (See 3B2 and 7.)

From Wells they went to Salisbury and from thence to Winchester, and so into Kent, where they hoped to have great aid, but they were deceived: for the Earl of Kent, George Bergaveny, John Brooke, Lord Cobham, Sir Edward Poynings, Sir Richard Guilford, Sir Thomas Bourchier, John Peche, William Scott, and a great number of people were ready to defend the country, which thing marvellously dismayed the Cornishmen, so that many of them fled the company. The captains brought their people to Blackheath, and there ordered their battles, either ready to fight with the king if he would assail them, or else assault the City of London. The king sent John, Earl of Oxford, Henry Bourchier, Earl of Essex, Edmond de la Pole, Earl of Suffolk, Sir Rise ap Thomas, and Sir Humphrey Stanley, noble warriors, with a great company of archers and horsemen, to environ the hill on either side, to the intent that all by ways being stopped, all hope of flight should be taken from them, and incontinently he himself being furnished with a great army, set forward out of the city, encamped himself in St. George's Field where he lodged that night, and on the next morning sent the Lord Daubney with a great company to set upon them early in the morning, which first got the bridge at Deptforde Strande, while the Earls set on them on every side, the Lord Daubney came into the field with his company, and without long fighting on the 22nd of June, the Cornishmen were overcome . . . there were slain of the rebels about 300, and taken of them, about 1,500 . . . the king wanted of all his number but 300 men, which were slain . . . The Lord Audley was drawn from Newgate to the Tower Hill in a coat of his own arms painted upon paper, reversed and torn and there beheaded . . . Flamocke and Joseph the blacksmith were drawn, headed and quartered at Tilburn, and their heads and quarters set up at London and other places, and at London Bridge foot.

44 Rebellion

Question

Using 4A2, 3 and 4 write your own account of the Cornish rebellion.

4B The Pilgrimage of Grace

Many believe the Pilgrimage of Grace presented the greatest threat to the Tudor monarchy. See if the documents provide any material to support this, if they show how it was dealt with, and what its motives seem to have been. (See 5C14 and 7B.)

1 REPORT OF CHAPUYS TO CHARLES V, 7 OCTOBER 1536

Five days ago in Lincolnshire, 50 miles from here, a great multitude of people rose against the King's commissioners, who levied taxes lately imposed by parliament and put down the abbeys. It is said some of the commissioners have been killed ... Cromwell, to whom the blame of everything is attached, and whose head the rebels demand ... it may be the way of stopping the demolition of the churches and the changes in matters of religion ...

2 THE PILGRIMS' OATH, 17 OCTOBER 1536

Ye shall not enter into this our Pilgrimage of Grace for the Commonwealth, but only for the love that ye do bear unto almighty God his faith, and to Holy church militant and the maintainance therof, to the preservation of the King's person and his issue, to the purifying of the nobility, and to expulse all villein blood and evil councillors against the commonwealth from his Grace and his Privvy Council of the same. And that ye shall not enter into our said Pilgrimage for no particular profit to yourself, nor to do any displeasure to any private person, but by counsel of the commonwealth, nor slay nor murder for no envy, but in your hearts put away fear and dread, and take afore you the Cross of Christ, and in your hearts His faith, the Restitution of the Church, the suppression of these Heretics and their opinions, by all the holy contents of this book.

3 HENRY VIII'S REPLY TO THE REBELS, 3 NOVEMBER 1536

First, as touching the maintainance of the Faith: the terms be so general that hard they be to be answered, but if they mean the Faith of Christ to which all Christian men be most obliged, we declare and protest ourself to be he that always do, and have minded to die and live in the purity of the same, and that no man can or dare set his foot by ours, in proving of the contrary; marvelling not a little that ignorant people will go about, or take upon them to instruct us (which something have been noted to be learned) what the right Faith should be ...
Now, touching the commonwealth: what king hath kept you all, his subjects, so long in wealth and peace, so long without taking or doing wrong, one to the other; so indifferently ministers justice to all, both high and low; so defended you from all outward enemies; so fortified the frontiers of this realm, to his no little and, in a manner, inestimable charges? What king hath given among you more general or freer pardons? What king hath been loather to punish his subjects, or showed more mercy amongst them?

4 HENRY VIII TO THE DUKE OF NORFOLK

Before you close up our said banner again you shall in any wise cause such dreadful execution to be done upon a good number of every town, village and hamlet that have offended in this rebellion, as well by the hanging them up in trees, as by the quartering them, and the setting up of their heads and quarters in every town, great and small, and in all such other places, as they may be a fearful spectacle to all other hereafter that would practise in any like manner.

5 ASKE'S DEPOSITION, MARCH 1537

The said Aske says: (1) That he grudged against the statue of suppressions, and so did all the country, because the abbeys in the North gave great alms to poor men and laudably served God ... And by the said suppression to service of God is much minished, great number of masses unsaid and consecration of the sacrament now not used in those parts, to the decrease of the Faith and spiritual comfort to man's soul, the temple of God ruffed and pulled down, the ornaments and relics of the church irreverently used, tombs of honourable and noble men pulled down and sold, no hospitality now kept in those parts . . . and the profits of the abbeys yearly go out of the country to the King; so that soon there will be little money left by reason of tenths and first fruits, the King's absence and the want of his laws . . . Also several of the abbeys were in the mountains and desert places, where the people be rude of conditions and not well taught the law of God, and when the abbeys stood the people not only had worldly refreshing in their bodies but spiritual refuge . . . by preaching, and many of their tenants were their fee'd servants, who now want refreshing both by meat, clothes and wages, and know not how to have any living . . . thus the suppression was greatly to the decay of the commonwealth and all those parts greatly grudged against it and still do . . . (2) To the statute of illegitimacy of the lady Mary the said Aske says that both he and all the wise men of those parts much grudged, seeing that on the mother's side she came of the greatest blood in Christendom . . . she ought to be favoured in this realm rather than otherwise, considering that her mother's ancestors have long been friends of the common wealth of this realm. Moreover it was thought that the divorce made by the archbishop of Canterbury was not lawful pending the appeal, and some even doubted the authority of his consecration . . . Moreover the lady Mary ought to be favoured for her great virtues and the statute annulled, lest the emperor should think he had cause to move war against the realm and stop the recourse of merchandise into Flanders . . .

As to the statute of Supremacy he says all men murmured at it and said it could not stand with God's law, giving various reasons . . . But the great bruit in all men's mouths then was that never King of England 'sith the Faith comyn within the realm' claimed any such authority, and that it should sound to be a mean of division from the unity of Catholic Church . . .

To the Statute of Uses, Aske says that to show his reasons would require great study in the law, that he has not of long time seen the said statute nor perused his books for such intent . . .

Not only he but in manner all men that rebelled blamed much divers bishops and preachers for division in preaching and variance in the Church of England, and thought that much of this insurrection arose by them. Also they blamed divers of the King's Council for the Statute of Suppression . . .

Questions

1 What point about the cause of grievance is being made in 4B1 which is similar to the one in 4A3 (paragraph one)?

2 How far does 4B2 support Chapuys' view (4B1) of the cause of the Lincolnshire uprising?
3 What does the second paragraph of 4B3 show you of Henry's view of kingship? Is it in any way contradicted by 4B4?
4 Does 4B5 show the Pilgrimage to have any non-religious purpose? Is there any echo of 4A1 in it or in 4B2? (See also 5C14.)

4C The Mid-Tudor Crisis

There are those who argue that as Wyatt's rebellion affected London it was the most dangerous of any Tudor uprising. See if you would agree.

1 ARTICLES OF THE REBELS 'IN DIVERS CAMPS BY THE EAST AND WEST OF EXETER'

1 We will have all the general councils and holy decrees of our forefathers observed, kept and performed, and whosoever shall gainsay them, we will hold as heretics.
2 We will have the laws of our sovereign lord King Henry VIII concerning the six articles to be used again as in his time they were.
3 We will have the sacrament hung over the high altar, and thus be worshipped as it was wont to be, and they which do not thereunto consent, we will have them die like heretics against the holy Catholic faith.
4 We will have the Mass in Latin as it was before, and celebrated by the priest without any man or woman communicating with him.
5 We will have the sacrament of the altar but at Easter delivered to the people, and then but in one kind.
6 We will that our curates shall minister the sacrament of baptism at all times, as well on week days as on the holy days.
7 We will have holy bread and holy water made every Sunday, palms and ashes at the other times accustomed, images to be set up again in every church, and all other ancient ceremonies held heretofore by our Mother the Holy Church.
8 We will not receive the new service because it is but like a Christmas game. We will have our old service of matins, Mass, evensong and procession as it was before; and we Cornishmen, whereof certain of us understand no English, utterly refuse the new English.
9 We will have every preacher in his sermon, and every

priest at the Mass pray, especially by name, for the souls in purgatory as our forefathers did.

10 We will have the Bible and all books of scripture in English called in again, for we be informed that otherwise the clergy shall not of long time confound the heretics.

11 We will have Doctor Moreman and Doctor Crispin, which hold our opinions, to be safely sent unto us, and to them we require the King's Majesty to give some certain livings to preach among us our Catholic faith.

12 We think it meet, because the Lord Cardinal Pole is of the King's blood, that he should not only have his pardon, but also be sent for from Rome, and promoted to be of the King's Council.

13 We will that no gentleman shall have any more servants than one to wait upon him, except he may dispend of a hundred marks in land, and for every hundred marks we think it reasonable that he should have a man.

14 We will that the half part of the abbey lands and chantry lands in every man's possession, however he came by them, be given again to the places where two of the chief abbeys were within every county where such half part shall be taken out; and there be established a place for devout persons, which shall pray for the King and the Commonwealth. And to the same we will have all the alms of the church box given for seven years.

15 For the particular griefs of our country, we will have them so ordered as Humphrey Arundell and Henry Bray, the King's Mayor of Bodmin, shall inform the King's Majesty, if they may have a safe conduct in the King's great seal to pass and repass with a herald of arms.

16 For the performance of these articles we will have four lords, eight knights, twelve esquires, and twenty yeomen pledges unto us until the King's Majesty have granted all these by Parliament.

2 CRANMER'S ANSWER TO THE FIFTEEN ARTICLES OF THE REBELS OF DEVON, 1549

When I first read your request, O ignorant men of Devonshire and Cornwall, straightways came into my mind a request, which James and John made unto Christ; to whom Christ answered: 'You ask you wot not what'. Even so thought I of you, as soon as ever I heard your articles, that you were deceived by some crafty papist, which devised those articles for you, to make you ask you wist not what.

As for the devisers of your articles, if they understand them, I may not call them ignorant persons, but, as they be indeed most rank papists and wilful traitors and adversaries both to God and to our sovereign lord the king, and to the whole realm. But I cannot be persuaded so to think of you, that in your hearts willingly you be papists and traitors; but that those be that have craftily seduced you, being simple and unlearned people, to ask you wot not what.

Wherefore my duty unto God, and the pity that I have of your ignorance, move me now at this time to open plainly and particularly your own articles unto you, that you may understand them, and no longer be deceived.

In your first article you require, that all the general councils and holy decrees of our forefathers may be observed and kept, and whosoever shall againsay them to be holden as heretics.

This you ask; but what you ask, I dare say, very few or none of you understand. For how many of you, I pray you, do know certainly which be called the general councils and holy decrees of the fathers, and what is in them contained? The holy decrees, as they call them, be nothing else but the laws and ordinances of the bishop of Rome; whereof the most part be made for his own advancement, glory, and lucre, and to make him and his clergy governors of the whole world, and to be exempted from all princes' laws . . .

3 REPLY TO PROTECTOR SOMERSET, WRITTEN IN EDWARD'S NAME, TO THE WESTERN REBELS

God hath made us your king by His ordinance and providence, by our blood and inheritance, by lawful succession, and by our coronation.

If ye would suspend and hang our doings in doubt until our full age, ye must first know, as king we have no difference of years . . . We are your rightful king, not by our age, but by God's ordinance, not only when we shall be one and twenty years of age, but when we were of ten years. We possess our crown not by years, but by the blood and descent from our father King Henry VIII.

Your pretence, which you say, moveth you to do thus, and wherewith you seek to excuse this disorder, we assure you is either false, or so vain, that we doubt not that, after that ye shall hereby understand the truth thereof, ye will all with one voice acknowledge yourselves ignorantly led, and by error seduced. And if there be anyone that will not, then assure you the same be rank traitors, enemies of our crown, seditious people, heretics, papists or such as care not what cause they have to provoke an insurrection, so they may do it, nor indeed can wax so rich with their own labours and with peace as they can do with spoils, with wars, with robberies and such like, yea with the spoil of your own goods.

4 CHRONICLE OF KING EDWARD VI

The people suddenly gathered together in Norfolk and increased to a great number, against whom was the Lord Marquis Northampton sent with the number of 1,060 horsemen, who, winning the town of Norwich, kept it one day and one night, and the next day in the morning with the loss of 100 men departed out of the town, among whom the Lord Sheffield was slain. There were taken divers gentlemen and servingmen to the number of thirty with which victory the rebels were very glad. But afterward, hearing that the Earl of Warwick came against them, they began to stay upon a strong plot of ground upon a hill near to the town of Norwich, having the town confederate with them. The Earl of Warwick came with the number of 6,000 men and 1,500 horsemen and entered the town of Norwich, which having won, it was so weak that he could scarcely defend it, and oftentimes the rebels came into the streets killing divers of his men and were repulsed again, yea, and the townsmen were given to mischief themselves. So, having endured their assaults three days and stopped their victuals, the rebels were constrained for lack of meat to remove, whom the Earl of Warwick followed with 1,000 Almains and all his horsemen, leaving the English footmen in the town, and overcame them in plain battle, killing 2,000 of them and taking Kett their captain, who in January following was hanged at Norwich and his head hanged out. Kett's brother was taken also and punished alike.

5 TROUBLE FOR MARY?

The Courtenay family was strong in the South-west. Courtenay was a descendant of Edward IV and was considered a suitable husband for either Mary or Elizabeth, though not by either of them! The following comment is by Antoine de Noailles at the French Embassy on 14 December 1553.

... from what I hear it only requires that my Lord Courtenay should marry her (1), and that they should go together to the counties of Devonshire and Cornwall. Here it can easily be believed that they would find many adherents, and they could then make a strong claim to the crown, and the Emperor and the Prince of Spain would find it difficult to suppress this rising.

1 *her* Elizabeth

6 MARY TUDOR'S SPEECH AT THE GUILDHALL, JANUARY 1554

I am come to you in mine own person to tell you that which already you see and know; that is how traitorously and rebelliously a number of Kentish men have assembled themselves against both us and you. Their pretence (as they said at the first) was for a marriage determined for us; to the which end to all the articles thereof ye have been made privy. But since, we have caused certain of our Privy Council to go again unto them ... and it appeared then unto our said Council that the matter of the marriage seemed to be but a Spanish cloak to cover their pretended purpose against our religion ...

Now, loving subjects, what I am ye right well know. I am your Queen, to whom at my coronation when I was wedded to the realm and laws of the same ... you promised your allegiance and obedience unto me ... My father as ye all know, possessed the same regal state which now rightly descended unto me, and to him always ye showed yourselves most faithful and loving subjects; and therefore I doubt not but ye will show yourselves likewise to me ... And I say to you, on the word of a prince, I cannot tell how naturally the mother loveth the child, for I was never the mother of any, but certainly if a prince and governor may as naturally and earnestly love her subjects as the mother doth love the child, then assure yourselves that I, being your lady and mistress, do as earnestly and tenderly love and favour you.

7 WRIOTHESLEY'S 'CHRONICLE'

From 1455 to 1518 Charles Wriothesley's (1508–62) Chronicle is a copy of Arnold's; from 1521 to 1559 it is original, often the work of an eye-witness. (See 6C9.)

The 25 day of January tidings were brought to the Lord Mayor, by Sir John Gage, Lord Chamberlain to the Queen, that Sir Thomas Wyatt, with certain rebels, were up in Kent, about Maidstone. Whereupon a court of Aldermen was called immediately in the afternoon; and that night the Lord Mayor rode to peruse the watch of the city, and so every night after two aldermen ride to peruse the said watches.

Also, that night, by the Council's commandment, the Lord Mayor secretly with the sheriffs apprehended the Lord Marquis of Northampton . . .

The 26 of January the Lord Marquis was sent from the Lord Mayor's house to the Tower of London by the Sword-bearer . . .

Also, this day the gates of the city began to be warded by the citizens.

The 27 of January the Lord Treasurer came to the Guildhall from the council to declare that the city should make out 500 footmen, well harnessed, to go against the rebels, whereupon a Common council was called in the afternoon to have their assents thereunto, which they granted, and had them ready that night among the Companies of the city . . . And the 28 of January, being Sunday, the said 500 men were assembled at Leadenhall, and there delivered to the Captains, and sent by water to Gravesend . . .

The 29 of January the Duke of Norfolk, with the Captain of the guard that were sent from the Queen, with certain other soldiers and yeomen of the guard, with the captains and soldiers that went out of the city, offered to assault Rochester Castle where the traitor Wyatt and his rebels lay, and the captains of the city with their soldiers fled to the rebels over Rochester Bridge and drew up the bridge, so that the Duke was fain to fly, and then the rebels took the Queen's ordnance and treasure.

The 30th of January Wyatt removed with his rebels from Rochester and came to Blackheath, and there camped with the Queen's ordnance, and lay in the town of Greenwich and there about. This day also ordnance was laid at every gate of the city.

The 31 January Wyatt removed to Greenwich and Deptford with his camp.

The first day of February a proclamation was made in the city of London with an herald, a trumpet, and the Common Crier . . . which was the traitor the Duke of Suffolk, which was fled westward, was discomforted, and his horsemen and baggage taken, and he and his two brethren fled in servingmen's coats. And also that Peter Carew and his uncle . . . were fled into France . . . And, further, that whosoever should take the traitor Wyatt should have a 100.l. lands to him and his heirs for ever.

The same day in the afternoon . . . all the Commons of the City were assembled in their liveries at the Guildhall. The Queen's Majesty, with her Lords and Ladies riding from Westminster to the said Guidhall, came thither by three of the clock . . . her Majesty came down into the great hall up into the place of the hustings, where was hanged a rich cloth of estate, she, standing under it, with her own mouth declared to the audience there assembled the wicked pretence of the traitor Wyatt, which was utterly to deprive her of her crown, and to spoil the City; which was so nobly and with so good spirit declared, and with so loud a voice, that all the people might hear her Majesty, and comforting their hearts with so sweet words that made them weep for joy to hear her Majesty speak . . .

The 2 of February . . . the citizens made preparation for a 1000 men of the householders of the said City, well harnessed, to defend the City, the Lord Mayor and Aldermen every one in his ward taking the muster of them . . .

The 3 day of February, being Saturday, in the afternoon, the traitor Wyatt with his rebels came into Southwark, and there trenched at the bridge foot, and set two pieces of ordnance against the gate at London Bridge. And then came the Lord William Howard, Lord Admiral, to the Lord Mayor, with a commission from the queen, and made a proclamation against the said Wyatt, and that the Queen had sent him to be Captain General, with the Lord Mayor, for the defence of the city, declaring to the citizens that he would die in the defence of it . . .

Sunday the 4th of February the Lord Admiral made strong defence on the bridge and warded with 300 of the citizens with him all the day till eight of the clock at night; and then relieved them with other 300 men to ward all night, and by five in the morning other 300 fresh men came to relieve them, and every morning and evening fresh relief was set.

The 6th of February, being Shrove Tuesday, afore six of the clock in the morning, Wyatt with his rebels went out of Southwark, and went to Kingston, over the bridge, and came toward Brentford . . .

Also the same day tidings came that the Duke of Suffolk and his brother were taken by the Earl of Huntingdon . . .

The 7th of February, being Ash-Wednesday, early in the morning, the Earl of Pembroke, Lieutenant of the Queen's army, with horsemen and footmen of the noblemen, gathered their armies together with the Queen's ordnance, and pitched their field by St. James beyond Charing Cross, to abide the said traitor Wyatt and his rebels. The Lord Mayor and the Lord Admiral set the citizens in good array at Ludgate, Newgate, and from Cripplegate to Bishopsgate, lest the rebels would draw to Finsbury field . . . Then Wyatt with his rebels came to the park pale by St. James about two of the clock in the afternoon, and Knevett, one of his captains with his rebels went by Tothill, through Westminster, and shot at the Court gates. But Wyatt, perceiving the great army of the Queen's camp, and ordnance bent against him, suddenly returned by the wall of the park at St. James, towards Charing Cross, with the lightest of his soldiers, where the Earl of Pembroke's men cut off his train and slew divers of the rebels; but Wyatt himself with divers other came in at Temple Bar, and so through Fleet Street ... crying 'a Wyatt! a Wyatt! God save Queen Mary!' But when he saw that Ludgate was shut against him, and the ordnance bent, he fled back again ... and by Temple Bar was taken, with the lord Cobham's son, and other of his captains and rebels, and brought to the court gate, and from thence sent by water to the Tower of London. And then all the Queen's host came through London in goodly array, and 'Te Deum' was sung in the Queen's Chapel for joy of said victory, and so few slain.

The 10th of February the Lord Mayor with other justices sat on the rebels by commission of Oyer and determiner at the justice hall in the Old Bailey, where that day were condemned of treason 82 persons of Kent and other places; and 32 were condemned to be drawn, hanged and quartered.

Also the same day in the afternoon the Duke of Suffolk, which was taken in Leicestershire, was brought through the City of London by the Earl of Huntingdon ... and so had to the Tower ...

The 17th of February the Duke of Suffolk was arraigned at Westminster and there condemned of treason ...

Friday the 23rd of February Lord Gray, Duke of Suffolk, was beheaded at the Tower Hill ...

The 15th March Wyatt, captain of the rebels, was arraigned at Westminster and there condemned of high treason ...

The 18th of March, being Palm Sunday, the Lady Elizabeth was taken to the Tower from Westminster by water privily ...

8 ELIZABETH, TO MARY, ON BEING TOLD SHE WOULD GO TO THE TOWER, 17 MARCH 1554

If ever any one did try this old saying that a king's word was more than another man's oath, I most humbly beseech your Majesty to verify it in me, and to remember your last promise and my last demand, that I be not condemned without answer and due proof, which it seems that I now am: for that without cause proved I am by your Council from you commanded to go unto the Tower, a place more wonted for a false traitor than a true subject: which though I know I deserve it not yet in the face of all this realm appears that it is proved; which I pray to God that I may die the shamefullest death that any died afore I may mean any such thing: and to this present hour I protest afore God, who shall judge my truth whatsoever malice shall devise, that I never practised, counselled, nor consented to anything that might be prejudicial to your person in any way or dangerous to the state by any means. Let conscience move your Highness to take some better way with me than to make me be condemned in all men's sight afore my deserts be known. I have heard in my time of many cast away for want of coming to the presence of their prince; and in late days I heard my lord of Somerset declare that if his brother had been suffered to speak with him he had never suffered; but the persuasions were made to him so great that he was brought in belief that he could not live safely if the admiral lived, and that made him give his consent to his death. Therefore ... I humbly crave to speak with your Highness which I would not be so bold to desire if I knew not myself most clear as I know myself most true. And as for the traitor Wyatt, he might peradventure write me a letter, but on my faith I never received any from him; and for the copy of my letter to the French king I pray God confound me eternally if I ever sent him word, message, token, or letter by any means: and to this my truth I will stand to my death.

Your Highness's most faithful subject.

Questions

1 Compare the Articles in 4C1 with Aske's deposition (4B5).
2 Compare 4C2 and 3 as answers to the Western rebels.
3 Who do you think provided Edward VI with information about Kett's rebellion (4C4)?
4 Why would de Noailles (4C5) favour a rising the King of Spain would find it hard to suppress?
5 a Do you think 4C6 bears out Wriothesley's comment in the tenth paragraph of 4C7?
  b What does Mary (4C6) think is the cause of Wyatt's rebellion?
6 What is the connection between 4C8 and 2D3?

4D The rising of the Northern Earls

By the time of Elizabeth's reign rebellions in England could be said to be less dangerous, whereas those in Ireland (see 10D) posed more of a threat.

Thomas Percy, the seventh Earl of Northumberland, was beheaded on the 22nd of August, 1572. Charles Neville, sixth Earl of Westmorland, was outlawed in 1571. He escaped to Scotland and then went to the Netherlands where he died. After this the power of the great feudal Northern nobility never recovered. Elizabeth did not sacrifice Cecil the way her father had Cromwell. The North had been subdued.

---

1 FORMAL PROCLAMATION OF THE EARLS, 15 NOVEMBER 1569

'We, the Earls of Northumberland and Westmorland, the Queen's true and faithful subjects, to all the same of the old Roman Catholic faith. Know ye that we with many others well disposed, as well of the nobility as others, have promised our faith for the furtherance of this sure good meaning. Forasmuch as divers disordered and ill-disposed persons about the queen's Majesty have by their crafty and subtle dealing, to advance themselves, overthrown in the realm the true and Catholic religion, and by the same abuseth the Queen, dishonoureth the realm, and now lastly seeketh to procure the destruction of the nobility. We therefore have gathered ourselves together to resist force by force, and rather by the help of God and of you good people, to reduce these things amiss, with the restoring of all ancient customs and liberties to God and this noble realm. And lastly, if we shall not do it ourselves, we might be reformed by strangers, to the great hazard of the state of this our country, whereunto we are all bound. God save the Queen.'

2 THE EARL OF SUSSEX, 24TH NOVEMBER 1569

... the Earls of Northumberland and Westmorland with their confederates have most undutifully and unnaturally ... entered into open and actual rebellion, and to cover their wicked and detestable attempts have abused and deluded many of Her Majesty's subjects in ... these parts ... sometimes affirming their doings to be with the advice and consent of the nobility of this realm, who indeed be wholly bent ... to spend their lives in dutiful obedience against them and all other traitors, sometimes pretending for conscience sake to seek to reform religion, where indeed it is manifestly known many of them never had care of conscience, or ever respected any religion, but continued a dissolute life, until at this present they were driven to pretend a popish holiness, to put some false colour upon their manifest treasons, directly against the commandment of God in holy scripture, the laws of this realm, and the ancient prerogative of the imperial crown of England, sometimes declaring that they be driven to take this matter in hand lest otherwise foreign princes might take it upon them, to the great peril of this realm, where indeed they ... have by all the wicked means they could practise with foreign princes to aid them in this wicked enterprise, and thereby sought ... to bring the whole realm to perpetual thralldom and misery under the subjection ... of foreign powers and potentates.

3 THE EARL OF NORTHUMBERLAND DURING INTERROGATION, 1572

Our first object was the reformation of religion and preservation of the person of the Queen of Scots, as next heir, failing issue of Her Majesty, which causes I believed were greatly favoured by most of the noblemen of the realm. I hoped my Lord Leicester, and especially my Lord Burghley ... would bring Her Majesty to the truth; but, being deceived, I can only pray God to indue her and them with His grace to know and fear him aright.

Questions

1 What has 4D1 in common with 4A1, 4B2, 4C1 and 5C14?
2 Does the statement of the Earl of Northumberland (4D3) bear out or add to the proclamation (4D1) of 15 November 1569?

5 The Court

Recent writing on the sixteenth century emphasises the importance of the court and, therefore, of those constantly with the monarch, as opposed to (in) the council. Faction fighting could be a feature of both and individual influence on the monarch might be exercised in either.

5A Royal Beasts

Heraldry was still important in the sixteenth century and symbols still mattered. (See 1C5 and 5B3.) Yorkists and Tudors added to the royal beast symbols, the heyday for which was in the fifteenth and sixteenth centuries. Two beasts, 'supporters', would normally 'support' (emblazon) a shield.

To the lion of England and the griffin of Edward III were added the falcon of the Plantagenets, favoured by Edward IV. Henry VII took over this, with other Yorkist symbols, on his marriage to Elizabeth of York, and it is also associated with Anne Boleyn. The Black Bull of Clarence and the White Lion of Mortimer both came to the Crown through Edward IV.

Henry VII added the Yale of Beaufort, derived from the Bohun antelopes, the white greyhound of Richmond and the Red Dragon of Wales. The unicorn was added with the accession of James VI to the English throne.

1 BEAUFORT YALES

The Beaufort Yales decorate the doorway of St. John's College, Cambridge.

52 *The Court*

2 TUDOR DRAGON AND GREYHOUND

The greyhound and the dragon support the shield of arms of Henry VII at King's College Chapel, Cambridge.

3 ANNE BOLEYN'S FALCON

The falcon symbol originates with Edward III. It was used by his sons, John of Gaunt and Edmund. Edward IV's younger son, Richard, had a white falcon as his badge. When Henry VII married Elizabeth the falcon became his family symbol as well. Henry VIII gave it to Anne Boleyn and it was also associated with the Earldom of Ormonde, granted to Anne's father in 1529. Elizabeth I used the badge herself. Here it is seen in an illuminated letter from 'The Ecclesiast', the text of Ecclesiates with commentary which was made for Anne while she was Queen.

Questions

Can you work out why the Beaufort symbol was a portcullis?

5B The Aristocracy

The monarch needed the backing of the aristocracy, but those of the blood royal could pose a threat. In the reigns of the first two Tudors it was dangerous to be of the old nobility, or to have a blood relationship to any previous monarch!

1 WARWICK IN 1468

This extract is from an old English chronicle known as 'Hearne's Fragment' which was written between 1516–22 by someone who claimed to have known Edward IV in the 1460s.

Sure and of truth it is the said Richard, Earl of Warwick, was sent into Normandy as ambassador with others, whose secret counsellings betwixt the French King and him alone brought him in suspicion of many things, inasmuch that his insatiable mind could not be content; and yet before him was there none in England of the half possessions that he had. For first he had all the Earldom of Warwick whole, with all the Spencers' lands, the Earldom of Salisbury, Great Chamberlain of England, Chief Admiral and Captain of Calais, and Lieutenant of Ireland, the which possessions amounted to the sum of 20,000 marks, and yet he desired more. He counselled and enticed the Duke of Clarence, and caused him to wed his eldest daughter Isabel, without the advice or knowledge of King Edward.

2 ON WARWICK

This extract is taken from Holinshed's Chronicles. (See 3B2.)

(He was) ever had in great favour of the commons of this land by reason of the exceeding household which he dayly kept in all countries wherever he sojourned or lay: and when he came to London he held such an house that six oxen were eaten at a breakfast, and every tavern was full of his meat, for who that had any acquaintance in that house he should have as much sod (1) and roast as he might carry away upon a long dagger.

1 *sod* boiled.

3 BATTLE OF BARNET, 1471

Montagu was the younger brother of the Earl of Warwick. Only in Warkworth's Chronicle (see 1B3) do we find the story of Montagu's treachery and details of the confusion between the emblem of the Earl of Oxford and that of Edward IV.

There was such a great mist that neither of them might see each other perfectly; there they fought, from four of the clock in the morning until ten of the clock in the forenoon. And divers times the Earl of Warwick's party had the victory, and supposed that they had won the field. But it happened so, that the Earl of Oxford's men had upon them their lord's livery, both before and behind, which was a star with streams, which was much like King Edward's livery, the sun with streams; and the mist was so thick that a man might not profitably judge one thing from another; so the Earl of Oxford's men shot and fought against the Earl of Oxford's men, weening and supposing that they had been King Edward's men; and anon the Earl of Oxford and his men cried 'treason! treason!' and fled away from the field with 800 men. The Lord Marquess Montague was agreed and appointed with King Edward, and put upon him King Edward's livery; and a man of the Earl of Warwick's saw that, and fell upon him, and killed him. And when the Earl of Warwick saw his brother dead, and the Earl of Oxford fled, he leapt on horseback, and fled to a wood by the field of Barnet, where there was no way forth; and one of King Edward's men had espied him, and one came upon him and killed him, and despoiled him naked. And so King Edward gat that field.

And after that the field was done, King Edward commanded both the Earl of Warwick's body and the Lord Marquess's body to be put in a cart, and returned him with all his host again to London; and there commanded the said two bodies to be laid in the church of Paul's, on the pavement, that every man might see them; and so they lay three or four days, and afterward were buried.

4 THE ACT OF ATTAINDER OF EDWARD, LATE DUKE OF BUCKINGHAM

Buckingham was descended from the youngest son of Edward III. His father had been killed after rebellion against Richard III. Attainder involved execution, forfeiture and disinheritance. It was a speedy process that could be reversed by letters patent under the great seal or by act of parliament.

Forasmuch as Edward, late Duke of Buckingham, late of Thornbury in the county of Gloucester, the 24th day of April in the fourth year of the reign of our Sovereign Lord the King that now is and divers times after, imagined and compassed traitorously and unnaturally the destruction of the most royal person of our said Sovereign Lord and subversion of this his realm, and then traitorously committed and did divers and many treasons against our said Sovereign Lord the King, contrary to his allegiance . . . of which treasons and offences the said late Duke . . . was severally indicted. And afterward for and upon the same treasons the 13th day of May the thirteenth year of the reign of our said Sovereign Lord the King at Westminster in the county of Middlesex before Thomas, Duke of Norfolk, for that time only being Great Steward of England by the King's letters patents, by verdict of his peers and by judgment of the said Steward against the said late Duke then and there given after the due order of the law and the custom of England was attained of high treason, as by records thereof more plainly appeareth. Wherefore be it ordained, enacted, and established by the King our Sovereign Lord, with the assent of the Lords spiritual and temporal and the Commons in this present Parliament assembled and by the authority of the same, that the said late Duke for the offences above rehearsed stand and be convicted, adjudged, and attainted of high treason, and forfeit to the King our Sovereign Lord and his heirs for ever all honours, castles, manors, lordships, hundreds, franchises, liberties, privileges, advowsons . . . lands, tenements, rents, services . . . whatsoever in England, Ireland, Wales, Calais, and Marches of the same, or elsewhere, whereof the said late Duke or any other person or persons to his use . . . were possessed . . . And over that, the said Edward to forfeit unto our said Sovereign Lord all goods and chattels . . .

5 CHARLES V ON THE EXECUTION OF BUCKINGHAM

A butcher's dog has killed the finest buck in England.

6 THE FRENCH AMBASSADOR, MARILLAC, TO THE CONSTABLE OF FRANCE, 21 MAY 1540

Lord Lisle was an illegitimate son of Edward IV. Henry VIII trusted him until 1540, when Cromwell seems to have framed him, aided by Lady Lisle's possibly Catholic sympathies and Henry's increasing suspicions of the Pole and Courtenay families and so of anyone of royal blood. Lord Lisle never left the Tower; when Henry decided to release him in 1542 he had a celebratory meal followed by a fatal heart attack.

Two days ago, at ten o'clock at night, my lord Lisle, Deputy of Calais, uncle of this King, was led prisoner to the Tower, where before had been committed three of his servants, and similarly today a chaplain of his who is come out of Flanders in a ship. The cause thereof hath not yet been so certified unto me that I can write it for truth; but it is bruited that he is accused of having had secret intelligence with the Cardinal Pole who is his nearest relative, and of other practices to deliver up to him the town of Calais. Howsoever it may be, the said Lord Lisle is in a very strait prison, and from the which none escape save by miracle.

7 DUKE OF SURREY, 1547

The Duke of Surrey was heir to the Duke of Norfolk. He and Wyatt (see 2B5) introduced the sonnet form into England. He was executed in 1547 for quartering the royal arms with his own, an act which Henry VIII, whose son Edward was still under age, took as a threat to his dynasty.

I know that the King wants to get rid of the noble blood around him and employ none but low people.

8 MELVILLE ON THE DUKE OF NORFOLK

See 3D6.

The Duke of Norfolk, the Earl of Sussex, and several other councillors were sent down to York to hear the Regent's accusation (1), and to be as judges between the King and Queens' Lords.
 . . .The Duke was then the greatest subject in Europe, not being a free Prince. For he ruled the Queen, and all those who were most familiar with her. He also ruled the

Council; and ruled two factions in England, both Protestants and Papists, with the city of London and whole Commons. The great men who were Papists were all his near kinsmen, whom he entertained with great wisdom and discretion; the Protestants had such proof of his godly life and conversation, that they loved him entirely . . .

The Duke of Norfolk . . . began to boast and speak plain language, 'That he would serve and honour the Queen his mistress so long as she lived, but after her decease he would set the crown of England upon the Queen of Scotland's head, as lawful heir.' And this he avowed to Secretary Cecil, desiring him to go and prattle that language again to the Queen . . .

The Duke of Norfolk understanding that his whole purposes were discovered, stood not to acknowledge to the Queen, 'That during her lifetime he would never offend her, but serve and honour her, and after her the Queen of Scotland, as in his opinion truest heir, and the only means for eschewing of civil wars, and great bloodshed that might otherwise fall out.' Now, albeit the Queen of England liked not that language; yet she would not appear to find fault with it for the time . . .

At that time the Duke commanded over all the north parts of England, where the Queen our mistress was kept, and so might have taken her out when he pleased . . .

. . . the Duke was sent for by the queen to come to Court. Whereupon first he posted in haste to secretary Cecil, to demand his counsel; for he reposed much upon him . . . The other made answer, 'That there was no danger; he might come and go at his pleasure, no man would or durst offend him': which made the Duke ride up quietly, only with his own train; whereas otherwise he would have been well accompanied. In the meantime Secretary Cecil informed the Queen, 'That the necessity of the time obliged her not to omit this occasion, but to take the matter stoutly upon herself, and incontinent command her guard to lay hands upon the Duke, or else no other durst do it; which if she did not at this time, her crown would be in peril.' The Queen following this counsel, the Duke was taken and secured, when he thought all England was at his devotion; who after long captivity was executed, ending his life devoutly in the Reformed Religion.

1 *accusation* against Mary Queen of Scots

9 THE TRIAL OF THE EARL OF ESSEX, 1601

A spacious court was made in Westminster Hall, where the Lord Treasurer Buckhurst sat as High Steward of England under a canopy of state; where sat also about the table the earls, barons, and judges of the land, according to their degrees . . .

Then the Lord High Constable of the tower, the Lieutenant of the Tower, and the gentleman-porter who carried the axe before the prisoners, came first in, and the prisoners followed and made their appearance at the bar, the gentleman porter with the axe standing before them, with the axe's edge from them . . . another proclamation was made, that the Serjeant-at-Arms to the queen's Majesty do return his precept of all the peers of Robert, Earl of Essex, and Henry, Earl of Southampton, which he delivered into the Court accordingly. Another proclamation was made, that all earls, viscounts, and barons of the realm of England which were peers of Robert, Earl of Essex, and Henry, Earl of Southampton, and summoned to appear this day, do make answer to their names, upon pain and peril that will fall thereon.

. . . Then the two Chief Judges and the Lord Chief Baron were sent in to them to deliver their opinions in law, which they did upon two points; the one 'that in cases where a subject attempteth to put himself into such strength as the King shall not be able to resist him, and to force and compel the King to govern otherwise than according to his royal authority and direction, it is manifest rebellion.' The other: 'That in every rebellion the law intendeth as a consequent the compassing the death and deprivation of the King, as forseeing that the rebel will never suffer that King to live or reign who might punish or take revenge of his treason or rebellion.'

After half an hour . . . the Serjeant-at-Arms called . . . Thomas, Lord Howard, who stood up bare-headed.

Lord Steward: 'My Lord Thomas Howard, whether is Robert, Earl of Essex, guilty of this treason whereupon he hath been indicted, as you take it upon your honour, or no?'

Whereupon the Lord Thomas Howard made answer, bending his body and, laying his left hand upon his right side, said, 'Guilty, my Lord, of high treason.' After which manner all the peers found him guilty . . . Being called over anew, they found Henry, Earl of Southampton, guilty of high treason also.

. . . Then the Lord High Steward, after a few exhortations to the Earls to prepare themselves for God, told them, seeing the law had found them guilty, it followed of course that he must proceed to judgment.

The Earl of Essex replied very cheerfully and said: 'Yea, my Lord, with a very good will I pray you go on.'

Then the Lord High Steward gave judgment as followeth: 'You must go to the place from whence you came, and there remain during her Majesty's pleasure; from thence to be drawn on a hurdle through London's streets and so to the place of execution, where you shall be hanged, bowelled, and quartered, your head and quarters to be disposed of at her Majesty's pleasure; and so God have mercy on your souls . . .'

. . . The Earl of Southampton obtained a reprieve, but the Earl of Essex was ordered for execution.

Questions

1 Using 5B1, 2 and 3, 2B3, 3A2 and 5C2 write a brief account of Warwick's career and character and his relationship with the House of York.
2 Look at 5B4 and 5. What does Charles V mean in 5B5? Do you think his view of who held responsibility for the execution of Buckingham was correct?
3 How true do you find the Duke of Surrey's comment in 5B7?
4 Is there any information in 5B8 which makes the idea of the Duke of Norfolk deciding to marry Mary Stuart rather surprising?

5C Upstarts

It was not safer to gain a position of influence even if you were not of the aristocracy. When reading this section see if the material fits in with your preconceptions about social mobility, or about social attitudes, in early modern England. (Bear 2B in mind.)

1 LETTER TO JOHN PASTON, MAY 5, 1450

The Pastons were a Norfolk family, originally yeomen, who had gained gentry status in the fifteenth century. John's father had become a successful and prosperous lawyer.

The de la Pole family fortunes had been made in the fourteenth century through trade in wine. William de la Pole, Duke of Suffolk, the favourite of Henry VI, was unpopular, partly because he favoured peace with France. He had a son who married Edward IV's sister and whose children were to prove troublesome as representatives of the 'white rose' to Henry VII and Henry VIII.

. . . On Monday next after May Day, there came tidings to London that, on Thursday before, the Duke of Suffolk came unto the coasts of Kent full near Dover, with his two ships and a little spynner (1), the which spynner he sent with certain letters by certain of his trusted men unto Calaisward, to know how he should be received; and with him met a ship called *Nicholas of the Towre* and by them that were in the spynner the master of the *Nicholas* had knowledge of the duke's coming. And when he espied the duke's ships he sent forth his boat to wit what they were, and the duke himself spake to them and said he was by the king's commandment sent to Calaisward. And they said he must speak to their master and so he, with two or three of his men, went with them in their boat to the *Nicholas*; and when he come, the master bade him 'Welcome, traitor', as men say; and further, the master desired to wit if the shipmen would hold with the duke, and they sent word they would not in no wise. Some say he wrote much thing to be delivered to the king, but that is not verily known. And some say he was arraigned in the ship, upon the impeachments and found guilty.

Also he asked the name of the ship, and when he knew it he remembered Stacy, that said if he might escape the danger of the Tower he should be safe; and then his heart failed him, for he thought he was deceived, and in sight of all his men he was taken out of the great ship into the boat: and there was an axe and a stoke (2), and one of the lewdest of the ship bade him lay down his head, and he should be fair ferd (3) with and die on a sword; and took a rusty sword, and smote off his head within half a dozen strokes, and took his gown of russet and his doublet of velvet mailed and laid his body on the sands of Dover. And some say his head was set on a pole by it.

1 *spynner* a small boat.
2 *stoke* block.
3 *ferd* dealt.

2 WILLIAM PASTON TO JOHN PASTON, 20 JANUARY 1460

Lord Rivers, the father of Elizabeth Woodville, married the widow of the Duke of Bedford, younger brother of Henry V. She was of the Burgundian ruling family and the social superior of her second husband. The Earl of March was the future Edward IV.

As for tidings, my Lord Rivers was brought to Calais and before the lords with eight score torches, and there my

Lord of Salisbury rated him, calling him knave's son, that he should be so rude as to call him and these other lords (1) traitors, for they shall be found the king's true liege men when he should be found a traitor. And my Lord of Warwick rated him and said his father was not but a squire, and brought up with King Harry V and sithen himself made by marriage and also made lord; and that it was not his part to have such language of lords, being of the king's blood. And my Lord of March rated him in like wise.

1 The Earls of Warwick, March and other Yorkist refugees.

3 BATTLE OF MORTIMER'S CROSS, 1461

This extract was taken from Gregory's Chronicle. (See 2A3.)

Also Edward Earl of March, the Duke of York's son and heir, had a great journey at Mortimer's Cross in Wales the second day of February . . . and there he put to flight the Earl of Pembroke (1), the Earl of Wiltshire. And there he took and slew of knights and squires to the number of 3,000.

And in that journey was Owen Tudor taken and brought unto Hereford, and he was beheaded at the market place, and his head set upon the highest grice (2) of the market cross, and a mad woman combed his hair and washed away the blood of his face, and she got candles and set them about him, burning more than a hundred. This Owen Tudor was father unto the Earl of Pembroke, and had wedded Queen Catherine, King Harry the VI's mother, thinking and trusting all the way that he should not be beheaded until he saw the axe and the block, and when that he was in his doublet he trusted on pardon and grace till the collar of his red velvet doublet was ripped off. Then he said, 'That head shall lie on the stock that was wont to lie on Queen Catherine's lap,' and put his heart and mind wholly unto God, and full meekly to his death.

1 *Earl of Pembroke* Jasper Tudor.
2 *grice* step of a cross.

4 WHY COME YE NOT TO COURT?

John Skelton had been Henry VIII's tutor. He was a protégé of the Howard faction (the family and friends of the Duke of Norfolk), whose influence was undermined by Wolsey, and lived in sanctuary in Westminster Abbey. He wrote this poem in 1522.

Why come ye not to court?
To which court?
To the king's court,
Or to Hampton Court?
Nay, to the King's court.
The King's court
Should have the excellence;
But Hampton Court
Hath the pre-eminence.
And Yorkes Place,
With my lord's grace,
To whose magnificence
Is all the confluence,
Suits and supplications,
Embassies of all nations.

5 BALLAD ABOUT WOLSEY

A great carl (1) he is and fat,
Wearing on his head a red hat.

1 churl, base fellow.

6 ANONYMOUS RHYME ON WOLSEY

Begot by Butchers, but by Bishops bred
How high his honour holds his haughty head!

7 THE BURIAL OF THE MASS

Jerome Barlow, a Greenwich Franciscan Friar, wrote 'The Burial of the Mass', which was printed in Strasburg in 1528. He was urged to write by an apostate friar, William Roye.

More like a god celestial
Than any creature mortal
  With worldly pomp incredible
Before him rideth two priests strong
And they bear two crosses long,
  Gaping in every man's face:
After them follow two laymen secular,
And each of them holdeth a pillar
  In their hands, stead of a mace.
Then followeth my lord on his mule
Trapped with gold under her cule (1),
  In every point most curiously;
On each side a poleaxe is born

Which in none other use are worn,
   Pretending some hid mystery.
Then hath he servants five or six score,
Some behind and some before,
   A marvellous great company,
Of which are lords and gentlemen
With many grooms and yeoman
   And also knaves among
Thus daily he proceedeth forth . . .

1 rump.

8 GEORGE CAVENDISH ON WOLSEY

Cavendish was one of twelve gentlemen ushers in Wolsey's household.

now will I declare unto you the order of his going into Westminster Hall, daily in the term of season. First, for his coming out of his privy chamber, he read most commonly every day two masses in his privy closet and there then said his daily service with his chaplain; and as I heard his chaplain say, being a man of credence and of excellent learning, that the cardinal what business of weighty matters soever he had in the day, he never went to his bed with any part of his divine service unsaid, yea not so much as one collect wherein I doubt not but he deceiveth the opinion of diverse persons . . . apparelled all in red, in the habit of a cardinal; which was either of fine scarlet, or else of crimson satin, taffeta, damask or cafia, the best that he could get for money; and upon his head a round pillion, with a noble of black velvet set to the same in the inner side; he had also a tippet of fine sables about his neck; holding in his hand a very fair orange, whereof the meat or substance within was taken out, and filled up again with the part of a sponge, wherein was vinegar, and other confections against the pestilent airs; the which he most commonly smelled into passing amongst the press, or else when he was pestered with many suitors . . . Then his gentlemen ushers cried and said, 'My Lords and masters, on before; make way for my Lord's Grace'. Thus passed he down from his chamber through the hall; and when he came to the hall door, there was attendant for him his mule, trapped all together in crimson velvet, and gilt stirrups.

9 LETTER FROM CHAPUYS, CHARLES V'S AMBASSADOR IN ENGLAND, TO CHARLES V, 25TH OCTOBER, 1529

Sire! The news here is, that the Cardinal who has long tottered, has at length come to his complete downfall. Having been dismissed from the Council, and deprived of his office as Chancellor, he has since also been constrained to make an inventory of all his moveables in his own hand, that nothing may be forgotten, and that he may be more easily convicted. It is said, that having of his own free will acknowledged his past errors and faults, he has presented all he had to the King, which is no trifling matter. Yesterday the King returned privately by water from Greenwich to view the said effects. He took with him only his Ladye Love, her mother and one gentleman of his chamber. The Cardinal notwithstanding his troubles, has always shewn a good face, until the day of St. Luke; when all his bravadoes have been turned into complaints and tears and sighs; and this, it is said, without ceasing day or night. When the King heard this, either moved with pity or thinking it inconvenient that he should die before a full disclosure and verification of several things had taken place, he sent him a ring for his consolation . . .

Sire! Two days after I had written the above, the Cardinal was judicially and definitely condemned by the great Council of the King, and declared a rebel to his authority, and guilty of high treason, in as much as in defiance of the Royal Authority and the privileges of the kingdom, he had obtained the bull of his Legatine authority, and had disposed by anticipation of several benefices in the patronage of the King and others. On this account, he has been deprived of all his offices and preferments with their dignities and prerogatives. All and each of his goods, moveables and immoveables, have been adjudged to the King, and he is sentenced to imprisonment in one of the Royal prisons here in London, until the King shall decide on his ultimate fate.

10 ON WOLSEY, 1555

Polydore Vergil (see 1B9) was in prison from April to December 1515 for remarks he had made about Wolsey in a letter in March. He also lost his collectorship of papal taxes, though he kept his livings, because of this. Therefore, he had a rather jaundiced view of the Cardinal. This extract is taken from his 'Anglica Historiae'.

The enjoyment of such an abundance of good fortune is to be reckoned most praiseworthy if it is showered upon sober, moderate and self-controlled men, who are not proud in their power, nor are made arrogant with their money, nor vaunt themselves in other fortunate circumstances. None of these characteristics could be described in Wolsey, who acquiring so many offices at almost the same time, became so proud that he considered himself the peer of Kings. He soon began to use a golden chair, a golden cushion, a golden cloth on his table, and, when he was walking, to have the hat, symbol of the rank of cardinal, carried before him by a servant, raised up like some holy idol or other, and to have it put upon the very altar in the King's chapel ... Thus Wolsey, with his arrogance and ambition, raised against himself the hatred of the whole people and, in his hostility towards nobles and common folk, procured their great irritation at his vainglory. His own odiousness was truly complete, because he claimed he could undertake himself almost all public duties.

11 HENRY VIII

Shakespeare and Fletcher's Henry VIII was probably written to be performed at the marriage of James I's daughter, Elizabeth, in 1612. This extract is from Act IV, Scene II.

Katherine:　　　He was a man
  Of an unbounded stomach, ever ranking
  Himself with princes; one that, by suggestion
  Tied all the kingdom; simony was fair play;
  His own opinion was his law: i' the presence
  He would say untruths; and be ever double
  Both in his words and meaning ...
  Of his own body he was ill, and gave
  The clergy ill example ...
Griffiths:　　　This cardinal
  Though from an humble stock, undoubtedly
  Was fashioned to much honour from his cradle.
  He was a scholar, and a ripe and good one;
  Exceeding wise, fair-spoken, and persuading;
  Lofty and sour to them that loved him not;
  But to those men that sought him sweet as summer,
  And though he were unsatisfied in getting,
  Which was a sin, yet in bestowing, madam,
  He was most princely: ever witness for him
  Those twins of learning that he raised in you,
  Ipswich and Oxford! one of which fell with him,
  Unwilling to outlive the good that did it;
  The other, though unfinish'd, yet so famous,
  So excellent in art, and still so rising,
  That Christendom shall ever speak his virtue.

12 EUSTACE CHAPUYS TO THE IMPERIAL CHANCELLOR, GRANVELLE, 1535

Master Cromwell, of whose origin and antecedents your Secretary Antoine tells me you desire to be informed, is the son of a poor blacksmith, who lived in a village ... and is buried in a common grave in the parish churchyard. His uncle ... was cook to the late Archbishop of Canterbury. The said Cromwell, in his youth, was an ill-conditioned scapegrace. For some offence he was thrown into prison, and was obliged afterwards to leave the country. He went to Flanders, and thence to Rome, and other places in Italy. Returning after a time to England, he married the daughter of a woolcomber, and lived in his father-in-law's house, carrying on the business. Afterwards he was a law-pleader, and thus became known to the Cardinal of York, who, perceiving his talents and industry, and finding him ready at all things, evil or good, took him into his service, and employed him in the demolition of five or six religious houses. On the Cardinal's downfall Cromwell acquitted himself towards him with marked fidelity ...

Cromwell contrived with presents and entreaties to obtain an audience of the King, whom he undertook to make the richest sovereign that ever reigned in England. He promised so fairly that the King at once retained him upon the council ... Since that time he has risen above everyone, except it be the lady, and the world says he has more credit with his master than ever the cardinal had. The cardinal shared his influence with the Duke of Suffolk and several others. Now there is not a person who does anything except Cromwell. The Chancellor is only his tool; and although he has, so far, refused to take the Great Seal himself, people say he will be persuaded to catch at it before long.

He can speak his own language remarkably well, and Latin and French, and Italian tolerably. For the rest, he is a person of good cheer, gracious in words and generous in actions; his equipage and his palace are magnificent.

13 LORD DARCY OF TEMPLEHURST TO CROMWELL, 1537

Templehurst was involved in the Pilgrimage of Grace. (See 4B.)

Cromwell, it is thou that art the very original and chief causer of all this rebellion and mischief and art likewise causer of the apprehension of us that be nobleman, and dost daily earnestly travail to bring us to one end and to strike off our heads; and I trust that, or thou die, though thou wouldst procure all the noblemen's heads within the realm to be stricken off, yet still there one head remain that shall strike off thy head.

14 PARLIAMENT ROLL, 1540

Thomas Cromwell, now Earl of Essex, whom your Majesty took and received into your trusty service, the same Thomas Cromwell then being a man of very base and low degree, and for singular Favour, Trust and Confidences which your Majesty bear and had in him, did not only erect and advance the same Thomas unto the state of an Earl, and enriched him with manifold gifts, as well of Goods, as of Lands and Offices, but also him the said Thomas Cromwell, Earl of Essex, did erect and make one of your most trusty Counsellors, as well concerning your Graces most supreme jurisdictions Ecclesiastical, as your most high secret affairs temporal. Nevertheless, your Majesty now of late hath found, and tried, by a large number of witnesses, being your faithful subjects and personages of great honour, worship and discretion, the said Thomas Cromwell . . . contrary to the singular trust and confidence your Majesty had in him, to be the most false, and corrupt Traitor, Deceiver, and Circumventor against your most Royal Person, and the Imperial Crown of this your realm, that hath been known, seen or heard of in all the time of your most noble reign . . . he hath caused many of your faithful subjects to be greatly infested with heresies, and other errors, contrary to the right laws and pleasure of Almighty God. And the same Thomas Cromwell . . . supposing himself to be fully able, by force and strength, to maintain and defend his abominable treasons, heresies and errors . . . in the last day of March in the 30th year of your most gracious reign . . . upon the demonstration . . . then and there made unto him, that there were certain new preachers, as Robert Barnes, clerk, and others, whereof part were committed to the Tower of London, for preaching and teaching of lewd learning against your Highness' proclamations; the same Thomas affirming the same preacher to be good . . . And moreover . . . the said Thomas Cromwell . . . hath had the nobles of your realm in great disdain, derision and detestation . . .

15 ELIZABETH TO WILLIAM CECIL, HATFIELD, 1558

'I give you this charge that you shall be of my Privy Council, and content yourself to take pains for me and my realm. This judgement I have of you, that you will not be corrupted by any manner of gift, and that you will be faithful to the state, and that, without respect to my private will, you will give me that counsel which you think best, and if you shall know anything necessary to be declared to me of secrecy, you should show it to myself only, and assure yourself I will not fail to keep taciturnity therein, and therefore henceforth I charge you.'

16 SIR THOMAS STUCLEY, ON CECIL, 1573

'Secretary Cecil may be called the King of England.'

17 LAMPOON ON ROBERT CECIL, WILLIAM'S SON, 1601

'Little Cecil trips up and down,
He rules both Court and Crown.'

Questions

1 Find the pun in the final sentence of 5C1.
2 What is ironic, in view of later events, about 5C2?
3 Why do you think 5C7 was printed in Strasburg rather than nearer home?
4 Using 5C4–11 describe Wolsey. Can you make any points in his favour?
5 What link was there between Wolsey and Cromwell (5C12)? Did they have much in common? Can you connect a sentence in 5C12 with the last sentence in 5C14?

5D Access to Elizabeth

The splendour, formality and hierarchical nature of the Tudor court are vividly described in the following documents.

1 THE QUEEN'S COURT, 1598

Paul Hentzer was tutor to a Silesian nobleman on a tour of England in 1598. His journal, from which this extract is taken, was first published in 1617.

We were admitted into the Presence Chamber, hung with rich tapestry and the floor, after the English fashion, strewed with hay; at the door stood a gentleman in velvet, with a gold chain, whose office was to introduce to the queen any person of distinction that came to wait on her. In the same hall were a great number of counsellors of state and gentlemen who waited the Queen's coming out, which she did from her own apartment when it was time to go to prayers. First came barons, earls, knights of the Garter, all richly dressed and bare-headed; next came the Chancellor, bearing the Seals in a red silk purse, between two others, one carrying the royal sceptre, the other the sword of state in a red scabbard with the point upwards; next came the queen, in the 65th year of her age, very majestic, her face fair but wrinkled, her eyes small yet black and pleasant, her nose a little hooked, her teeth black (from the English habit of too great use of sugar). She had in her ears two pearls with very rich drops; she wore false hair and that red; upon her head she had a small crown and she had on a necklace of exceeding fine jewels. Her air was stately, her manner of speaking mild and obliging. That day she was dressed in white silk, bordered with pearls the size of beans, and over it a mantle of black silk shot with silver threads, with a long train carried by a marchioness. As she went along she spoke very graciously to one and another in English, French and Italian; whoever speaks to her is kneeling, but now and again she raises some with her hand. Wherever she turned her face as she was going along, everybody fell down on their knees. The ladies of the court followed, very handsome and well-shaped, for the most part dressed in white. She was guarded on each side by 50 gentlemen with gilt battle-axes.

... We saw her table set with the following solemnity; a gentleman entered the room bearing a rod and with him one with a table-cloth which, after they had both kneeled three times with the utmost veneration, he spread upon the table. Then came two others, one with the rod again, the other with a salt-cellar, a plate and bread, which they placed on the table with the same ceremonies. At last came a countess dressed in white silk who, after she had bowed three times in the most graceful manner, approached the table and rubbed the plates with bread and salt. Then the Yeomen of the Guard entered, bare-headed, clothed in scarlet with a gold rose upon their backs, bringing in a course of 24 dishes, served on gilt plates. These were placed on the table while a lady-taster gave each of the guards a mouthful to eat of the particular dish he had brought, for fear of any poison. During the time that this guard, which has the tallest and stoutest men that can be found in all England, were bringing dinner, twelve trumpets and two kettle-drums made the hall ring for half an hour. At the end of this ceremonial, the Queen's ladies appeared and with great solemnity lifted the food off the table and carried it into the Queen's inner and private chamber, for the Queen dines and sups alone with very few attendants.

... We were led into two chambers, called the Presence or Chambers of Audience, which shone with tapestry of gold and silver and silk of different colours: under the canopy of state are these words, embroidered in pearl: '*Vivat Henricus Octavus*'. Here is besides a small chapel, richly hung with tapestry, where the Queen performs her devotions. In her bed-chamber, the bed was covered with very costly coverlids of silk. All the other rooms being very numerous, are adorned with tapestry of gold, silver and velvet, in some of which were woven history pieces; there were also numbers of cushions ornamented with gold and silver; in short, all the walls of the palace shine with gold and silver.

2 THE QUEEN DINES

Thomas Platter, author of this account, was a Swiss tourist who visited Nonesuch palace in 1599.

Now when the queen had returned to her chamber, her guardsmen wearing tabards, red, if I remember, with the royal arms on their backs embroidered in gold, carried two tables into the room with trestles, and set them down where the queen had been sitting. Then another two entered each bearing a mace and bowed three times; first at their entrance, and by the door, then in the centre of the room and lastly in front of the table, and after they had laid it they withdrew again. Soon two more guards in tabards appeared bowing with plates and other things which they laid on the table. Following them came another two bowing, and placed the carving-knives, bread and salt upon the table. Then a gentleman bearing a mace entered, together with a charming gentlewoman or lady-in-waiting, who bowed very gracefully, as described above, thrice to the empty table, at the same time a gentleman with a mace arrived with another gentleman and all four stood before the table.

Then straightway came the queen's guardsmen with red tabards folded back, one behind the other, and if I am not mistaken, a weapon at their sides, each one bearing a single covered dish of food. They are all very tall, fine, strong men, and all similarly attired, so that I never in my life saw their like. I believe there must have been forty of them.

When they handed over the food a gentleman removed the cover, while the lady-in-waiting served and carved a large piece off, which she gave to the guard who carried it in, and who was supposed to eat the portion, though they generally took it out or merely tasted a morsel.

Two of them brought wine and beer which was also poured out and tasted. And after this long table had been fully laid and served and the same obeisance and honours performed as if the queen herself had sat there, whatever dishes there were, were offered to the queen in her apartment for her to make her choice. These were sent into her and she ate of what she fancied, privily however, for she very seldom partakes before strangers, and the remainder was carried out again to the lords' table; and the guards brought other fresh dishes, which were served like the former, and I observed amongst them some very large joints of beef, and all kinds of game, pasties and tarts. After the third course had been thus brought in, served and removed again, and the dessert prepared and cleared off, the queen's musicians appeared in the presence chamber with their trumpets and shawms (1), and after they had performed their music, everyone withdrew, bowing themselves out just as they had come in, and the tables were carried away again.

1 an early kind of wind instrument.

Questions

1 How far does 5D1 bear out the description of Elizabeth in 2A30?
2 Compare the descriptions of Elizabeth's court life in 5D1 and 2.

6 Government

As you look at the material in this chapter try to decide where the power of government lay in the sixteenth century and how effective government was.

6A Theory

The views expressed in this section could be seen as reactions to the Wars of the Roses, or to threats to stability in Tudor England. The English Reformation (see chapter 7), with the emphasis on Royal Supremacy that was its unique feature, led to great stress being laid on the exaltation of monarchy.

1 THE TREE OF COMMONWEALTH

Edmund Dudley (1462?–1510) was a lawyer and speaker who worked with Empson to enforce Henry VII's policy of weakening the feudal barons through financial exactions. He was so unpopular that on the accession of Henry VIII he was thrown into the Tower on a trumped-up charge of treason. While there, hoping to ingratiate himself with the new king, he produced a treatise in favour of absolute monarchy. He was beheaded on Tower Hill, 18 August 1510. This extract is taken from his 'Tree of Commonwealth'.

... all Dukes, Erles, Barons, knightes, esquiers, and other gentlemen by office or auctorite, nede to lyve in a good conformyte, that is to saie, euery man after the honour and degre that god and his prince hath callid hym vnto, and after that part or porcion to leade his lyef, and not maligne or envie his superiors nor disdaign or sett at nought his inferiors. But euery man to know other with his dewtie and to helpe and guyde as his power may extend ...

2 THE OBEDIENCE OF A CHRISTIAN MAN

William Tyndale (d. 1536) was brought to Henry's attention by Anne Boleyn. Despite his views expressed here, Tyndale denounced Henry VIII's divorce. He was under the delusion it was a machination of Wolsey. This extract is taken from his 'Obedience of a Christian Man' of 1528. (See 7B1–2.)

It is better to suffer oon tyrant than many, and to suffer wronge of oon than of every man. Yea, and it is better to haue a tyrant unto thy kinge then a shadoo ... For a tyrant, though he do wronge unto the goode, yet he punisheth the evil and maketh all men obey ... A kinge that is as softe as silke and effeminate ... shall be more grievous unto the realme then a right tyrant.

3 HOMILY ON OBEDIENCE, 1547

The first book of homilies, from which this is taken, was produced by Cranmer in 1547. It was a series of sermons to be preached by those not licensed by their bishop to give their own. Great stress was laid on royal ecclesiastical supremacy.

Almightie God hath created and appooyncted all thynges, in heaven, yearth, and waters, in a most excellent and perfect ordre ... In the yearth he hath assigned kynges, princes, with other governors under them, all in good and necessarie ordre ... Every degree of people, in their vocacion, callyng, and office, hath appointed to them their duetie and ordre. Some are in high degree, some in lowe, some kynges and princes, some inferiors and subjectes, priestes and laymen, masters and servauntes, fathers and children, husbandes and wifes, riche and poore, and every one have nede of other . . . Take awaie kynges, princes, rulers, magistrates, judges, and such states of god's ordre, no man shall ride or go by the high way unrobbed, no man shal slepe in his awne house or bed unkilled, no man shall kepe his wife, children, and possessions in quietnesse . . .

4 MIRROR FOR MAGISTRATES, 1559

'Mirror for Magistrates', edited by William Baldwin, was history with a moral: the fickleness of fortune and the just punishment of vice. It was published in 1559 and reprinted six times in the next 18 years. It was imitated and added to well into the seventeenth century.

Full little know we wretches what we do
When we presume our princes to resist.
We war with God against His glory too,
That placeth in His office whom he list.
Therefore was never traitor yet but missed
The mark he shot at, and came to fearful end,
Nor ever shall till God be forced to bend.

Who that resisteth his dread sovereign lord,
Doth damn his soul by God's own very word.
A Christian subject should with honour due
Obey his sovereign though he were a Jew.

5 INSCRIPTION AT GRAFTON MANOR, WORCESTER, 1567

Plenti and grase be in this plase;
Whyle everi man is plesed in his degre
There is both pease and uniti;
Salaman saith there is none acorde
When everi man would be a lorde.

6 THOMAS WILSON, 1578

Thomas Wilson (1525?–81), a scholar and MP, was employed on embassies to Portugal and to the Netherlands and became Secretary of State in 1577.

Unhappie is that cowntrie where the meaner sorte hath the greatest swaye, for that in a base multitude is never seen any good cownsel, or stayed judgement. God keepe englande from any soche confused authoritie, and maynteyne us with our annoynted soverayne, whose onelie power under Christ is the safetie of us al.

7 SHAKESPEARE'S 'TROILUS AND CRESSIDA', ACT I, SCENE III

Ulysses:
When that the general is not like the hive
To whom the foragers shall all repair,
What honey is expected? Degree being vizarded,
The unworthiest shows as fairly in the mask.
The heavens themselves, the planets and this centre
Observe degree, priority and place,
Insisture, course, proportion, season, form,
Office and custom, in all line of order;
And therefore is the glorious planet Sol
In noble eminence enthroned and sphered
Amidst the other; whose medicinable eye
Corrects the ill aspect of planets evil,
And posts, like the commandment of a king,
Sans check to good and bad: but when the planets
In evil mixture to disorder wander,
What plagues and what portents! what mutiny!
What raging of the sea! shaking of earth!
Commotion in the winds! frights, changes, horrors,
Divert and crack, rend and deracinate
The unity and married calm of states
Quite from their fixture! O, when degree is shaked,
The enterprise is sick! How could communities,
Degrees in schools and brotherhoods in cities,
Peaceful commerce from dividable shores,
The primogeniture and due of birth,
Prerogative of age, crowns, sceptres, laurels,
But by degree, stand in authentic place?
Take but degree away, untune that string,
And, hark, what discord follows! each thing
Meets in mere oppugnancy . . .
Strength should be lord of imbecility
And the rude son should strike his father dead:
Force should be right; or rather, right and wrong,
Between whose endless jar justice resides,
Should lose their names, and so should justice too.
Then everything includes itself in power,
Power into will, will into appetite;
And appetite, an universal wolf,
So doubly seconded with will and power,
Must make perforce an universal prey
And last eat up himself . . .
This chaos, when degree is suffocate,
Follows the choking.

Questions

Which documents in 6A stress the need for an established hierarchy and which concentrate on the need to obey the king? Which ones stress both?

6B Institutions

Think about the relative roles and importance of Monarch, Parliament and Council as you look at these documents.

1 THE KING'S PREROGATIVE, 1548

William Stanford (1509–1558) was a lawyer and MP. His 'Exposicion of the Kinges Prerogative' was much used by later legal writers.

'*Prerogativa*' is as much to say a privilege or preeminence that any person hath before another, which, as it is tolerable in some, so it is most to be permitted or allowed in a prince or sovereign governor of a realm. For besides that he is the most excellentest and worthiest part or member of the common body of the wealth, so is he also (through his good governance) the preserver, nourisher and defender of all the people, being the rest of the same body . . . For which cause the laws do attribute to him all honour, dignity, prerogative and preeminence, which prerogative doth not only extend to his own person but also to all other possessions, goods and chattels. As that his person shall be subject to no man's suit, his possessions cannot be taken away from him by any violence or wrongful disseisin, his goods and chattels are under no tribute, toil nor custom, nor otherwise distrainable . . .

2 DE REPUBLICA ANGLORUM, 1565

Sir Thomas Smith was English ambassador to France 1562–6, Fellow of Queens', Public Orator and Regius Professor of Civil Law at Cambridge. 'De Republica Anglorum' was published in 1583, six years after his death.

The monarch of England, king or queen, hath absolutely in his power the authority of war and peace, to defy what prince it shall please him and to bid him war, and again to reconcile himself and enter into league or truce with him, at his pleasure or the advice only of his Privy Council. His Privy Council be chosen also at the prince's pleasure . . . the prince doth participate to them all, or so many of them as he shall think good, such letters . . . as be sent to himself or his secretaries, and keepeth so many embassies and letters sent unto him secret as he will . . . In war time and in the field the prince hath also absolute power, so that his word is law; he may put to death . . . whom he shall think so to deserve, without process of law . . . The prince useth also absolute power in crying . . . the money of the realm by his proclamation only. The money is always stamped with the prince's image and title. The form . . . weight, fineness and baseness thereof is at the discretion of the prince . . . For all other measures and weights . . . they have accustomed to be established and altered by Parliament, and not by the prince's proclamation only. The prince useth also to dispense with laws made, whereas equity requireth a moderation to be had, and with pains for transgression of laws where the pain of the law is applied only to the prince. But where the forfeit . . . is part to the prince, the other part to the declarator, detector or informer, there the prince doth dispense for his own part only . . . The prince giveth all the chief and highest offices or magistracies of the realm, be it of judgment or dignity, temporal or spiritual, and hath the tenths and first fruits of all ecclesiastical promotions, except in the Universities and certain colleges which be exempt. All writs, executions and commandments be done in the prince's name . . . the supreme justice is done in the king's name and by his authority only. The prince hath the wardship and first marriage of all those that hold lands of him in chief.

3 COMMYNES ON THE KING AND PARLIAMENT

See 2A4.

The king cannot undertake (a campaign) without assembling his parliament, which is like our three estates. It is a very just and laudable institution, and therefore, the kings are stronger and better served when they (consult parliament) on such a matter. When these estates are assembled (the king) declares his intentions and asks for aid from his subjects; he cannot raise any tax in England except for an expedition to France or Scotland or some other comparable cause. They will grant them very willingly and liberally – especially for crossing to France!

4 LETTER FROM THOMAS CROMWELL, 1523

I, amongst other, have indured a parliament, which continued by the space of seventeen whole weeks, where we communed of war, peace, strife, contention, debate, murmur, grudge, riches, povery, penury, truth, falsehood, justice, equity, deceit, oppression, magnanimity, activity, force, attempraunce, treason, murder, felony ... and also how a commonwealth might be edified and also continued within our realm. Howbeit, in conclusion, we have done as our predecessors have been wont to do, that is to say, as well as we might, and left where we began.

5 CROMWELL TO THE MAYOR, SHERIFF AND COMMONALTY OF CANTERBURY, 18 MAY 1536

In my hearty wise I commend me unto you ... forasmuch as the King's pleasure and commandment is that Robert Darknall and John Bryges should be elect and chosen citizen or burgess for that city, by reason whereof my lord chancellor and I by our letters written unto you advertised you thereof, and ye, the same little or nothing regarding but rather contemning, have chosen other at your own wills and minds contrary to the King's pleasure and commandment in that behalf, whereat the King's Highness doth not a little marvel; wherefore, in avoiding further displeasure that might thereby ensue, I require you on the King's behalf that notwithstanding the said election ye proceed to a new and elect those other, according to the tenor of the former letters to you directed for that purpose, without failing to do so as the King's trust and expectation is in you and as ye intend to avoid his Highness displeasure at your peril. And if any person will obstinately gainsay the same, I require you to advertise me thereof that I may order him as the King's pleasure shall be in that case to command. Thus fare ye well ...

6 LETTER TO THOMAS CROMWELL, MARCH 1539

My lord admiral has showed me that your pleasure is to have a friend of yours to be one of the burgesses of the Parliament for the borough of Gatton in the shire of Surrey, whereof Sir Roger Copley is owner; wherein your lordship shall have your pleasure ... I had promised it unto a friend of mine, which, since I know your lordship's pleasure, at my desire is contented to leave it. So that now, if I might know the name of your lordship's friend, I shall send it to Mr Copley to the intent that he may cause the indentures to be made between the sheriff and him for the same.

7 ACTS OF THE PRIVY COUNCIL, GREENWICH, 10 JANUARY 1552

... A letter to the Mayor and burgess of Reading to elect a new burgess of Parliament instead of John Seymour, by them chosen in the place of William Grey, late deceased ...

8 GREENWICH 19 JANUARY 1552

... A letter to the Sheriff of Essex and Hertfordshire to elect a new knight of the shire, in lieu of Sir Henry Parker deceased, at the next county day, and to use the matter in such sort as Mr Sadleir may be elected and returned, for that he seemeth most fittest of any other person thereabouts ...

9 ELECTION RETURN, 1572

This Election return was made by Dame Dorothy Packington, lord of the borough of Aylesbury (enfranchised by charter 1554).

Know ye, me, the said Dame Dorothy Packington, to have chosen, named, and appointed my trusty and well-beloved Thomas Lichfield and George Burden esquires to be my burgesses of my said town of Aylesbury. And whatsoever the said Thomas and George, burgesses, shall do in the service of the Queen's Highness in that present parliament to be holden at Westminster ... I, the same Dame Dorothy Packington, do ratify and approve to be my own act, as fully and wholly as if I were or might be present there.

10 LORD KEEPER, SIR JOHN PUCKERING, TO PARLIAMENT, 1593

'Her Majesty hath ever more been most loth to call for the assembly of her people in Parliament and hath done the same but rarely and only upon most just, weighty and great occasions ... Her Most Excellent Majesty would have you all to know that . . . of her own disposition, she would yet still forbear, as she hath done, to draw you often together.'

11 SIR FRANCIS WALSINGHAM TO THE EARL OF LEICESTER, APRIL 1586

I have let my lords (of the Council) here understand how unkindly your lordship taketh it that you hear so seldom from them, and that since your charge there (the Low Countries) you never received any letter of advice from them. They answer, as it is truth, that, her Majesty retaining the whole direction of the causes of the country to herself and such advice as she receiveth underhand, they know not what to write or to advise. She can by no means, as I have heretofore written unto your lordship, endure that the causes of that country should be subject to any debate in Council, otherwise than as she herself shall direct, and therefore men forebear to do that which otherwise they would.

12 WILLIAM CECIL, LORD BURGHLEY, TO ROBERT CECIL, 1596

In such matters as I differ in opinion from her Majesty I will not change my opinion by affirming the contrary, for that were to offend God . . . but as a servant I will obey her Majesty's commandment and no wise contrary the same . . . after that I have performed my duty as a councillor.

Questions

1 How far does the material in 6B support the view of the Tudor monarchy or an absolute monarchy?
2 What picture of elections emerges from 6B5–9?
3 What idea of the power and privileges of Parliament are given by 6B3 and 6B10?
4 What of Elizabeth's attitude emerges from 6B10, 11 and 12?

6C Law and Order

His failure to maintain law and order contributed to Henry VI's downfall. Later rulers tried to avoid his weakness in this respect. Try to work out what means they had to impose their will and what methods they used.

1 PETITION TO THE KING, 1472

'in divers parts of this realm great abominable murders, robberies, extortions, oppression and other manifold maintainences, forcible entries . . . affrays, assaults be committed and done by such persons as either be of great might, or else favoured under persons of great power, in such wise that their outrageous elements as yet remain unpunished, insomuch that of late divers persons have been slain, some in Southwark, here nigh about the City, and some here at Westminster Gate, no consideration that your high presence is had here at your Palace of Westminster, nor that your high court of Parliament is here sitting, and is in a manner contumelious contempt of your highness . . . to the great emboldening of all rioters and misgoverned persons.'

2 THE BISHOP OF ROSS ON THE BORDERERS

The Borderers were those living in the North of England on the Scottish border.

. . . For as in time of war, they are readily reduced to extreme poverty by the almost daily inroads of the enemy, so, on the restoration of peace, they entirely neglect to cultivate their lands, though fertile, from the fear of the fruits of their labour being immediately destroyed by a new war. Whence it happens that they seek their subsistence by robberies, or rather by plundering and raping, for they are particularly averse to the shedding of blood; nor do they much concern themselves whether it be from Scots or English that they rob and plunder.

3 DEED OF RICHARD III CREATING HIS SON PRINCE OF WALES, 1483

'the land of Wales lies in a corner and differs in language and manners from the other people of the realm, for which reason it requires a special lord immediately under the king.'

4 A CRIMINAL ACT OF 1534

Forasmuch as the people of Wales and marches of the same, not dreading the good and wholesome laws and statutes of this realm, have of long time continued and persevered in perpetration and commission of divers and manifold thefts, murders, rebellions, wilful burning of houses and other scelerous deeds and abominable malefacts, to the high displeasure of God, inquietation of the King's well-disposed subjects and disturbance of the public weal; which malefacts and scelerous deeds be so rooted and fixed in the same people that they be not like to cease unless some sharp correction and punishment for redress and amputation of the premises be provided according to the demerits of the offenders . . .

5 AN ACT AGAINST VAGABONDS AND BEGGARS, 1495

It is worth noting that legislation dealing with begging and vagrancy came in before the dissolution of the monasteries (see also 6C6).

Forasmuch as the King's Grace most entirely desireth amongst all earthly things the prosperity and restfulness of this his land and his subjects of the same to live quietly and surefully to the pleasure of God and according to his laws, willing and always of his pity intending to reduce them thereunto by softer means than by such extreme rigour . . . considering also the great charges that should grow to his subjects for the bringing of vagabonds to the gaols . . . and the long abiding of them therein . . . His Highness will by the authority of this present Parliament it be ordained and enacted, that where such misdoers should be by examination committed to the common gaol . . . that the sheriff, mayors, bailiffs, high constables, and petty constables . . . within three days after this Act proclaimed, make due search, and take or cause to be taken all such vagabonds, idle and suspect persons, living suspiciously, and them so taken to be set in stocks, there to remain by the space of three days and three nights and there to have none other sustenance but bread and water; and after the said three days and three nights to be had out and set at large and then to be commanded to avoid the town; And if eftsoons he be taken in such default in the same town or township, then he to be set in the like wise in stocks by the space of six days with like diet as is before rehearsed; and if any person or persons give any form of meat or drink to the said misdoers being in stocks in the form aforesaid . . . that then they forfeit for every time so doing 12d.

And it is also ordained . . . that all manner of beggars not able to work . . . go, rest, and abide in his hundred where he last dwelled, or there where he is best known or born, there to remain . . . without begging out of the said hundred, upon pain to be punished as is beforesaid.

6 BEGGARS ACT OF 1531

Where in all places throughout this realm of England vagabonds and beggars have of long time increased and daily do increase . . . by the occasion of idleness, mother and root of all vices, whereby hath insurged and sprung . . . continual thefts, murders, and other heinous offences . . . to the great displeasure of God, the inquietation and damage of the King's people, and to the marvellous disturbance of the common weal of this realm . . . Be it therefore enacted . . . that the Justices of the Peace . . . shall make diligent search and enquiry of all aged, poor, and impotent persons which live or be compelled to live by alms of the charity of the people that be or shall be hereafter abiding . . . within the limits of their division . . . and the said Justices of Peace . . . shall have the power and authority by their discretions to enable to beg, within such . . . limits as they shall appoint, such of the said impotent persons which they shall find and think most convenient within the limits of their division to live of the charity and alms of the people, and to give in commandment to every such aged and impotent beggar that none of them shall beg without the limits to them so appointed, and shall also register and write the names of every such impotent beggar in a bill or roll indented, the one part to remain with themselves and the other part by them to be certified before the Justices of Peace at the next Sessions after such search . . . And if any such impotent person so authorised to beg do beg in any other place than within such limits that he shall be assigned unto, that then the Justices of Peace shall . . . punish all such persons by imprisonment in the stocks by the space of two days and two nights, giving them but only bread and water, and after that cause every such impotent person to be sworn to return again . . . where they be authorised to beg in.

7 LICENCING ACT, 1552

Forasmuch as intolerable hurts and troubles to the common wealth of this realm doth daily grow and increase through such abuses and disorders as are had and used in common ale-houses and other houses called tippling-houses; It is therefore enacted ... That the Justices of Peace within every shire, city, borough, town, corporate, franchise, or liberty within this realm, or two of them at the least, whereof one of them be of the Quorum, shall have full power and authority, by virtue of this Act, within every shire ... where they be Justices of Peace to remove, discharge, and put away common selling of ale and beer in the said common ale-houses and tippling-houses in such town or towns and places where they shall think meet and convenient; And that none ... shall be admitted or suffered to keep any common ale-house or tippling-house but such as be thereunto admitted and allowed in the open Sessions of the Peace, or else by two Justices of the Peace, whereof the one to be of the Quroum: And that the said Justices ... shall take bond and surety from time to time by recognisance of such as shall be admitted and allowed hereafter to keep any common ale-house or tippling-house, as well for and against the using of unlawful games as also for the using and maintenance of good order and rule to be had and used within the same, as by their discretion shall be thought necessary and convenient ... And the said Justices shall certify the same recognisance at the next Quarter Sessions of the Peace to be holden with the same shire ... where such ale-house or tippling-house shall be; the same recognisance there to remain of record before the Justices of Peace of that shire ... upon pain of forfeiture to the King for every such recognisance taken and not certified, £3. 6. 8 ... Provided alway, that in such towns and places where any fair ... shall be kept, that for the time only of the same fair ... it shall be lawful for every person ... to use the common selling of ale or beer ... as hath been done in times past ...

8 DE REPUBLICA ANGLORUM

Sir Thomas Smith's 'De Republica Anglorum' was written in 1565 and first published in 1583. (See 6B2.)

... the Justices of Peace be men elected out of the nobility, higher and lower, that is the dukes, marquises, barons, knights, esquires, and gentlemen, and of such as be learned in the laws, such and in such number as the Prince shall think meet, and in whom for wisdom and discretion he putteth his trust, inhabitants within the county; saving that some of the higher nobility and chief magistrates for honour's sake are put in all or in most of the commissions of all the shires of England. They have no time of their rule limited but by Commission from the Prince alterable at pleasure.

At the first they were but four, after eight now they come commonly to 30 or 40 in every shire, either by increase of riches, learning or activity in policy and government. So many more being found which have either will or power or both, are not too many to handle the affairs of the common wealth in this behalf ...

The Justices of the Peace be those in whom at this time for the repressing of robbers, thieves, and vagabonds, of privy complots and conspiracies, of riots and violences, and all other misdemeanours in the common wealth the Prince putteth his special trust. Each of them hath authority upon complaint to him made of any theft ... murder, violence, complots, riots, unlawful games, or any such disturbance of the peace and quiet of the realm, to commit the persons whom he supposeth offenders to the prison ... till he and his fellows do meet. A few lines signed in his hand is enough for that purpose: these do meet four times in the year ... to enquire of all the misdemeanours aforesaid.

The Justices of the Peace do meet also at other times by commandment of the Prince upon suspicion of war, to take order for the safety of the shire, sometimes to take muster of harness and able men, and sometimes to take order for the excessive wages of servants and labourers, for excess of apparel, for ... evil orders in alehouses ... for punishment of idle and vagabond persons ...

9 SPECIAL COMMISSION OF OYER AND TERMINER, 18 APRIL 1577

This document is in the 'bag of secrets', a hotch-potch of legal cases collected in the nineteenth century. In 1576 the gypsies described in it had been found to have forged papers and they and their associates were hanged. A commission of 'oyer and terminer' was the term used when JPs of the quorum (for instance, of 40 JPs four would be so designated) were commissioned to deal with cases of treason, murder and any felonies.

Thursday, 18 April, 19 Elizabeth. *Bucks.* Indictment found at Aylesbury, against *Rowland Gabriel*, *Laurence Bannester*, *Thomas Gabriel*, and *Christopher Jackson*, all late of Medmenham in the county of Bucks, Yeomen; and being of the age of 14 years and upwards, for that they for one month and upwards, viz., from the *1 February, 19 Elizabeth*, until the *17 March then next*, at Medmenham, and in other parts of the same county did feloniously keep company with *Richard Jackson*,

William Gabriel, *George Jackson*, and *Katherine Deago*, Widow, and other vagabonds, to the amount of sixteen and upwards, vulgarly called and calling themselves Egyptians, and counterfeiting, transforming, and altering themselves in dress, language, and behaviour to such vagabonds called Egyptians, contrary to the statute.
Thursday, 18 April, 19 Elizabeth. *Bucks*. Another Indictment against the said *Richard Jackson*, *William Gabriel*, *George Jackson*, and *Katherine Deago*, for keeping company for the space of one month and upwards with the persons named in the first Indictment, being gypsies, &c.

. . . the said *Rowland Gabriel*, *Laurence Bannester*, *Thomas Gabriel*, *Christopher Jackson*, *William Gabriel*, *George Jackson*, and *Katherine Deago*, are brought to the bar, and being severally arraigned, plead Not Guilty.

. . . Verdict, GUILTY.

10 A MAGISTRATE'S DUTIES, 1581

William Lambarde (1536–1601) was a JP for Kent and wrote 'Eirenarcha' from which this extract is taken, to explain a magistrate's duties. It was often reprinted.

Ye shall swear that, as justice of peace in the county of Kent, in all articles in the Queen's Commission to you directed, ye shall do equal right to the poor and to the rich after your cunning, wit and power, and after the laws and customs of the realm and statutes thereof made; and ye shall not be of counsel with any quarrel hanging before you; and that you hold your sessions after the form of statutes thereof made and the issues, fines and amercements that shall happen to be made and all forfeitures which shall fall before you ye shall cause to be entered without any concealment or embezzling and truly send them to the Queen's exchequer. Ye shall not let for gift or other cause, but well and truly ye shall do your office of justice of the peace in that behalf, and that you take nothing for your office of justice of peace to be done, but of the Queen, and fees accustomed and costs limited by statute; and ye shall not direct nor cause to be directed any warrant (by you to be made) to the parties, but ye shall direct them to the bailiffs of the said county or other the Queen's officers or ministers, or other indifferent persons to do execution thereof. So help you God and by the contents of this book.

11 ORDER FROM THE PRIVY COUNCIL TO THE LORDS LIEUTENANT OF NORFOLK AND SUFFOLK, 27TH JULY 1588

'see watches kept in every thoroughfare town to stay and apprehend all vagabonds and rogues are like to pass up and down to move disorders; and if any such be found with any manifest offence tending to stir troubles or rebellion, to cause such to be executed by martial law.'

Questions

1 What evidence is provided in 6C4–11 of the efforts of Tudor governments to keep law and order?
2 Do the JPs have a role apart from the maintenance of law and order?
3 Can you guess why the gypsies and their associates in 6C9 caused such worry? Do any of the names give a clue? You might look also at 3D, 7D and 10C.

6D Finance

In the past, as today, some might say, people wanted the government to carry out certain policies, but were unwilling to foot the bill. See if these documents give any idea of how government money was found and what it was spent on.

1 HOLINSHED ON 1490

See 3B2.

King Henry, sorely troubled in his mind . . . determining no more with peaceable message, but with open war to determine all controversies betwixt him and the French King, called his high court of Parliament and there declared the cause why he was justly provoked to make war against the Frenchmen, and thereupon desired them of their benevolent aid of men and money toward the maintenance thereof. The cause was so just that every man allowed it and to the setting forth of the war taken in hand for so necessary an occasion, every man promised his helping hand. The king commended them for their true and faithful hearts. And to the intent that he might spare the poorer sort of the commons (whom he ever desired to keep in favour) he thought good first to exact money of the richest sort by way of a benevolence.

Which kind of levying was first devised by King Edward the Fourth ... King Henry, following the like example, published abroad that by their open gifts he would measure and search their benevolent hearts and good minds towards him, and he that gave little to be esteemed according to his gift. By this it appeareth that whatsoever is practised for the prince's profit and brought to a precedent by matter of record, may be turned to the great prejudice of the people, if rulers in authority will so adjudge and determine it. But by this means King Henry got innumerable great sums of money, with some grudge of the people, for the extremity shewed by the commissioners in divers places.

2 FABYAN CONCORDENCE OF HISTORIE, 1473

This year this King, intending to make a voyage over sea into France, called before him his lords severally, both spiritual and temporal, to know their good minds, what of their free wills they would aid and depart with him toward the said voyage. And after he had so known their good disposition to himward, he then sent for the Mayor of London and his brethren, the aldermen, and them severally examined and exhorted to aid and assist him toward the said great journey, of which the mayor for his part granted £30, and of the aldermen some 20 marks, and the least £10. And that done, he sent for all the trusty commoners within the said city, and them exhorted in like manner, which for the more party granted to him the wages of half a man for a year, the which amounted to £4 11s. 4d. And after that he rode about the more part of the land, and used the people in such fair manner that he raised thereby notable sums of money, the which way of the levying of this money was after named a benevolence.

3 ACT FOR THE FEUDAL AID, 1504

Forasmuch as the King our Sovereign Lord is rightfully entitled to have two reasonable aids according to the laws of this land, the one aid for the making knight of the right noble Prince his first begotten son Arthur, late Prince of Wales deceased, whose soul God pardon, and the other aid for the marriage of the right noble Princess his first begotten daughter Margaret, now married unto the King of Scots; and also that his Highness hath sustained and borne great and inestimable charges for the defence of this his realm, and for a firm and a perpetual peace with the realm of Scotland, and many other countries and regions, to the great weal, comfort, and quietness of all his subjects; the Commons in this present Parliament assemblied, considering the premises, and that if the same aids should either of them be levied and had by reason of their tenures according to the ancient laws of this land, should be to them doubtful, uncertain, and great inquietness for the search and none knowledge of their several tenures and of their lands chargeable to the same, have made humble petition to his Highness graciously to accept and take of them the sum of £40,000 ... upon the which petition and offer so made his Grace benignly considering the good and loving mind of his subjects ... of his mere motion and abundant grace, and for the tender zeal and love that his Highness beareth to his said nobles and subjects ... by this present Act doth remit, pardon, and release ... all his right, title, and interest which his Grace hath ... by reason of the said aids or either of them. And also his Grace ... right well pleased with the said loving offer and grant of his subjects by them so made ... hath pardoned, remitted and released the sum of £10,000 ... and is content to accept ... the sum of £30,000 only in full recompence and satisfaction ...

4 HARPSFIELD'S LIFE OF THOMAS MORE

Harpsfield (1519?–1575) based his life of More, published in 1557, on material from Roper. A Roman Catholic, he was in the Tower from 1559.

... he was chosen a Burgess of the Parliament, in the later days of king Henry the seventh. At which time was there concluded a marriage between James, the king of Scots, and Lady Margaret, eldest daughter of the said king. And because great charges would grow to the king by reason of setting and sending forth the said Lady, he demanded of the Parliament about three fifteenths, as it hath been reported. Now considering the continual custom almost of all times and of all Princes at least from Henry the first ... and as well the great and present as the long durable commodity as it was then likely should ensue to this realm by the marriage, it was thought there would be small reluctation or repining against this Parliament.

Howbeit Master More ... disliked upon the said payment, and shewed openly his mind therein, and with such reasons and arguments debated and inforced the matter that the residue of the lower house condescended to his mind, and thereby was the Bill overthrown ...

The remembrance of this displeasure sank deeply into the king's heart, and bred great and heavy indignation against Master More, ready upon any small occasion to burst out against him. But yet did the king forbear, as well lest he might seem thereby to infringe and break the ancient liberty of the Parliament house for free speaking touching the public affairs (which would have been taken odiously) as also for that Master More had then little or nothing to lose. But yet there was a causeless quarrel devised against his father, whereby he was committed to the Tower, from whence he could not get himself out until the king had got out of his purse a fine of one hundred pounds.

5 AN ACT OF THE SUBSIDY OF TONNAGE AND POUNDAGE, 1559

I In their most humble wise show unto your most excellent Majesty, your poor and obedient subjects and Commons in this your present Parliament assembled, That where as well your noble Grandfather of worthy memory, King Henry the Seventh ... as other your right noble and famous progenitors, kings of this your realm of England, time out of mind, have had and enjoyed unto them by authority of Parliament, for the defence of the same now your realm, and the keeping and safeguard of the seas for the intercourse of merchandize, coming in or going out of the same your realm ... we, your said poor Commons, by the advice and consent of the Lords spiritual and temporal in this your present Parliament assembled, and by the authority of the same, to the intent aforesaid, give and grant to you our supreme Liege Lady and Sovereign, one subsidy called Tonnage, that is to say, of every ton of wine ... that shall or is come into your realm, by way of merchandise, the sum of 3s ... and also one other subsidy called Poundage, that is to say, of all manner of goods and merchandizes of every merchant, denizen, and alien ... carried out of this your realm or brought into the same by way of merchandize, of the value of every 20s. of the same goods and merchandize, 12d., and so after the rate; and of every 20s value of tin and pewter vessel carried out of this your realm by any and every merchant-alien, 12d over and above the 12d aforesaid.
II Except ... all manner of woollen cloth made within this your realm of England, and by any merchant-denizen, and not born alien, carried out of this your said realm; and all manner of wools ... and hides ... also carried out of this your realm; and all ... manner of fresh fish and bestial coming into the same your realm.
III And further we ... grant unto you ... of every merchant-denizen for every sack of wool £1.13s.4d ... and of every merchant-stranger ... £3.6s.8d.

6 CIRCULAR LETTER FROM THE COUNCIL TO THE LORDS-LIEUTENANT OF THE COUNTIES, 1588

After our very hearty commendations to your good lordship, we doubt not but both to your lordship and also to others that have any charge this last year in any part of government within this realm it is manifest, how necessary it was that this realm was defended both by sea and land in such sort as had been seen against the common potent enemy attempting to have invaded and made a conquest of the same: wherein the Queen's Majesty with the assistance of God's special favour and by expenses of great treasures, which she had most princely reserved for the maintenance of the state of this her realm, hath received great honour to herself, to her people singular comfort and safety, and hereby her enemies repulsed with great losses, ignominy and dishonour: yet nevertheless her Majesty in her wisdom seeth it necessary to make new preparations for the strengthening of all her forces, both by sea and land, to serve to withstand the new attempts of the enemy this year following ...

And for the more speedy help to this, it is thought by her Majesty and us of her council, that presently means be made to provide some convenient sum of money by way of loan ... of her good and faithful subjects, as heretofore hath been yielded unto her Majesty in times of less need and danger, and yet always fully repaid. And ... we have thought meet by her Majesty's direction to commend the care hereof to your lordship, having charge by her Majesty, as her lieutenant in the said shire; praying your lordship that without any delay your lordship will consider either by your own knowledge or with secret conference with some such as you think to be well affected to this service and are of knowledge to inform your lordship therein, how of each particular person, being men of lands or wealth in goods, such particular sums might be reasonably required by her Majesty's letter under her privy seal by way of loan in that whole county ...

7 LETTER TO THOMAS LAWLEY FROM ELIZABETH I

Trusty and well-beloved, we greet you well. Whereas for the better withstanding of the intended invasion of this realm, upon the great preparations made by the King of Spain both by sea and land the last year, the same having been such as the like was never prepared at any time against this realm, we were enforced for the defence of the same and of our good and loving subjects to be at infinite charges both by sea and land, especially for that same intended invasion tended directly to the conquest of the realm; and finding also by such intelligences as we daily receive that the like preparations are now making for the like intent the next year by the said King, for the withstanding whereof it shall be necessary for us to prepare both by sea and land, which cannot be performed without great charges. We have therefore thought it expedient, having always found our good and loving subjects most ready upon such like occasion to furnish us by way of a loan of some convenient portions of money agreeable with their estates (which we have a mind always to repay), to have recourse to them in like manner at this present. And therefore having made choice in the several parts of our realm of a number able to do us this kind of service (which is not refused betwixt neighbour and neighbour), amongst this number we have also particularly named you, Thomas Lawley, for your ability and good will you bear to us and our realm, to be one. Wherefore we require you to pay to our use the sum of £25 to such person as by our lieutenant of that county shall be named to you by his hand writing. And these our letters of privy seal . . . shall be sufficient to bind us, our heirs and successors, duly to repay the said sum . . .

Given under our privy seal at our palace of Westminster the xxth day of February in the xxxIst year of our reign.

8 DEBATES ON MONOPOLIES

The following extracts are from Townsend's Journals of 1601 detailing committee meetings of November 21 and 25.

(November 21) *Sir Robert Wroth*: There have been divers patents granted since the last parliament; these are now in being, viz. the patents for currants, iron, powder, cards, horns, ox-shin bones, train-oil, transportation of leather, lists of cloth, ashes, bottles, glasses, bags, shreds of gloves, aniseed, vinegar, sea-coals, steel, aquavitae, brushes, pots, salt, salt-petre, lead, accedence, oil, calamint stone, oil of blubber, fumathoes, or dried pillchers in the smoke, and divers others.

Upon reading of the patents aforesaid, Mr. Hackwell of Lincoln's Inn stood up and asked thus: Is not bread there?

(November 25) *The Speaker*: It pleased her Majesty to command me to attend upon her . . . from whom I am to deliver to you all her Majesty's most gracious message, sent by my unworthy self . . . that partly by intimation of her council, and partly by divers petitions that have been delivered unto her both going to chapel and also walking abroad, she understood that divers patents, that she had granted, were grievous to her subjects; and that the substitutes of the patents had used great oppression. But, she said, she never assented to grant anything which was '*malum in se*'. And if in the abuse of her grant there be anything evil, which she took knowledge there was, she would herself take present order of reformation thereof. I cannot express to you the apparent indignation of her Majesty towards these abuses . . . She said her kingly prerogative was tender; and . . . desireth us not to . . . doubt of her careful reformation . . . some should be presently repealed, some suspended, and none put into execution but such as should first have a trial according to the law for the good of the people.

Questions

1 a Do 6D1 and 2 give help in deciding whether 'the new monarchy' (chapter 2) began with Edward IV or Henry VII?
  b What do they show about the king's need of money?
  c How do they relate to 6D6 and 7?
2 What picture of Henry VII emerges from 6D2–4?
3 Explain the term *denizen*, which is used several times in 6D5.
4 Does 6D8 confirm or modify the impression you gained from 6B3 and 10–12 of the relative power of monarch and parliament?

7 Religion

Came reformation fast or slow?
From above or from below?

This jingle I have made up reflects the current debate on the Reformation. Were the changes in the church imposed on the nation by the monarch, or the result of the popular growth of Protestantism? Revisionist historians favour the view that changes in the Church were imposed by the monarch rather than reflecting an upsurge of Protestant opinion among the people. In the reign of Henry VII it was unclear whether Protestant ideas were spreading due to Lollardy (based on Wyclif's teaching), or to Luther's influence. (In the reign of Richard II, Wyclif had been protected by John of Gaunt. But under Henry VIII, as under the Lancastrians, the Lollards – seen as Wyclif's followers – came to be persecuted as heretics.)

7A Henry VII

See if these three documents incline you to believe Reformation came from 'below' and if you can get any idea of the beliefs of early Tudor heretics.

1 STEPHEN SWALLOW'S WORDS ADMITTED BEFORE THE ARCHBISHOP OF CANTERBURY, 1489

Swallow's words suggest he was a Lollard.

'the Pope is an old whore, sitting upon many waters, having a cup of poison in his hand. Also that the Pope is Antichrist, and all cardinals, archbishops, bishops, priests and religious men be the disciples of Antichrist ... That the Church of Rome is the synagogue of Satan.'

2 ROBERT FABYAN'S 'GREAT CHRONICLE OF LONDON', 1494

See 1C3.

Upon the xxviii day of April was an old cankered heretic, weak-minded for age, named Joan Boughton, widow, and mother unto the wife of Sir John Young, which daughter, as some reported, had a great smell of an heretic after the mother, burnt in Smithfield. This woman was iiii score years of age or more, and held viii opinions of heresy which I pass over, for the hearing of them is neither pleasant nor fruitful. She was a disciple of Wyclif, whom she accounted for a saint, and held so fast and firmly viii of his xii opinions that all the doctors of London could not turn her from one of them. When it was told to her that she should be burnt for her obstinacy and false belief, she set nought at their words but defied them, for she said she was so beloved with God and His holy angels that all the fire in London should not hurt her. But on the morrow a bundle of faggots and a few reeds consumed her in a little while; and while she might cry she spake often of God and Our Lady, but no man could cause her to name Jesus, and so she died. But it appeared that she left some of her disciples behind her, for the night following, the more part of the ashes of that fire that she was burnt in were had away and kept for a precious relic in an earthen pot.

3 FROM 'REGISTRUM DE RICARDI MAYEW', 1505

This is taken from a bishop's register.

In the name of God, Amen. I, John Crofte, of the paryshe of Erdisley, withyn the diocese of Hereford, wilfully knowledge before you ... commissaries of the reverend father in Godde, Richard, byshop of Hereford ... that I have hadde in my ward and kepyng diverse bookys conteynyng heresies and errouris ageyn Cristen feyth and the determination of all holy churche, which bookys I have radde and declared oftyn tymes prively and opynly, holidays and festfull dayes, before many diverse persons, redyng, declaryng and techyng agaynst the blessed sacrament of the awter othirwise then me oghte to have done, also agaynste the sacrament of confession to prestis and penance for satisfaction of syn, also agaynst the solemnization of the sacrament of matrimony, callyng it exorzismes and coninzations. Also, I have redde and declared agaynst oure holy father, the pope, showyng that he hath not the power of byndyng and lowsyng that Criste gave to Petur, but in usurping that power upon him he makyth hymselfe Antecriste. Also I have redde and taught agayn the veneration and worshipyng of images standyng in churchis, calling them maummetis, and agayn the shrynyng of seyntis bonys in goold and sylver, and hangyng aboute thaym the same. These errouris, heresies, and false opynyons afore rehearsed, dampned and reproved by autorite of all holy church, in especiall, and all other in generall, I forswere, abjure, and forsake . . .

Question

If you did not believe reformation came from 'below' what arguments could you cite to support this view after looking at 7A1–3?

7B Henry VIII

Ask yourself if the following documents support the idea that the English Reformation was imposed from 'above'. (See 4B.)

1 OBEDIENCE OF A CHRISTIAN MAN, 1528

William Tyndale (d. 1536) translated the New Testament, Pentateuch and Job, using the vulgate and the work of Erasmus and Luther. He was lured away from the house of the Merchant Adventurers and put to death for heresy. Extracts 1 and 2 are from his book 'Obedience of a Christian Man and how Christian Rulers ought to govern'.

'If the Scripture were in the mother tongue,' they will say, 'then would the lay people understand it every man after his own ways.' Wherefore serveth the curate but to teach them the right way? Wherefore were the holidays made but that the people should come and learn? Are ye not abominable schoolmasters in that ye take so great wages, if ye will not teach? If ye would teach, how could ye do it so well and with so great profit as when the lay people have the Scripture before them in their mother tongue? For then should they see, by the order of the text, whether thou juggledest or not. And they would believe it because it is the Scripture of God, though thy living be never so abominable. Where now, because your living and your preaching are so contrary and because they grope out in every sermon your open and manifest lies and smell your insatiable covetousness, they believe you not when you preach truth. But alas, the curates themselves (for the most part) wot no more what the New or Old Testament meaneth than do the Turks. Neither know they of any more than that they read at masse, matins and evensong, which yet they understand not. Neither care they but even to mumble up so much every day (as the pie and popinjay speak they wot not what) to fill their bellies with all. If they will not let the lay-man have the word of God in his mother tongue, yet let the priest have it, which, for a great part of them, do understand no Latin at all; but sing and say patter all day with the lips only that which the heart understandeth not.

2 FROM TYNDALE'S PREFACE TO HIS TRANSLATION OF GENESIS, 1530

. . . our wily and malicious hypocrites . . . say, some of them, that it is impossible to translate the scripture into English; some, that it is not lawful for the lay-people to have it in their mother-tongue; some, that it would make them all heretics; as it would, no doubt, from many things which they of long time have falsely taught; and that is the whole cause whereof they forbid it, though they other cloaks pretend: and some . . . say that it would make them rise against the king, whom they themselves . . . never yet obeyed . . .

A thousand books had they lever to be put forth against their abominable doings and doctrine, than that the scripture should come to light. For as long as they may keep that down, they will so darken the right way with the mist of their sophistry, and so tangle them that either rebuke or despise their abominations, with arguments of philosophy, and with worldly similitudes and apparent reasons of natural wisdom, and with wresting the scripture unto their own purpose, clean contrary unto the process, order, and meaning of the text; and so delude them in descanting upon it with allegories, and amaze them, expounding it in many senses before the unlearned lay-people, (when it hath but one simple literal sense, whose light the owls cannot abide) that, though thou feel in thine heart, and art sure, how that all is false that they say, yet couldst thou not solve their subtle riddles.

Which thing only moved me to translate the new Testament. Because I had perceived by experience how that it was impossible to establish the lay-people in any truth, except the scriptures were plain laid before their eyes in their mother-tongue, that they might see the process, order and meaning of the text: for else, whatsoever truth is taught them, these enemies of all truth quench it again . . .

3 MEMOIRS OF SIR JAMES MELVILLE (1535–1617), FIRST PUBLISHED 1683

See 3D6.

King Henry VIII of England being discontent with the Pope, for refusing to grant the divorce from his wife, Queen Catherine of Castile; for revenge he looked through his fingers at the preachers of the Reformed Religion, who had studied in Dutchland under Martin Luther, and were lately come to England. In process of time the hatred betwixt the King and the Pope came to so great a length, that he proclaimed himself 'Head of the kirk of England', and discharged St. Peter's pennies to be paid from that time forth; with a strict command to all his subjects no manner of way to acknowledge the Pope. He obtained the said divorce from his own clergy, marrying another; which occasioned to him the hatred of the Pope, the Emperor and King of Spain, and all their assistants.

4 AN ACT MAKING THE KING HEAD OF THE CHURCH

Albeit the King's Majesty justly and rightfully is and ought to be the supreme head of the Church of England, and so is recognised by the clergy of this realm in their Convocations; yet nevertheless for corroboration and confirmation thereof, and for increase of virtue in Christ's religion within this realm of England, and to repress and extirp (1) all errors, heresies and other enormities and abuses heretofore used in the same, be it enacted by authority of this present Parliament that the King our Sovereign Lord, his heirs and successors kings of this realm, shall be taken, accepted and reputed the only Supreme Head in earth of the Church of England called 'Anglicana Ecclesia', and shall have and enjoy annexed and united to the imperial crown of this realm as well the title and style thereof, as all honours dignities, preeminences, jurisdictions, privileges, authorities, immunities, profits and commodities, to the said dignity of Supreme Head of the same Church belonging and appertaining. And that our said Sovereign Lord, his heirs and successors . . . shall have full power and authority from time to time to visit, repress, redress, reform, order, correct, restrain, and amend all such errors, heresies . . . which by any manner spiritual authority or jurisdiction ought or may lawfully be reformed, repressed, ordered . . . most to the pleasure of Almighty God, the increase of virtue in Christ's religion, and for the conservation of the peace, unity, and tranquility of this realm: any usage, custom, foreign laws, foreign authority, prescription, or anyother thing or things to the contrary hereof notwithstanding.

1 root out.

5 ON THE ACT OF SUPREMACY

Gardiner, Bishop of Winchester, was a conservative ready to accept royal ecclesiastical supremacy. His 'de vera obedienta' was a major tract of the late 1530s on obedience to the monarch – a theme insisted upon by Cromwell.

It seems worth while for me to look here at a question which is commonly studied, and is spoken of at this time in almost all men's hands and mouths: whether the agreement of the English is based upon God's law, when they declare and proclaim the most victorious and most noble prince Henry VIII, King of England and France, defender of the faith and Lord of Ireland, to be the Supreme Head of the Church of England; and by which they give him authority, by free election in the open court of Parliament, to make use of his own right and to call himself Supreme Head of the Church of England in name as well as deed.

There was nothing new in this: they only wished to have the power that God's law gives a prince more clearly expressed and given a fitter name. The purpose was to eliminate that false opinion from the minds of the common people by which the false pretended power of the bishop of Rome had for years blinded them to the great limitations on the king's authority – which all men are bound to wish and use all their power to see kept safe, restored and defended from wrongs . . .

Seeing the Church of England consists of the people that are included in the word 'kingdom', and the king is called their head, since he is called the head of the kingdom of England, shall he not also be the head of the same men when they are called the Church of England?

6 A LETTER FROM CRANMER TO LORD LISLE, 27 APRIL 1535

. . . it is not the person of the Bishop of Rome which usurpeth the name of the pope is so much to be detested, but the very papacy and see of Rome, which both by their laws suppressed Christ and set up the Bishop of that see as a god of this world . . . And this is the chief thing to be detested in that See; that is hath brought the professors of Christ into such an ignorance of Christ. And besides this, he hath consumed and wasted innumerable goods of all Christendom for the maintenance of that estate, to the intolerable impoverishment of all Christian realms; which said dominion and power, with other corrupt doctrines by them invented, is the thing rather to be abhorred than the person; yea, and the person also, if he prosecute to maintain the same.

7 AN ACT EXTINGUISHING THE AUTHORITY OF THE BISHOP OF ROME, 1536

Forasmuch as notwithstanding the good and wholesome laws, ordinances, and statutes heretofore enacted . . . for the extirpation, abolition, and extinguishment, out of this realm and other his Grace's dominions, seignories, and countries, of the pretended power and usurped authority of the Bishop of Rome, by some called the Pope, used within the same or elsewhere concerning the same realm, dominions, seignories or countries, which did obfuscate and wrest God's holy word and testament a long season from the spiritual and true meaning thereof, to his worldly and carnal affections, as pomp, glory, avarice, ambition, and tyranny, covering and shadowing the same with his human and political devices, traditions and inventions, set forth to promote and establish his only dominion, both upon the souls and also the bodies and goods of all Christian people, excluding Christ out of his kingdom and rule of man his soul as much as he may, and all other temporal kings and princes out of their dominions which they ought to have by God's law upon the bodies and goods of their subjects; whereby he did not only rob the King's Majesty, being only the Supreme Head of this his realm of England immediately under God, of his honour, right and preeminence due unto him by the law of God, but spoiled his realm yearly of innumerable treasure, and with the loss of the same deceived the King's loving and obedient subjects, persuading to them, by his laws, bulls . . . as . . . many were seduced and conveyed unto superstitious and erroneous opinions; so that the King's Majesty, the Lords spiritual and temporal, and the Commons . . . were forced . . . for the public weal of this realm to exclude that foreign pretended power, jurisdiction, and authority, used and usurped within this realm . . . yet it is come to the knowledge of the King's Highness . . . how that divers seditious and contentious persons, being imps of the said Bishop of Rome . . . do . . . preach . . . the advancement and continuance of the said Bishop's feigned . . . authority . . .

8 CUTHBERT TUNSTAL TO REGINALD POLE, 1536

Cuthbert Tunstal was another Orthodox bishop ready to accept royal supremacy. Reginald Pole, grandson of George, Duke of Clarence, and distant cousin to Henry VIII, could not agree. In 1553, because of his royal blood, Pole was considered to be a possible husband for Mary I. He became her Archbishop of Canterbury instead.

You suppose that the King's grace . . . in taking upon him the title of Supreme Head . . . intendeth to separate his church of England from the unity of the whole body of Christendom . . . You do err too far. His full purpose and intent is to see the laws of Almighty God purely and sincerely kept and observed in his realm, and not to separate himself or his realm any wise from the unity of Christ's Catholic Church.

9 AN ACT OF 1556

This is 'An Act whereby all religious houses of monks, canons and nuns which may not dispend manors, lands, tenements and hereditaments above the clear yearly value of £200 are given to the King's Highness, his heirs and successor, for ever'.

Forasmuch as manifest sin, vicious, carnal and abominable living, is daily used and committed among the little and small abbeys, priories and other religious houses of monks, canons and nuns, where the congregation of such religious persons is under the number of 12 persons, whereby the governors of such religious houses and their convent spoil, destroy, consume and utterly waste as well their churches, monasteries, priories, principal houses, farms, granges, lands ... as the ornaments of their churches and their goods and chattels to the high displeasure of Almighty God, slander of good religion, and to the great infamy of the King's Highness and the realm if redress should not be had thereof; and albeit that many continual visitations hath been ... for an honest and charitable reformation of such unthrifty, carnal and abominable living, yet ... their vicious living shamelessly increaseth and ... by a cursed custom so rooted and infested ... so that without such small houses be utterly suppressed and the religious persons therein committed to great and honourable monasteries ... there can be no reformation in this behalf. In consideration whereof the King's most royal Majesty, being supreme head in earth under God of the Church of England, daily finding and devising the increase, advancement and exaltation of true doctrine and virtue in the said church, to the only glory and honour of god and in the total extirping and destruction of vice and sin ... considering also that divers and great solemn monasteries of this realm wherein ... religion is right well kept and observed, be destitute of such full numbers of religious people as they ought and may keep, hath thought good that a plain declaration should be made ... to the Lords ... as to ... the Commons ... whereupon the ... Lords and Commons by a deliberation finally be resolved that it is ... much more to the pleasure of Almighty God and for the honour of this his realm that the possessions of such religious houses, now being spent, spoiled and wasted for increase and maintenance of sin, should be used and converted to better uses, and the unthrifty religious persons so spending the same to be compelled to reform their lives; and thereupon most humbly desire the King's Highness that it may be enacted by the authority of this present Parliament, that his Majesty shall have and enjoy to him and to his heirs for ever all and singular monasteries, priories and other religious houses of monks, canons and nuns, of what kinds or diversities of habits, rules or orders so ever they be called or named, which have not in lands and tenements, rents, tithes, portions and other hereditaments above the clear yearly value of two hundred pounds; and in like manner shall have and enjoy all the sites and circuits of every such religious houses, and all and singular the manors, granges, lands, rents, services, tithes, pensions, portions, churches, chapels, advowsons, patronages, annuities ... and other hereditaments appertaining ... to every such monastery, priory or religious house not having ... the said clear yearly value of two hundred pounds ...

And ... the King's Highness shall have and enjoy to his own proper use all the ornaments, jewels, goods, chattels and debts which appertained to any of the chief governors of the said monasteries or religious houses ...

In consideration ... his Majesty is pleased and contented of his most excellent charity to provide to every chief head and governor of every such religious house during their lives such yearly pensions or benefices as for their degrees and qualities shall be reasonable and convenient ... the chief governors ... of honourable great monasteries shall take ... into their houses ... such number of the persons of the said convents as shall be assigned by the King ...

10 HALL'S CHRONICLE

See 1B1 and 1D5.

The fourth day of February the King held his High court of Parliament at Westminster, in the which was many good and wholesome statutes and laws made and concluded. And in this time was given unto the King by the consent of the great and fat abbeys all religious houses that were of the value of 300 mark and under, in hope that their great monasteries should have continued still. But even at that time one said in the Parliament House that these were as thorns, but the great abbots were putrified old oaks, and they must needs follow.

11 PROCEEDS FROM THE DISSOLUTION OF THE MONASTERIES

These figures are taken from the acounts of Thomas Pope, Treasurer of the Court of Augmentations, 24 April 1536 to Michaelmas, 1538.

	£
From receivers of purchased lands	27,732 2 9
From sale of gold and silver plate	6,987 8 11
From fines for exemption from suppression	5,948 6 8
From sale of lands	29,847 16 5

Religion

From fines for leases	1,006 17 0
From other sources	95 4 4
TOTAL RECEIPTS	71,617 16 1½
Less:	
Expenses, pensions, debts of monastic houses etc	12,701 14 7¾
Errors and auditing cost	60 13 2
TOTAL DEDUCTIONS	12,762 7 9¾
BALANCE OUTSTANDING	58,855 8 3¾

12 DAVELGARTHEN

Davelgarthen was an image of a saint in St. Asaph's, believed locally to ride into hell and release the souls of the damned. Friar Forest, Catherine of Aragon's confessor, publically opposed Henry's divorce. In 1532 he took the oath of supremacy, but, in 1538, he became the only orthodox Catholic accused of heresy by Protestants in sixteenth century England. The rest were treated as traitors. A wooden image of Davelgarthen was on the scaffold when he was burnt.

David Davelgarthen,
As sayeth the Welshmen,
Fetched outlaws out of the Hell.
Now he is come, with spear and shield,
In harness to burn at Smithfield,
For in Wales he may not dwell.
And Forest the friar,
that obstinate liar.
That wilfully shall be dead,
In his contumacy
the Gospel doth deny,
and the King to be Supreme Head.

13 INJUNCTIONS TO THE CLERGY, 1538

Cromwell issued injunctions in his capacity as vicegerent to the Supreme Head of the Church of England.

... that ye shall provide ... one Book of the whole Bible of the largest volume in English, and the same set up in some convenient place within the said Church that ye have use of, whereas your Parishioners may most commodiously resort to the same and read it; the charge of which Book shall be ratably born between you, the Parson, and the Parishoners aforesaid, that is to say the one half by you, and the other half by them.

Item: That ye shall discourage no man privily or apertly from the reading or hearing of the said Bible, but shall expressly provoke, stir, and exhort every person to read the same, as that which is the very lively word of God, that every Christian man is bound to embrace, believe, and follow, if he look to be saved: admonishing them nevertheless to avoid all contention, altercation therein, and to use an honest sobriety in the inquisition of the true sense of the same, and refer the explication of the obscure places to men of higher judgement in Scripture.

Item: That ye shall every Sunday and Holy Day through the year openly and plainly recite to your Parishoners, twice or thrice together or oftener, if need require, one particle or sentence of the Pater Noster, or creed in English to the intent that they may learn the same by heart. And so from day to day, to give them one little lesson or sentence of the same, till they have learned the whole Pater Noster and creed in English by rote. And as they be taught every sentence of the same by rote, ye shall expand and declare the understanding of the same unto them, exhorting all parents and householders to teach their children and servants the same, as they are bound in conscience to do. And that done, ye shall declare unto them the Ten Commandments, one by one, every Sunday and Holy-day, till they likewise be perfect in the same ...

14 HENRY VIII TO HOUSE OF LORDS, CHRISTMAS EVE 1545

'no Prince in the world more favoureth his subjects than I do you, nor no subjects or commons more love and obey their sovereign lord then I perceive you do me ... what charity is amongst you, when one calleth the other heretic and Anabaptist, and he calleth him again Papist, hypocrite and Pharisee ... Some be too stiff in their old Mumpsimus, other be too busy and curious in their new Sumpsimus ... I, whom God hath appointed his Vicar and high minister here, will see these divisions extinct and these enormities corrected, according to my duty ... not to dispute and make Scripture a railing and a taunting stock against priests and preachers, as many light persons do. I am very sorry to know and hear how unreverently that most precious jewel, the word of God, is disputed, rhymed, sung and jangled in every alehouse and tavern, contrary to the true meaning and doctrine of the same.'

80 *Religion*

15 'THE POPE SUPPRESSED BY HENRY VIII', A CONTEMPORARY WOODCUT

Religion   81

16 EDWARD VI AND THE POPE, ARTIST UNKNOWN

In this picture the dying Henry VIII points to his son. The Duke of Somerset, on Edward's left, has Warwick and Cranmer to his left. The defeated Pope has the words 'Idolatry and Superstition' behind him. He has been overcome by the Bible. The destruction of idols is shown in the top right of the picture. The painting is possibly from 1548, after orders for the destruction of religious images had been given.

Questions

1 How far do the documents in 7A and B support the argument that there was popular pressure for reform of the church?
2 **a** Why did Tyndale think the Bible should be available in English (7B1–2)?
   b What arguments does he claim were used by the opponents of a vernacular Bible?
   c How does he regard the clergy? (See too 6A2.)
3 Using all the documents in 7B see what motives you can find for the reformation in England and Wales. What seem to have been the major changes in the church in Henry VIII's reign?
4 How effective are 7B15 and 16 as propaganda to a largely illiterate population? See how many similarities you can find between them.

7C Edward VI and Mary I

The extent to which England was Protestant by 1558 is the subject of yet another dispute between historians. (See 4C2.)

1 HOOPER TO BULLINGER, 1549

Hooper (d. 1555) was a Marian martyr, despite opposing the accession of Lady Jane Grey. His Protestant views drove him from England 1539–49. He was a favourite Bishop of Edward VI.

How dangerously our England is afflicted by heresies . . . There are some who deny that man is endued with a soul different from that of a beast, and subject to decay. Alas, not only are those heresies reviving among us that were formerly dead and buried, but new ones are springing up every day. There are such libertines and wretches who are daring enough in their conventicles not only to deny that Christ is the Messiah and saviour of the world, but also to call that blessed seed a mischevious fellow and deceiver of the world. On the other hand, a great portion of the kingdom so adheres to the popish faction, as altogether to set at nought God and the lawful authority of magistrates; so that I am greatly afraid of a rebellion and civil discord.

2 ACTES AND MONUMENTS OF THE CHRISTIAN RELIGION

John Foxe (1516–87), a Marian exile, wrote 'Actes and Monuments of the Christian Religion' on his return. It deals with martyrs up to his own day and stresses the continuity of the protestant tradition in England from Wyclif onwards. First published in 1563, there were new editions in 1570, 1576 and 1583. After the Bible it was the most popular book in England for a century.

In November (1553) the people, and especially the churchmen, perceiving the queen so eagerly set upon her old religion, they likewise for their parts, to show themselves no less forward to serve the queen's appetite (as the manner is of the multitude, commonly to frame themselves after the humour of the prince and time present) began in their choirs to set up the pagaent of St. Katherine, and of St. Nicholas, and of their processions in Latin, with all their old solemnity with their gay gardeviance (gear) and grey amices.

3 ROBERT PARKYN, PRIEST OF ALLDWYCH LE STREET IN YORKSHIRE, 1553

Then began holy church to rejoice in god, singing both with heart and tongue, *Te Deum laudamus*, but heretical persons, (as there was many) rejoiced nothing threat. Ho, it was joy to hear and see how those carnal priests (which had led their lives in fornication with their whores and harlots) did lour and look down, when they were commanded to leave and foresake their concubines and harlots and do open penance according to the canon law, which then took effect.

4 WRIOTHESLEY'S 'CHRONICLE'

See 4C7.

Monday the 2 of April, 1554, the Parliament began at Westminster . . . the queen's Majesty riding in her parliament robes from her palace of Whitehall to St. Peter's church with all her lords spiritual and temporal in their robes, and there heard mass of the Holy Ghost and a sermon . . .

Sunday the 8 of April was a villainous fact done in Cheap early. . . . A dead cat having a cloth like a vestment of the priest at mass with a cross on it afore, and another behind put on it; the crown of the cat shorn, a piece of paper like a singing cake out between the forefeet of the said cat bound together, which cat was hanged on the post of the gallows in Cheap beyond the Cross in the parish of St. Matthew, and a bottle hanged by it; which cat was taken down at 6 of the clock in the morning and carried to the Bishop of London, and he caused it to be shewed openly in the sermon time at Paul's Cross in the sight of all the audience there present.

The Lord Mayor, with his brethren the aldermen of the City of London, caused a proclamation to be made that afternoon that whosoever could utter or shew the author of the said fact should have £6.13.4d. for his pains, and a better reward with hearty thanks. But at that time, after much enquiry and search made, it could not be known, but divers persons were had to prison for suspicions of it.

5 VENETIAN AMBASSADOR, 1555

'many persons are of opinion that the example afforded by the nobility who ... showed their great readiness to assist at the thanksgiving and high mass, will do no less now to confirm the people in their obedience to the church than any sermon preached last year.'

6 UNNAMED LADY TO BONNER, BISHOP OF LONDON, 1555

'The blood of the martyrs is the seed of the gospel; when one is put to death a thousand doth rise for him.'

Questions

1 What different views is Hooper objecting to in 7C1?
2 Which documents in 7C support the view that England was still a Catholic country in the mid-sixteenth century, and which the view that it was Protestant? Are there other possible interpretations of this material?

7D The Elizabethan Settlement?

While reading this section see if you think the Settlement of 1559 was Catholic or Protestant, if it settled anything, and if you can get any idea of Elizabeth's views.

1 SIR JOHN HAYWARD'S 'ANNALS OF THE FIRST FOUR YEARS OF QUEEN ELIZABETH'

See 2A24.

1559. Not onely images, but roode-loftes, relickes, sepulchres, bookes, banneres, coopes, vestments, altar-cloathes wer, in diverse places, committed to the fire, and that with such shouting, and applause of the vulgar sort, as if it had beene the sacking of some hostile city.

2 GODDRED GYLBY'S PREFACE TO HIS TRANSLATION OF AN EPISTLE OF CICERO, 1561

Men are now a days here in England glutted as it wer with gods worde, and therfore almost ready to vomit up again yt which thei have receyved, lothing ye sermons and despising the preachers, some turning to curious arts ... som Atheistes ...

3 APOLOGY OF THE CHURCH OF ENGLAND

John Jewel (1522–71), a Marian exile, and Bishop of Salisbury in 1560, wrote 'Apologia pro Ecclesia Anglicana' in 1562. Alice Bacon (Francis's mother) translated this from Latin into English in 1564.

We have come as near as we possibly could to the Church of the apostles and of the old ... bishops and fathers, which Church we know hath ... been sound and perfect ... a pure virgin, spotted as yet with no idolatry nor with any foul or shameful fault; and have directed according to their customs and ordinances not only our doctrine but also the sacraments and the forms of common prayer.

4 THE PURITAN ARTICLES IN CONVOCATION, 1563

Strype (1643–1735) amassed many Tudor documents and edited Stowe's Survey. This extract is taken from his 'Annals of the Reformation'.

I That all the Sundays in the year and the principal feasts of Christ be kept holy days; and all the other holy days to be abrogated.
II That in all parish churches the minister in common prayer turn his face towards the people; and there distinctly read the divine service appointed, where all the people assembled may hear and be edified.
III That in ministering the sacrament of baptism, the ceremony of making the cross in the child's forehead maybe omitted, as tending to superstition.
IV That forasmuch as divers communicants are not able to kneel during the time of the communion, for age, sickness, and sundry other infirmities, and some also superstitiously both kneel and knock; that order of kneeling may be left to the discretion of the ordinary within his jurisdiction.
V That it be sufficient for the minister, in time of saying divine service and ministering the sacraments, to use a

surplice; and that no minister say service or minister the sacraments but in a comely garment or habit.
VI That the use of organs be removed.

5 THE PAPAL BULL AGAINST ELIZABETH, 1570

... Elizabeth, the pretended queen of England and the servant of crime, ... with whom as in a sanctuary the most pernicious of all have found refuge. This very woman, having seized the crown and monstrously usurped the place of the Supreme Head of the Church in all England together with the chief authority ... belonging to it ... has once again reduced this kingdom ... to a miserable ruin.

... She has removed the royal Council, composed of the nobility of England, and filled it with obscure men, being heretics; oppressed the followers of the Catholic faith ... abolished the sacrifice of the mass, prayers, fasts ... and has ordered that books of manifestly heretical content be propounded to the whole realm ... She had dared to eject bishops, rectors of churches and other Catholic priests from their churches and benefices, to bestow these and other things ecclesiastical upon heretics, and to determine spiritual causes ... has forbidden the prelates, clergy and people to acknowledge the Church of Rome ...

... Therefore, resting upon the authority of Him whose pleasure it was to place us ... upon this supreme justice-seat, we do out of the fullness of our apostolic power declare the aforesaid Elizabeth to be a heretic and favourer of heretics, and her adherents in the matters aforesaid to have incurred the sentence of excommunication and to be cut off from the unity of the body of Christ.

And moreover her to be deprived of her pretended title to the aforesaid crown and of all lordship, dignity and privilege whatsoever.

And also the nobles, subjects and the people of the said realm and all others who have in any way sworn oaths to her, to be forever absolved from such an oath and from any duty arising from lordship, fealty and obedience ... We charge and command all and singular the nobles, subjects, peoples and others aforesaid that they do not dare obey her orders, mandates and laws. Those who shall act to the contrary we include in the like sentence of excommunication.

6 CASES IN THE ARCHIDIACONAL COURT OF ESSEX

15 April, 1584 *Contra Ricardum Yawlinge, de Woodham Mortimer*:

... for being absent from his parish church vi weeks, and saith that he will not come to church unless there be a sermon preached; for he saith that public service read in church is no service unless there be a sermon ... Further that he is not so well edified by reading as by preaching.

7 November, 1586 *Contra Matheum Fisher, de Romford*:

... for playing at stool ball in service time, and gave cruel words to the churchwardens for demanding xiid of him for his absence.

26 April, 1585 *Contra Ricardum Atkis, curatum de Romford*:

... for that he was so drunk the 21st of March last, being Sunday, that he could neither examine the youth in the Catechism, nor say evening Prayer; but would have said one lesson twice ... Dominus excommunicavit eum.

22 October, 1600 *Thomas Peryn, de Rayleigh*:

... for a common drunkard and a railer and chider, to the grief of the godly and great danger of his soul.

1584 *Contra Nicholaum Lynch, de Theydon Bois*:

... He shall openly before the congregation penitently confess that he is heartily sorry for offending Almighty God; and that he hath abused the congregation in procuring the banns openly to be asked in the church between him and Joan Roberts, and not proceeding in the marriage.

7 EDMUND CAMPION'S STATEMENT OF FAITH AT THE END OF HIS TRIAL, 1580

Campion (1540–81), 'diamond of England' (according to William Cecil), was an outstandingly able academic, who gave up a promising career for his faith, and accompanied Persons on the first Jesuit mission to England in 1580. This mission, coupled with the work of William Allen's seminary at Douai and its successors, doomed Elizabeth's hope of the gradual extinction of Roman Catholicism in England. The presence of well-trained missionary priests kept the faith alive. There is now some criticism of them for focusing their mission on the upper ranks of society.

'It was not our death that ever we feared. But we knew that we were not the lords of our own lives, and therefore for want of answer would not be guilty of our deaths. The only thing that we have now to say is, if that our religion do make us traitors, we are worthy to be condemned; but otherwise are, and have been, as good subjects as ever the Queen had.

'In condemning us you condemn all your own ancestors – all the ancient priests, bishops and kings – all that was once the glory of England, the island of saints, and the most devoted child of the See of Peter.

'For what have we taught, however you may qualify it with the odious name of treason, that they did not uniformly teach? To be condemned with these lights – not of England only, but of the world – and by their degenerate descendants, is both gladness and glory to us.

'God lives; posterity will live; their judgement is not so liable to corruption as that of those who are now going to sentence us to death.'

Answer of the Lord Chief Justice: 'You must go to the place from whence you came, there to remain until ye shall be drawn through the open City of London upon hurdles to the place of execution, and there be hanged and let down alive, and your privy parts cut off, and your entrails taken out and burnt in your sight; then your head to be cut off and your bodies divided into four parts, to be disposed of at her Majesty's pleasure. And God have mercy on your souls.'

8 JOHN GERARD'S AUTOBIOGRAPHY, 1564–1588

Gerard, a Catholic, was asked to write his autobiography for the benefit of Jesuit novices.

My parents had always been Catholics, and on that account had suffered much . . . I was only a boy of five and my brother not much more when we were taken away . . . and placed in a strange house among heretics. It was the time my father and two other gentlemen were imprisoned in the Tower of London because they had plotted to rescue Mary Queen of Scots and restore her to her throne . . . At the end of three years my father paid . . . for his release; and as soon as he was free he called us home again. Our faith was unaffected, for he had taken good care to put us in charge of a Catholic tutor.

Later, when I was about twelve, I was sent to Oxford, where my tutor was . . . a good and learned man and a Catholic in sympathy and conviction. But I stayed less than a year, for at Easter time they tried to force us to go to church and receive the Protestant sacrament. So I went back to my father's house . . .

. . . With some other Catholics I set sail *[for France about 9 years later]*. The wind, however, was against us and after five days at sea we were forced to put into port at Dover. There we were all arrested . . . and sent to London under custody. The others were imprisoned by warrant of the Queen's Privy Council, but although I confessed myself a Catholic and refused to attend service I was left free [thanks to] some members of the Council who seemed to be friendly to my family . . . [they] sent me to my maternal uncle, a Protestant, to be kept in custody. At the end of three months he petitioned the Council for my full release . . . But when he was asked if I had 'gone to church', as they say, he had to admit that all his efforts to me me go had failed.

The Council then sent me [with a letter] to the Bishop of London, John Aylmer, Bishop of London 1577–94 who [read the letter and] asked me whether I was ready to discuss my religion with him. I told him that I had no doubts about my faith and I did not want to.

'In that case,' said the Bishop, 'you will at least have to stay a prisoner here.'

. . . He gave orders that his chaplain's bed should be brought into my room . . . as he didn't stop blaspheming and cursing the saints and the Church, I was forced to defend my religion. We spent practically the whole night arguing . . .

After two days they gave up hope and sent me back to the Council with what they had told me was a letter of recommendation . . . The Council read it and at once ordered me to be imprisoned until I became a law-abiding subject – to their way of thinking a recalcitrant subject is one who does not submit to their heresy . . . So I was sent to the Marshalsea and there met a large number of Catholics and several priests who with a light heart were awaiting sentence of death . . . And I was there from the beginning of Lent until the end of Lent in the following year . . .

During this period we were brought before the Assizes on two occasions. We were . . . fined according to the statute for refusing to attend church. I was made to pay two thousand florins . . .

From time to time our cells were entered and a search made for altar plate, *Agnus Deis*, and relics. Once . . . a traitor . . . disclosed our hiding holes to the prison authorities, who came and almost filled a cart with the books and altar plate that they took away. In my own cell they found all that was needed for saying Mass, since next door there was a good priest imprisoned and we had found a way of opening the door between us, and we had Mass very early every morning. Later we made up our losses . . .

In the next year the insistent requests of my friends secured my liberation, but they had to give sureties in cash that I would not attempt to fly the country, while for my part I had to bind myself to report at the prison at the end of every three months. Three or four times these sureties had to be renewed before I could go ahead with my plans. At last ... a very dear friend of mine came forward and offered to go bail for me if I should fail to appear at the agreed time. Later, after I had left England, he Anthony Babington paid more than the surety – he forfeited his life, being one of the most distinguished in that group of fourteen gentlemen who were executed in the cause of Mary Queen of Scots ...

Free at last, I made my way to France ...

1588

... The Spanish Fleet had exasperated the people against the Catholics; everywhere a hunt was being organised for Catholics and their houses searched; in every village and along all the roads and lanes very close watches were kept to catch them. The Earl of Leicester ... had sworn that by the end of the year there would be no Catholic left in the country ...

After crossing the sea we sailed up the English coast. On the third day ... we ordered the ship to cast anchor off the point until nightfall ... we were taken ashore in the boat and dropped there ...

As soon as my companion had left I came out of the wood by a different path. I had gone only a short distance when I saw some country folk coming toward me. Walking up to them I asked whether they knew anything about a stray hawk ... I wanted them to believe that I had lost my bird and was wandering about the countryside in search of it ... And they would not be surprised because I was ... unfamiliar with the lanes ... They told me they had not seen a falcon recently and they seemed sorry that they could not put me on its track. So ... I went off as if I were going to search for it in the trees and hedges round about. In this way I got off the road without arousing their suspicions ... Whenever I saw anybody in the fields I went up to him and asked my usual questions about the falcon, concealing all the time my real purpose, which was to avoid the villages and public roads and get away from the coast where I knew watchers guarded the thoroughfares and kept out strangers. Most of the day went like this and in all I managed to cover eight or ten miles ... I turned for the night into an inn in a village I was passing, thinking they were less likely to question a man they saw entering an inn.

I got some food and ... told them I wanted to buy a pony ... On horseback I hoped to move more quickly and more safely too – people travelling on foot are often taken for vagrants and liable to arrest, even in quiet times.

The next morning ... I rode straight into a group of watches at the entrance to a village. They ... asked me who I was and where I came from, I ... explained that my falcon had flown away and I had come here to see whether I could recover it ... They insisted I had to come before the Constable and the Officer of the Watch, both of whom happened ... to be in church ...

I told them to go and tell the officer that I was here ... the officer came out at once with some attendants and started to examine me ... He asked me first where I came from and I named a number of places which I had learned were not far away. Then he asked me my name, employment, home, and the reason for my coming, and I gave the answers that I had given before. Finally on asking whether I was carrying any letters, I invited him to search me and satisfy himself, but he did not do it. He insisted, however, that it was his duty to take me before the Justice of the Peace and I said that if he thought it was really necessary I was ready to go, but I was anxious to hurry on for I had been away from my master long enough already ... the man looked at me ...

'You've got the look of an honest fellow. Go on then in God's name. I won't hold you back any longer.'

... Going round the city walls I came to the gate ... I saw the inn.

I was there only a short time when in walked a man ... He began talking about some Catholic gentlemen imprisoned in the city and mentioned by name a man, one of whose relatives had been with me in the Marshalsea Prison ... After he had gone out I asked the man I had been talking to who he was.

'He is a very good fellow, except for the fact that he is a Papist.'

'How do you know this?' I asked.

'He has spent many years in the city gaol. There are a lot of Catholic gentlemen there and this man was released only a short time ago.'

'Was he released,' I asked, 'because he has given up his faith?'

'No, and he never will. He is a most pig-headed man. He is merely out on bail and has to report to the prison whenever he is summoned. There is some business he does for a gentleman in prison which brings him here frequently.'

I kept quiet until the man returned and when the others had gone out I told him I wanted to have a word with him ... I had heard he was a Catholic, I said, and was very pleased to hear it because I was one ... I told him that I wanted to get to London and that if he could do me the kindness of introducing me to any people who were known on the road so that I could join on to them and pass as one of their party, he would be doing good work ...

However he knew of no one . . . so I asked him whether he could give me the name of a name whom I might hire as an escort. He said . . . he knew a gentleman who was in town just then who might be able to help me out of my difficulties.

. . . He led me into a busy mart . . . The gentleman he had told me about was waiting there, having selected this place because it gave him a chance to look at me . . . Eventually he came up to us and told my friend in a whisper that he thought I was a priest. Then [he led us out to the cathedral, where] he put a lot of questions to me, finally asking me to tell him straight whether or not I was a priest, and if I was he promised to give me all the help I needed . . . I asked my guide who the gentleman was and when he told me his name and position I realised what a good friend Providence had given me. I admitted at once that I was a Jesuit priest and had recently arrived from Rome. Straight away he got me a change of clothes and a good horse and took me out to a country house . . .

Braddocks 1594

On Easter Monday . . . as we were preparing everything for Mass before daybreak we heard, suddenly, a great noise of galloping hooves. The next moment . . . the house was surrounded by a whole troop of men . . . We barred the doors; the altar was stripped, the hiding-places opened and all my books and papers thrown in. It was most important to pack me away first with all my belongings. I was for using the hiding-place near the dining-room; it was farther away from the chapel the most suspected room in the house and it had a supply of provisions . . . Also there was more chance there of overhearing the searchers' conversation and picking up some information that might prove useful to us . . . and it was also a well built and safe place. However the mistress of the house was opposed to it. She wanted me to use the place near the chapel; I could get into it more quickly and hide all the altar things away with me. As she was very insistent I agreed, although I knew I would have nothing to eat if the search was a long one. We hid away everything that needed hiding . . .

I was hardly tucked away when the puirsuivants broke down the door and burst in. They fanned out through the house, making a great racket. The first thing they did was to shut up the mistress of the house in her own room with her daughters, then they locked up the Catholic servants in different places in the same part of the house. This done, they took possession of the place and began to search everywhere, even lifting up the tiles of the roof to examine underneath them and using candles in the dark corners. When they found nothing they started knocking down suspicious-looking places. They measured the walls with long rods and if the measurements did not tally they pulled down the section they could not account for. They tapped every wall and floor for hollow spots; and on sounding anything hollow they smashed it in . . .

Arrest 1594

The next day I was brought before the commissioners . . .

They first asked me my name and station in life. When I gave them the name I was using, one of them called out my true name, and said I was a Jesuit . . . I said I would be quite frank and give straight answers to all questions concerning myself, but added I would say nothing which would involve others. I told them my name and profession, saying I was a Jesuit priest . . .

'Who sent your over here?' they asked.

'The Superiors of the Society.'

'Why?'

'To bring back wandering souls to their Maker.'

'No, you were sent to seduce people from the Queen's allegiance to the Pope's, and to meddle in State business.'

'Regarding things of State, they are no concern of ours and we are forbidden to have anything to do with them. This prohibition is general to all Jesuits; and there is, besides, a special prohibition included in the instructions given to the Fathers sent on this mission. As for the allegiance due to the Queen and the Pope, each has our allegiance and the allegiances do not clash. The history of England and of all other Christian states shows this.'

'How long have you been acting as a priest in this country?'

'About six years.'

'How did you land? And where? Whom have you lived with since then?'

I answered that I could not reply to these questions with a good conscience, particularly the last one.

. . . However, they urged that it was precisely on these points that they wanted to satisfy themselves, and they ordered me to answer in the Queen's name.

I answered:

'I honour the Queen, and I will obey her and you in all that is lawful. But on this point you must hold me excused. If I name any person who had harboured me or mention any house where I have found shelter, innocent people will suffer for the kindness they have done me. Such is your law, but for my part I would be acting against charity and justice, which you will never persuade me to do.'

'If you won't answer,' they retorted, 'then we will have to force you to' . . .

On the third or perhaps it was the fourth day I was taken out to my second examination . . . there was another man who for many years now had conducted examinations under torture. His name was Topcliffe. He was a cruel creature and thirsted for the blood of Catholics . . .

Topcliffe had on his court dress with a sword hanging at his side. He was old and hoary and a veteran in evil . . . Topcliffe looked up at me and glared.

'You know who I am? I am Topcliffe. No doubt you have often heard people talk about me?'

He said this to scare me. And to heighten the effect he slapped his sword on the table close to his hand as though he intended to use it . . .

Now at times like this I always answered with deference, but when I saw that he was trying to frighten me I was deliberately rude to him. He realised he was going to get nothing more out of me, so he took his pen and wrote out a most clever and mendacious report on the examination.

'Here, look at this paper,' he said, 'I am placing it before the Privy Council. It shows you up as a traitor, and on many counts.'. . .

'The examinee was sent to England by the Pope and by the Jesuit, Persons, on a political mission to pervert the Queen's loyal subjects and to seduce them from the Queen's allegiance . . . If, therefore, he refuses to disclose the places where he has stayed and the persons with whom he has been in contact the presumption is that he has done much mischief to the state.'

And so it went on . . . As I wanted him to let the Council see my answer, I told him that I would reply in writing. Topcliffe was delighted . . .

He was hoping to trip me up in what I wrote, or at least to get a sample of my handwriting. If he had this he could prove that certain papers . . . belonged to me. I saw the trap and wrote in a feigned hand.

'. . . I am forbidden to meddle in State affairs and I have never done and never will. My endeavour has been to bring back souls to the knowledge and love of their Creator, to make them live in due obedience to God's laws and man's, and I hold this last to be a matter of conscience. I humbly beg that my unreadiness to reply to questions concerning persons I know may not be put down to contempt of authority. I am forced to act thus by God's commandments. To do otherwise would be a sin against justice and charity.'

While I was writing the old man became more and more angry. He shook with passion and wanted to tear me away from the paper . . .

Then I signed very close up to the line so that he had no space to add anything. He saw that he was beaten and in his frustration he blurted out threats . . .

I stayed chained up for three months or a little more. As only my priesthood could be proved against me, some of my friends tried to get me moved to a better prison; and this they achieved by bribing . . .

I looked on this change to the Clink as a translation from Purgatory to Paradise. I no longer heard obscene . . . songs, but, instead, I had Catholics praying in the next cell . . . I could have freer dealings with them through a hole made in the wall, which they had covered over and concealed with a picture. Through this hole they handed me . . . letters from some of my friends, and at the same time gave me paper, pen and ink . . .

Through this same hole I also made my confession and received the Blessed Sacrament. But there was no need to carry on like this for long, for some Catholics in the prison contrived to make a key that would open my door. Then every morning before the warder came round . . . they came and took me to another part of the prison, where I said Mass and gave the sacraments to the Catholics confined in that section. All of them had keys of their own doors . . .

Another time I was examined . . . Topcliffe said:

'Speak the truth. Have you or have you not reconciled people to the Church of Rome?'

I saw his bloody purpose clearly, for this was expressly forbidden under the penalty of high treason . . . But I knew that I was already compromised because of my priesthood, so I answered forthrightly:

'Yes, I have reconciled people to the Church and I am sorry I have not brought this blessing to more.'

'Well,' said Topcliffe. 'And how many more would you wish to have reconciled if you had had the chance? A thousand, say?'

'Yes, certainly,' I answered. 'A hundred thousand. And more than that, if I could.'

'It would be enough to raise an army against the Queen,' said Topcliffe.

'The men I should reconcile,' I said, 'would be the Queen's men. They would not be against her. We hold that obedience is due to those in authority.'

'All the same,' answered Topcliffe, 'you teach rebellion. Look, I have a Bull of the Pope here. It was made out to Sanders when he went to Ireland to raise rebellion among the Queen's subjects. Here it is, read it for yourself.'

'There is no need to read it,' I answered. 'It is probable enough that if the Pope sent him he had authority. But I have none. We are expressly forbidden to meddle in politics. I never have done so and never will.'

'Take it,' he said. 'Read it. I want you to read it.'

. . . Seeing the name Jesus stamped at the top I kissed it reverently.

'What!' cried Topcliffe. 'You kiss the Pope's Bull?'

'I kissed the name of Jesus . . . But if, as you say, it is really a Bull of the Pope, then I reverence it on that account too.'

As I said this, I kissed the embossed paper a second time . . .

Another time they had me up for examination . . . in . . . the Guildhall. Topcliffe was there . . . Turning to me they asked:

'Do you recognise the Queen as the true and lawful Queen of England?'

'I do,' I answered.

'And in spite of the fact that she has been excommunicated by Pius V,' said Topcliffe.

'I recognise that she is Queen,' I replied, 'though I know too that there has been an excommunication.'

I was aware, of course, the Pope had stated that the excommunication had not yet come into force in England: its application had been withheld until it could be made effective.

Then Topcliffe asked:

'What would you do if the Pope were to send over an army and declare that his only object was to bring the kingdom back to its Catholic allegiance? And if he stated at the same time that there was no other way of re-establishing the Cathlolic faith; and commanded everyone by his apostlic authority to support him? Whose side would you be on then – the Pope's or the Queen's?'

. . . 'I am a loyal Catholic and I am a loyal subject of the Queen. If this were to happen, and I do not think it at all likely, I would behave as a loyal Catholic and as a loyal subject.' . . .

April 1597

They led me away and took me to the Tower of London . . .

On the third day the warder came to my room . . . he said the Lords Commissioners had arrived with the Queen's Attorney-General and that I had to go down to them at once . . .

They put no questions about individual Catholics – they were all about political matters – and I answered on the general lines I had always done before. I said that matters of state were forbidden to Jesuits . . .

They then asked me about the letters I had recently received . . .

'Didn't you receive a packet a short time ago,' said Wade, Secretary of the privy council, 'and hand it over to so and so to give to Henry Garnet?' . . .

'You say,' said the Attorney-General, 'you have no wish to obstruct the Government. Tell us, then, where Father Garnet is. He is an enemy of the state, and you are bound to report on all such men.'

'He isn't an enemy of the state,' I said. 'On the contrary, I am certain that if he were given the opportunity to lay down his life for his Queen and country, he would be glad of it. But I don't know where he lives, and if I did, I would not tell you.' . . .

They then produced a warrant for putting me to torture . . .

They took me to a big upright pillar . . . driven into the top of it were iron staples for supporting heavy weights. Then they put my wrists into iron gauntlets and ordered me to climb two or three wicker steps. My arms were then lifted up and an iron bar was passed through the rings of one gauntlet, then through the staple and rings of the second gauntlet. This done, they fastened the bar with a pin to prevent it slipping, and then, removing the wicker steps one by one from under my feet, they left me hanging by my hands and arms fastened above my head. The tips of my toes, however, still reached the ground, and they had to dig away the earth from under them . . . a gripping pain came over me. It was worst in my chest and belly, my hands and arms. . . . The pain was so intense that I thought I could not possibly bear it . . .

Sometime after one o'clock, I think, I fell into a faint. How long I was unconscious I don't know, but I don't think it was long, for the men held my body up or put the wicker steps under my feet until I came to. Then they heard me pray and immediately they let me down again. And they did this every time I fainted – eight or nine times that day – before it struck five . . .

A little later they took me down. My legs and feet were not damaged but it was a great effort to stand upright.

They led me back to my cell . . .

In the morning . . . my warder came to say that Wade had arrived . . . I put on a cloak with wide sleeves – I could not get my swollen hands through the sleeves of my own gown – and I went down.

. . . Wade said to me:

'I have been sent here in the name of the Queen and her Secretary, Cecil. They say they know . . . Garnet meddles in politics and is a danger to the state. And this the Queen asserts on the word of a Sovereign and Cecil on his honour . . .'

'They cannot be speaking from experience,' I answered . . .

In the same way as before we went to the torture chamber.

The gauntlets were placed on the same part of my arm as last time. They would not fit anywhere else, because the flesh on either side had swollen into small mounds, leaving a furrow between; and the gauntlets could be fastened in the furrow. I felt a very sharp pain when they were put on.

. . . I was hung up in the same way as before, but now I felt a much severer pain in my hands but less in my chest and belly. Possibly this was because I had eaten nothing that morning.

. . . This time it was longer before I fainted, but when I did they found it so difficult to bring me round they thought I was dead, or certainly dying, and summoned the Lieutenant . . . When I came to myself, I was no longer hanging but sitting on a bench with men supporting me on either side . . . and my teeth had been forced open with a nail or some iron instrument and hot water had been poured down my throat . . .

I was hung up again. The pain was intense . . . the Governor of the Tower . . . ordered me to be taken down. It seemed I had been hanging only an hour in this second period today . . .

My warder brought me back to my room . . . He brought me some food . . . the little I did eat he had to cut up into small pieces. For many days after I could not hold a knife in my hands – that day I could not even move my fingers . . . He had to do everything for me . . .

At the end of three weeks . . . I was able to move my fingers, and to hold a knife in my hand . . . I asked my warder to buy me some large oranges . . . I presented him with them, but I was thinking of another use . . .

My finger exercises consisted of cutting up the orange peel into small crosses; then I stitched the crosses together in pairs . . . making them into rosaries. All the time I stored the juice from the oranges in a small jar.

My next move was to ask the warder to take some of the crosses and rosaries to my friends in my old prison . . . Though I could now hold a pen in my hand, I could scarcely feel . . . My sense of touch did not revive for five months, and then not completely.

As I did not dare to ask my warder for a pen . . . I asked whether I could have a quill for picking my teeth. The warder gave permission . . . I made a toothpick, taking care that it looked long enough for the warder not to suspect that I had cut a piece off . . . I asked him for some paper to wrap the rosaries in, and, lastly, I obtained his leave to write a few lines in charcoal, begging my friends to pray for me. All this he allowed . . . but, in fact, on the same sheet of paper I wrote to my friends in orange juice, telling them to reply in the same way . . . and to give the warder a little money . . .

My friends received the rosary wrapped in the paper . . . They went to a room upstairs and putting the paper by the fire, read what I had written. They replied . . . sending me a gift . . . which provided them with a pretext for the paper . . .

At the end of three months I asked whether he would allow me to write some letters in pencil and he gave me permission. I always handed him my letters unsealed . . . He admitted that he could not read and . . . carried everything . . . to my friends. Finally he allowed me some ink, and took . . . letters to and fro.

. . . But he begged me not to ask him to go to the Clink so often, because he would eventually come under suspicion and both of us would suffer.

9 THE PURITAN 'SURVEY OF THE MINISTRY' FOR ESSEX, 1586

A survey of sixteen hundreds of thereabouts in the county of Essex, containing benefices . . . 335.

Wherein there are of ignorant and unpreaching ministers 173, of such as have two benefices apiece, 61, of non-residents that are single beneficed 10, preachers of scandalous life, 12.

Non-Residents.
Bartholemew Barefoote, very young in years, presented to his benefice by his father, a non-resident.
The parson of Quenden, double-beneficed, he lieth absent from his place where there has been neither divine service nor preaching since Christ-tide last past.
Bancks, parson of Moreton and canon of Christ Church in Oxon, who by reason of his age is not able to preach nor distinctly to read, yet he provideth none among his people to do good. Witness, Robert Ogley.
Preachers of Scandalous Life in Essex.
Mr. Ampleforth, vicar of Much Baddow, had a child by his own sister . . . he is also suspected of popery . . . he is one doth falsify the Scriptures.
Mr. Goldringe, parson of Langdon Hill, he was convicted of fornication, a drunkard.
Mr. Ocklei, parson of Much Burstead, a gamester.
Mr. Durden, parson of Mashbury, a careless man, a gamester, an ale-house haunter, a company keeper with drunkards and himself sometimes drunk.
Witnesses, Richard Reynolds, John Argent, etc.
Mr. Cuckson, vicar of Linsell, unable to preach, he hath been a pilferer.
Mr. Mason, parson of Rawrey, had a child by his maid

Religion 91

and is vehemently suspected to have lived incontinently with others, and was brought for the same before a justice of the peace.

10 OUR BISHOPS, 1588

Martin Marprelate, a puritan pamphleteer, printed material on a secret press 1587–9. See if you can tell why he chose this pen-name from this epistle of 1588.

Right poisoned, peresecuting, and terrible priests . . .

. . . Our L. Bps . . . with the rest of that swinish rabble are petty Antichrists, petty popes, proud prelates, intolerable withstanders of reformation, enemies of the gospel, and most covetous, wretched priests . . .

. . . Our Bp. and proud, popish, presumptuous, profane, paltry, pestilent, and pernicious prelates . . . are first usurpers . . .

. . . Therefore all the L. Bishops in England, Ireland, and Wales . . . are petty popes and petty usurping Antichrists, and I think if they will still continue to be so that they will breed young popes and Antichrists . . . neither they nor their brood are to be tolerated in any Christian commonwealth, quoth Martin Marprelate . . .

Is it any marvel that we have so many swine, dumb dogs, non-residents, with their journeymen the hedge priests, so many lewd livers, as thieves, murderers, adulterers, drunkards, cormorants, rascals, so many ignorant and atheistical dolts, so many covetous popish Bps. in our ministry, and so many and so monstrous corruptions in our church, and yet likely to have no redress; seeing our impudent, shameless, and wainscot-faced bishops, like beasts, contrary to the knowledge of all men and against their own consciences, dare in the ears of her Majesty affirm all to be well where there is nothing but sores and blisters, yea, where the grief is even deadly at the heart . . . I am ashamed to think that the Church of England should have these wretches for the eyes thereof, that would have the people content with bare reading only and hold that they may be saved thereby ordinarily. But this is true of our Bishop and they are afraid that anything should be published abroad whereby the common people should learn that the only way to salvation is by the word preached . . .

11 ARCHBISHOP WHITGIFT TO BISHOP WICKHAM OF LINCOLN, 1587

Whereas I am credibly informed that divers, as well parish Churches as Chapels of Ease, are not sufficiently furnished with Bibles, but some have either none at all, or such as be torn and defaced, and yet not of the translation authorised by the Synods of Bishops: These are therefore to require you strictly in your visitations, or otherwise, to see that all and every the said Churches and Chapels in your diocese be provided of one Bible or more, at your discretion, of the translation allowed aforesaid, and one book of Common prayer, as by the laws of this realm is appointed. And for the performance thereof, I have caused her Highness's Printer to imprint two volumes of the said translation of the Bible aforesaid, a bigger and a less: the largest for such Parishes as are of ability, and the lesser for Chapels and very small parishes, both of which are now extant and ready . . .

12 LAWS OF ECCLESIASTICAL POLITY

Hooker (1554?–1600) was writing to defend the church from Presbyterian rather than Catholic attack. The first five books of his series of eight on 'Laws of Ecclesiastical Polity' were published in 1593 (in his lifetime), and the remaining three books in the 1660s, when they were of great influence.

. . . the first state of things was best, in the prime of Christian religion faith was soundest, the Scriptures of God were then best understood by all men . . . The glory of God and the good of the Church was what the Apostles aimed at and therefore ought to be the mark whereat we also level. But . . . what reason is there in these things to urge the state of one only age as a pattern for all to follow? It is not, I am right sure, their meaning that we should now assemble our people to serve God in close and secret meetings; or that common brooks or rivers should be used for places of baptism . . . or that all kinds of standing provision for the ministry should be utterly taken away and their estate made again dependent upon the voluntary devotion of men. In these things they easily perceive how unfit that were for the present, which was for the first age convenient enough.

13 NICHOLAS BRETON, 1603

My parishioners . . . are a kind of people that love a pot of ale better than a pulpit . . . who, coming to divine service more for fashion than devotion, are contented after a little capping and kneeling, coughing and spitting, to help me sing out a psalm, and sleep at the second lesson.

Questions

1 What picture of Elizabethan England emerges from 7D? Is it Catholic or Protestant?
2 Does the greatest threat to the Church Settlement come from Puritan or Catholic views?
3 Look at 7D8 and consider
   a How effective was the government in dealing with what it viewed as a Catholic threat?
   b What means lay at the government's disposal?
   c What impression of Gerard's character, especially his truthfulness, emerges?
4 What impression of clergy and laity emerges from chapter 7 as a whole?

8 Social and Economic Issues

The sixteenth century was a period of population increase and, as a consequence, of inflation. Can you see any similarities with our own times?

8A Mortality

The population increase was checked to some extent by a new disease known as 'the sweat'.

1 REGISTRUM ANNALIUM COLLEGII MERTONENSIS, 1485

See 3B6.

In the same year, about the end of August and the beginning of September, a marvellous and unprecedented sickness broke out in the University, which beginning suddenly with an unexpected sweat, deprived many of their lives. By about the end of September this mortality was spread abroad almost without warning through the whole country. In the city of London three mayors died within ten days; and so borne on the breeze from east to west it struck down with extraordinary slaughter almost all the nobility, except however the lords spiritual and temporal. All either died or escaped within the twenty-four hours: but so great and so cruel a massacre of wise and prudent men has not been heard of in our history for many centuries. This mortality did not last more than a month or six weeks, at any rate with the exception of a few cases.

2 CONTINUATION OF THE CROYLAND CHRONICLE, AUGUST 1485

See 2A6.

The king's opponents, having landed at Milford Haven, made their way through rugged and indirect tracks in the northern part of that province, where William Stanley was holding the sole command. Whereon the king sent word to Lord Stanley, requesting him immediately to come before him at Nottingham. For the king feared lest, as it really happened, the mother of the said Earl of Richmond whom Lord Stanley had married, might induce her husband to go over to the party of her son. He excused himself, alleging he was ill of the sweating sickness, and could not come. His son, who had secretly prepared to desert from the king, was detected and taken prisoner.

3 POLYDORE VERGIL'S 'ANGLICA HISTORIA', 1485–1537

See 1B9.

In the same year, immediately after Henry's landing in the island, a new kind of disease swept the whole country; it was a baleful affliction and one which no previous age had experienced. A sudden deathly sweating attacked the body and at the same time head and stomach were in pain from the violence of the fever. When seized by the disease, some were unable to bear the heat and . . . removed the bedclothes or . . . undressed themselves; others slaked their thirst with cold drinks; yet others endured the heat and stench (for the perspiration stank foully) and by adding more bedclothes provoked more sweating. But all alike died, either as soon as the fever began or not long after, so that of all the persons infected scarcely one in a hundred escaped death. And those who survived twenty-four hours after the sweating ended (for this was the period when the fever raged) were not then free of it, since they continually relapsed and many thereafter perished. Finally, however, the disease itself revealed a remedy. For some who sweated once, when they subsequently endured the sweating again, observed the things which had alleviated the first attack, and made use of them as a remedy, each time adding something useful to the cure.

Hence those who fell victim a third time to the disease learnt how to cure themselves and easily escaped the virulence of the fever by profiting from their previous observations. As a result it came about (after, it is true, a disastrous loss of life) that an effective remedy was evolved for all, which is as follows. Anyone who is attacked by the sweating by day should retire to bed, dressed just as he is; should lie quietly and not move from it; for exactly twenty-four hours. Meanwhile he should add more bedclothes, not thereby to provoke the fever, but so that he should perspire gently and naturally. He should take nothing to eat . . . but may drink enough . . . warmed to quench his thirst . . . care should chiefly be taken not to allow even an arm to be exposed . . . for this is fatal.

4 DESPATCHES OF SEBASTIAN GIUSTINIAN FROM THE COURT OF HENRY VIII

Guistinian was Venetian ambassador to Henry VIII and a friend of More.

London, August 6, 1517.
. . . this new malady . . . makes very quick progress, proving fatal in twenty-four hours at the farthest, and many are carried of in four or five hours. The patients experience nothing but a profuse sweat, which dissolves the frame, and when once the twenty-four hours are passed, all danger is at an end.

London, August 27, 1517.
. . . his Majesty is at a place called Windsor, alone with his physician and the reverend Master Dionysius memo and three of his favourite gentlemen; nor does he admit any one, for fear of this disease, which is now making very great progress in the land, so that many of those who accompanied the King have died, and it is said that his Majesty means to change his quarters. The Cardinal also has been ill of this malady until now, this being the fourth time that he has had it.

5 THE CHRONICLE OF EDWARD VI, JULY 1551

At this time came the sweat into London, which was more vehement than the old sweat. For if one took cold, he died within three hours, and if he escaped, it held him but nine hours or ten at the most. Also, if he slept the first six hours, as he should be very desirious to do, then he raved and should die raving.

. . . It grew so much – for in London the tenth day there died seventy in the liberties, and this day 120 and also one of my gentlemen, another of my grooms, fell sick and died – that I removed to Hampton Court with very few with me.

6 JOHN STRYPE

See 7D4.

What diseases and sicknesses everywhere prevailed! The like whereof had never been known before, both for the lasting and mortality of them: which being hot burning fevers, and other strange diseases began in the great dearth of 1556, and increased more and more the two following years. In the summer 1557 they raged horribly throughout the realm and killed an exceeding great number of all sorts of men . . . In some places corn stood and shed on the ground for lack of workmen. In the latter end of the year quartan agues were so common among men, women, and young children also, that few houses escaped; and these agues were not only common but to most people very dangerous, especially such as had been sick of the burning fevers before. In 1558, in the summer, about August, the same fevers raged again in such manner as never plague or pestilence, I think . . . killed a great number. The winter following also the quartan aguees continued in the same manner.

7 DR PERNE, VICE-CHANCELLOR, TO LORD BURGHLEY, CHANCELLOR OF CAMBRIDGE UNIVERSITY, 1574

Although we must confesse that our synnes is the principall cause of this and of all other plages sent by allmightie God, Yet the secondarie cause and meanes is that God did use to bringe the same, so far fourth as I do understand, is not the corruption of the ayer as the Phisitians saieth at this tyme, but partlie by the apparell of one that came from London to Midsomer fayer and dyed of the plage in Barnwell, where the plage hath been and is now most vehement. The other cause as I conjecture, is the corruption of the King's dytch the which goeth through Cambridge, and especially in those places where there is most infection the which I will procure, so sone as we have any hard frost, to be clensed.

8 THE FUGGER NEWSLETTERS

See 3D3.

Antwerp, October 18, 1592.
Last week 198 people died of the plague in London.

Antwerp, May 2, 1593.
English letters of the 254th ult. state that the plague has not yet died out in London. This week 34 people have died of it.

Cologne, July 23, 1593.
It was announced in London on the 17th inst. that 149 people died of the plague that week. It is feared it may spread further.

Antwerp, August 15, 1593.
London letters of the 19th July record that during that week there had been 666 deaths in the city, of which 454 were from the plague. Many people are leaving town, in consequence and going to their country seats.

Antwerp, September 25, 1593.
Letters of the 10th from London announce that there are about a thousand deaths of the plague weekly in the city and outside it some five hundred, and there is no sign of any end to the mortality.

Antwerp, November 7, 1593.
From London in England we hear that the plague has somewhat abated.

Antwerp, November 23, 1593.
There were 420 deaths of the plague in London that week and this is still a large number.

Questions

1 Does 8A2 in any way cast doubt on the accuracy of 8A3?
2 How far are 8A1–5 in agreement?
3 In whose reign was the rise in population temporarily halted?
4 a What differing explanations for the spread of disease are given in 8A7?
   b In what ways can that extract be said to mark the transition from a mediaeval to a modern attitude to illness?
5 Judging from the symptoms described in the documents, what disease do you think 'the sweat' might have been?

8B Sex and Status

As you look at the documents in this section, try to decide what a woman's role was in this period, both in theory and practice.

About ten years ago there was academic debate as to whether the gentry were in the ascendant or in decline in the sixteenth century. Can you find material in this section to support either viewpoint?

1 'THE LACE LADY', 1484

This is the memorial brass for Margaret Peyton at Isleham Parish church, Cambridgeshire.

96 *Social and Economic Issues*

2 'AN ENGLISH WOMAN', HANS HOLBEIN THE YOUNGER, 1547

3 AVICE TYNDALL, 1571

Avice Tyndall, of Thornbury, Avon, is shown wearing a robe over an embroidered petticoat with a small sash at the waist and sleeves puffed at the shoulder. She also wears a Paris head, or French hood – a close fitting cap with a curved border in front which fits over the ears – and a hanging veil behind.

Avice Tyndall
1571
Thornbury

4 KATHERINE PARR TO HENRY VIII

'what great imperfection and weakness by our first creation is allotted unto us women, to be ordained and appointed as inferiors and subject unto men as our head ... Since therefore God hath appointed such a natural difference between men and women, and Your Majesty being so excellent in gifts and ornaments of wisdom, and I a silly poor woman, so much inferior in all respects of nature unto you, how then cometh it now to pass that Your Majesty, in such diffuse causes of religion, will seem to require my judgment?'

5 LETTER TO A FRIEND AT SALAMANCA FROM A COURTIER WHO ACCOMPANIED PRINCE PHILIP TO ENGLAND, 1554

All the women here wear petticoats of coloured cloth without admixture of silk, and above come coloured robes of damask, satin or velvet, very badly cut. Their shoes are sometimes of velvet, but more often of leather, and they wear black stockings and show their legs up to the knee when walking. As their skirts are not long they are passably immodest when walking, and even when seated. They are neither beautiful nor graceful when dancing, and their dances only consist in strutting or trotting about. Not a single Spanish gentleman has fallen in love with one of them nor takes any interest in them, and their feelings for us are the same. They are not the kind of women for whom Spaniards feel inclined to take much trouble or spend their substance, which is an excellent thing for the Spaniards. There are no distractions here except eating and drinking, the only variety they understand ...

Who, in any other land, ever saw women riding forth alone as they do here, where many of them manage their horses with consummate skill and are as firm in the saddle as any man?

6 FIRST BLAST OF THE TRUMPET AGAINST THE MONSTROUS REGIMENT OF WOMEN, 1559

When the Scottish reformer, John Knox, wrote against 'The monstrous regiment of women' it was Mary of Guise, Mary Stuart and Mary Tudor he had in mind. None the less, Elizabeth was displeased. He wrote the following piece in 1559.

'to promote a woman to bear rule, superiority, dominion or empire above any realm, nation or city is repugnant to nature; contumely to God, a thing most contrary to his revealed will and approved ordinance; and finally, it is the subversion of good order, of all equity and justice ... for no man ever saw the lion make obedience and stoop before the lioness, neither yet can it be proved that the hind takes the conducting of the herd among the harts.'

7 DE REPUBLICA ANGLORUM

Sir Thomas Smith's 'De Republica Anglorum' was written in 1565 and published after his death in 1583. (See 6B2.)

'women, as those whom nature hath made to keepe home and to nourish their familie and children, and not to medle with matters abroad, nor to beare office in a citie or common wealth no more than children and infantes.'

8 NEDERLANDTSCHE HISTORIE, 1575

Van Meteren was a Dutch merchant in London (c. 1558–1612) who wrote 'Nederlandtsche Historie'.

Wives in England are entirely in the power of their husbands, their lives only excepted. Therefore, when they marry, they give up the surname of their father and of the family from which they are descended, and take the surname of their husbands, except in the case of duchesses, countesses and baronesses, who, when they marry gentlemen of inferior degree, retain their first name and title, which, for the ambition of the said ladies, is rather allowed than commended. But although the women there are entirely in the power of their husbands, except for their lives, yet they are not kept so strictly as they are in Spain or elsewhere. Nor are they shut up: but they have the free management of the house or housekeeping ... They go to market to buy what they like best to eat. They are well dressed, fond of taking it easy, and commonly leave the care of household matters and drudgery to their servants. They sit before their doors, decked out in fine clothes, in order to see and be seen by the passers-by. In all banquets and feasts they are shown the greatest honour; they are placed at the upper end of the table, where they are the first served; at the lower end they help the men. All the rest of their time they employ in walking and riding, in playing at cards or otherwise, in visiting their friends and keeping company, conversing with their equals (whom they term gossips) and their neighbours, and making merry with them at child-births, christenings, church-ings and funerals; and all this with the permission of knowledge of their husbands, as such is the custom. Although the husbands often recommend to them the pains, industry and care of the German or Dutch women, who do what the men ought to do both in the house and in the shops, for which services in England men are employed, nevertheless the women usually persist in retaining their customs. This is why England is called the Paradise of married women. The girls who are not yet married are kept more rigorously and strictly than in the Low Countries.

The women are beautiful, fair, well-dressed and modest, which is seen there more than elsewhere, as they go about the streets without any covering either of huke (1) or mantle, hood, veil, or the like. Married women only wear a hat both in the street and in the house; those unmarried go without a hat, although ladies of distinction have lately learnt to cover their faces with silken masks or vizards, and feathers, for indeed they change very easily, and that every year, to the astonishment of many.

1 *huke* a kind of cape or cloak with a hood.

9 AN ACT AGAINST THE WEARING OF COSTLY APPARELL, 1510

Forasmuch as the great and costly array and apparell used within this realm contrary to good statutes thereof made hath been the occasion of great impoverishing of divers of the king's subjects and provoked many of them to rob and do extortion and other unlawful deeds to maintain thereby their costly array: in eschewing whereof, be it ordained by the authority of this present parliament that no person of what estate, condition or degree that he be use in his apparell any cloth of gold of purple colour or silk of purple colour but only the King, the Queen, the King's Mother, the King's Children, the King's Brothers and Sisters upon pain to forfeit the said apparell wherwith soever it be mixed, and for using the same to forfeit xx. pound: and that no man under the estate of a Duke use in any apparell of his body or upon his horses any cloth of gold or tissue upon pain to forfeit the same apparell wherewith soever it be mixed and for using the same to forfeit xx. mark; and that no man under the degree of an Earl wear in his apparell any sables upon pain to forfeit the same apparell. And that no man under the degree of a Baron use in his apparell of his body or of his horses any cloth of gold or cloth of silver or tinsel satin nor no silk or cloth mixed or broidered with gold or silver upon pain of forfeiture of the same apparell, albeit that it be mixed with any other silk or cloth, and using of the same to forfeit x. mark. And that no man under the degree of a Lord or a Knight of the Garter wear any woollen cloth made out of this realm of England, Ireland, Wales, Calais or the Marches of the same or Berwick, upon pain to forfeit the said cloth and for using of the same to forfeit x. pound. And that no man under the degree of a Knight of the Garter wear in his gown or coat or any other his apparell any velvet of the colour of crimson or blue upon pain to forfeit the same gown or coat or other apparell and for using of the same to forfeit xl. shillings.

10 LETTER ABOUT MORE, FROM ERASMUS TO ULRICH VON HUTTEN, 23 JULY 1519

I have never seen any one less dainty about what he eats. Until he grew up, he was quite content with water, as his father had been before him. But not to make his companions uncomfortable, he used to drink out of a pewter cup, usually the thinnest small beer, and often nothing but water. Wine he sometimes touched with the tips of his lips, since it is the English custom to pledge one another in a loving cup; to avoid seeming to shun it altogether, also to accustom himself to what is commonly done. He used to choose beef and salt fish and bread made of coarse and fermented flour, rather than the delicacies which most people enjoy . . . His favourist dishes are made of milkfoods and fruit, and particularly of eggs.

In dress he likes simplicity, and never wears silk or purple or chains of gold, unless required . . .

He has always liked equality and hated despotism . . . around the quietest throne is . . . rivalry and luxury and sham, with marks of mastery and servitude . . .

From his earliest years he followed after good learning. As a young man he took up Greek literature and philosophy – to the distress of his father, an upright man and usually of sound sense; who being himself an authority on English Law, thought fit to check these studies by cutting off all supplies, and indeed More was almost disowned, because he seemed to be deserting his father's profession. The study of law has little in common with true learning, but in England those that succeed have a great position; and with good reason, for it is from their ranks that the nobility is for the most part filled. Complete mastery of the law is said to require the strenuous labour of many years . . .

In the City of London, his birthplace, he has been for some years a judge in civil cases; an office which has little work (the court only sits on Thursday mornings till dinnertime) but confers great honour.

11 EDWARD VI, 1551

the grasier, the fermour, the merchaunt become landed men, and call themselves gentlemen, though they be churles . . . the artificer will leave the towne, and . . . will live in the countrie: yea, and more than that, will be a justice of peax, and will thinke skorne to have it denied him, so lordly be they now adaies.

12 ON ENGLAND

William Harrison's (1534–93) description of England was written in 1577 and revised 1586–7. It prefaced Holinshed's Chronicle.

1577: 'We in England divide our people commonlie into foure sorts, as gentlemen, citizens or burgesses, yeomen, and artificers, or laborers. Of gentlemen the first and cheefe (next the king) be the prince, dukes, marquesses, earls, viscounts, and barons; and these are called the nobilitie; they are also named lordes and noble men; and next to them be knights and esquires, and simple gentlemen . . . Citizens and burgesses have placed next to gentlemen, who be those that are free within the cities, and are of some substance to beare office in the same . . . Our yeoman are those, which by our lawyers are called 'Legales homines', free men borne English, and may dispend of their owne free land in yearlie revenue, to the summe of fortie shillings sterling . . . the fourth and last sort of people in England are daie labourers, poore husbandmen, and some retailers . . . copie holders, and all artificers . . .

. . . Who soever studieth the lawes of the realm, who so studieth in the universitie or professeth physicke and the liberall sciences, or beside his service in the roome of a capteine in the warres, can live ydlely and without mannuell labour, and theretoo is able and will bear the port, charge, and countenance of a gentleman, he shall be called master, which is the title that men give to esquires and gentlemen, and reputed for a gentleman. Which is so much the lesse to be disalowed of, as that the prince dooth loose nothing by it, the gentlemen being so much subject to taxes and publike paiments as is the yeoman or husbandman.'

1587: 'Now all the wealth of the land dooth flow unto our common lawiers, of whome, some one having practised little above thirteene or fourteene yeares is able to buie a purchase of so manie 1000 pounds.'

13 THOMAS WILSON, 'THE STATE OF ENGLAND', 1600

See 6A6.

. . . within these 40 or 50 years . . . since the clergy hath been trodden down . . . and since the long continuance of peace hath bred an inward canker and rest in men's minds, the people doing nothing but jar and wrangle one with another, these lawyers by the ruins of neighbours' contentions are grown so great, so rich and so proud that no other sort dare meddle with them. Their number is so great now that, to say the truth, they can scarcely live by one another.

Questions

1 What attitude to women is shown in 8B4, 6 and 7? Is it borne out by material in Chapter 2 and Chapter 6?
2 How far are 8B5 and 8 in agreement?
3 What do 8B10, 12 and 13 show about the position of lawyers?
4 How far do 8B9–11 give the idea of a hierarchical society? Does reading them strengthen or qualify the view of social mobility given by 5C?

8C London and the Land

1 INDICTMENT OF THE BISHOP OF NORWICH, 1482

'for not repairing the highway in the parish of St. Martin in the Fields lying between his inn and the inn of the Bishop of Durham, which way is so overflowed with water that the lords both spiritual and temporal, the king's justices ... all persons journeying by the way to Westminster to administer and observe the laws are often hindered.'

2 MANCINI ON LONDON, 1483

See 1B8.

On the banks of the Thames are huge warehouses for imports, and numerous cranes of remarkable size to unload merchandise from the ships. From the district on the east, adjacent to the Tower, three paved streets lead towards the other quarter in the direction of the walls on the west; they are almost straight and are the busiest streets in the city. The one closest to the river, below the others, is devoted to various staple commodities, both liquid and solid minerals, wines, honey, pitch, wax, flax, robes, thread, grain, fish, and other rather sordid goods. In the street running between the other two you will find hardly anything for sale except clothes. And in the third street, which is level and touches the centre of the town, the traffic is in more precious goods such as gold and silver cups, dyed stuffs, various silks, carpets, tapestry, and much other exotic merchandise ... There are also many other populous districts with numerous trades, for whatever there is in the city it all belongs to craftsmen and merchants. Their houses are not, as is usually the case, encumbered with merchandise only at the entrance, but there are spacious depositories in the inmost areas where goods are heaped, stowed and packed away like honey in a cone.

3 FRANCISCUS ON LONDON, 1497

This letter was sent from Andreas Franciscus, Venetian Ambassador to Henry VIII, to his friend, Jacobus Sansonus.

All the streets are so badly paved that they get wet at the slightest quantity of water, and this happens very frequently owing to the large numbers of cattle carrying water, as well as on account of the rain, of which there is a great deal in this island. Then a vast amount of evil smelling mud is formed, which does not disappear quickly but lasts a long time, in fact nearly the whole year round.

4 DESPATCH OF SEBASTIAN GIUSTINIAN

See 8A4.

Richmond, May 5 1517

... after Easter a certain preacher, at the instigation of a citizen of London ... commenced abusing the strangers in the town, and their mode of life and customs, alleging that they not only deprived them of their industry, and of the emoluments derivable thence, but disgraced their dwellings, taking their wives and daughters ... exhorting them not to suffer ... this sort of persons to inhabit their town, by which means he so irritated the populace that from that day they commenced threatening the strangers that on the 1st of May they would cut them to pieces and sack their houses.

... On the night preceding the first of May, the London apprentices ... with a number of bandits, amounting in all to 2,000, rose and went to divers parts of the city inhabited by French and Flemish artificers and mechanics, whose houses they sacked, and wounded many of them, though it is not understood that any were killed. They next proceeded to the dwelling of his Majesty's French secretary, which they sacked ... they also sacked a number of houses of French artificers in the neighbourhood of his residence. They next went to the house of the Florentine, and Lucchese, and Genoese merchants, whom they insulted; but as the said dwellings were well supplied with men and arms and artillery, they could not do them any harm. Against the houses of the Venetians ... no demonstration was made, as they have ever comported themselves with so much equity and decorum, that there was no wishing to harm them. The house of the Spanish ambassador likewise received some insult, but not of importance ...

Much greater mischief and bloodshed would have taken place, had precautionary measures not been adopted beforehand, I believe by the right reverend Cardinal, who was forewarned, and also by the other lords, who on that night came with a considerable force ...

5 HALL ON EVIL MAY DAY

See 1D5.

Evil May Day, 8 Henry VIII. In this season the Genowayes, Frenchmen, and othe straungers, sayde and boasted them selfes to be in suche favour with the Kyng and hys counsayll, that they set naughte by the rulers of the citie: and the multitude of straungers was so great aboute London, that the poore Englishe artificers could skace get any lyvynge; and mooste of the straungers were so proude that they disdayned, mocked, and oppressed the Englishmen, which was the beginning of the grudge. For amonge all other thynges there was a carpenter . . . which bought two stockdoves in Chepe, and as he was about to paye for them, a Frencheman tooke them oute of hys hands, and sayde they were not meate for a carpenter. 'Well,' sayde the Englisheman, 'I have bought them, and now payd for them, and therefore I wil have them.' 'Naye,' sayde the Frencheman, 'I will have them for my lorde the ambassador,' and . . . the Frencheman called the Englisheman knave, and went away with the stockdoves . . . The straungers came to the French ambassadour and . . . the carpenter was sent to pryson . . .

Also a Frenchman had slayne a man. Howbeit the Frenchmen were not alonely oppressors of the Englishemen, for a Lombarde . . . entised a manne's wyfe . . . to come to his chamber with her husbande's plate, whiche thynge she dyd. After when her husband knewe it, he demanded hys wyfe, but aunswer was made he shoulde not have her; then he demanded his plate, and in lyke maner aunswer was made that he shoulde neither have plate nor wyfe. And when he had served an accion agaynste the straunger in the Guylde hall, the straunger so faced the Englisheman that he faynted in his sute. And then the Lombard arrested the poore man for his wyfe's boorde, while he kept her from her husband in his chamber. This mocke was much noted, and for these and many other oppressions done by them, there encreased suche a malice in the Englishemennes harts, that at the last it brast oute.

6 SERMON ON PLOUGHERS, 1549

Hugh Latimer (1485?–1555) author of the following extract, was converted to Protestantism by Bilney who was Bishop of Worcester (1536–9). He opposed enclosure and worked with Hales' 'commonwealth men'. In 1553 he was given notice of a summons but refused to go into exile and was martyred. Note that his father was involved in suppressing the Cornish Revolt of 1497. (See 4A.)

. . . Now what shall I say of these rich artisans of London? . . . Shall I call them proud men of London, malicious men of London, merciless men of London? No, no, I may not say so, they will be offended with me then. Yet must I speak . . . But London cannot abide to be rebuked; such is the nature of man . . . But London was never so ill as it is now. In times past men were full of pity and compassion, but now there is no pity; for in London their brother shall die in the streets for cold, he shall lie sick at their door . . . and perish there for hunger. In times past when any rich man died in London, they were wont to help the poor scholars of the university with exhibition. When any man died, they would bequeathe great sums of money towards the relief of the poor. When I was a scholar at Cambridge myself, I heard very good report of London and knew many that had relief of the rich men of London; but now I can hear no such good report and yet I enquire of it and hearken for it, but now charity is waxed cold, none helpeth the scholar nor yet the poor. And in those days what did they when they helped the scholars? Many they maintained and gave them livings that were very papists and professed the pope's doctrine; and now the knowledge of God's word is brought to light, and many earnestly study and labour to set it forth, now almost no man helpeth to maintain them. Oh! London! London! repent, repent . . . Amend therefore; and ye that be prelates, look well to your office, for right prelating is busy labouring and not lording. Therefore preach and teach and let your plough be doing; ye lords, I say, that live like loiterers, look well to your office; the plough is your office and charge. If you live idle and loiter, you do not your duty, you follow not your vocation . . . How . . . hath it happened that we have had so many hundred years so many unpreaching prelates, lording loiterers, and idle ministers?

7 THE TREASURER OF FLUSHING, 1573

Yow receave many strangers into the realme . . . and the realme by them receaveth many comodyties, as connynge in many syences wherein before yow were altogether ignorant.

8 THOMAS JOHNSON, 1596

What coountrie . . . is there at this presente that nourisheth so many aliens from all parts of the world as England doth?

102 Social and Economic Issues

9 ROUS ON ENCLOSURES

Rous was a pioneer in his research on enclosures. He presented petitions to Parliament against them. His 'Historia Regum Anglie' was written between 1480 and 1486. (See 1B5.)

... royal roads are obstructed by enclosures ... streams are obstructed ... woods and undergrowth grow and in them rooks flourish as never before, constantly consuming all kinds of grain crop, they also provide congenial lairs for wild beasts such as wolves and foxes which eat sheep, rabbits and birds ... And where royal roads run through decayed villages often by the gate ... the most savage robbers lurk, who rob men and rape women; they also ambush, seize, rob, beat, wound, tie up or do brutally take captive, mutilate without mercy, and kill God's faithful flock and the king's subjects, without regard for age or sex ...

10 POPULAR RHYME AGAINST ENCLOSURE, COVENTRY, 1496

The cyte is bound that should be free
The right is holden from the cominalte
Our comiens that at lammas (1) open shuld be cast
They be closed in and hegged full fast.

1 *lammas* a harvest festival when loaves made from the first ripe corn were consecrated.

11 AN ITALIAN VIEW OF ENGLISH FARMERS, 1497

This extract is taken from a letter which was sent to Jacobus Sansonus from his friend Andreas Franciscus, Venetian Ambassador to Henry VIII (see 8C3) in 1497.

'the farmers are so lazy and slow that they do not bother to sow more wheat than is necessary for their own consumption; they prefer to let the ground be transformed into pasture for the use of sheep that they breed in large numbers.'

12 THE FIRST BOOKE OF UTOPIA, 1516

In this extract More is writing as a Christian humanist, he is criticising a self-interested government that is not concerned with the welfare of the community, but with profit and power. 'Utopia' was on the Papal Index.

... Your sheep that were wont to be so meek and tame, and so small eaters, now ... be become so great devourers and so wild, that they eat up ... the very men themselves. They consume ... whole fields, houses and cities. For look in what parts of the realm doth grow the finest and therefore dearest wool, these noblemen and gentlemen, yea, and certain abbots ... not contenting themselves with the yearly revenues and profits, that were wont to grow to their ... predecessors of their lands, nor being content that they live in rest and pleasure nothing profiting, yea, much annoying the weal public, leave no ground for tillage, they enclose all into pastures; they throw down houses; they pluck down towns, and leave nothing standing, but only the church to be made a sheep house. And as though you lost no small quantity of ground by forests, chases ... parks, those good holy men turn all dwelling places and all glebeland into desolation and wilderness. Therefore that one covetous and insatiable cormorant may compass about and enclose many thousand acres of ground together within one pale or hedge, the husbandmen be thrust out of their own ... they must needs depart away, poor silly wretched souls, men, women ... children, widows ... and their whole household small in substance and much in number, as husbandry requireth many hands. Away they trudge ... out of their ... houses, finding no place to rest in ... All their household stuff ... they be constrained to sell it for a thing of nought. And when they have wandered abroad till that be spent, what can they do else but steal, and then justly ... be hanged, or else go a begging. And yet then also they be cast in prison as vagabonds, because they go about and work not: whom no man will set to work, though they ... willingly profer themselves ... For one herdman ... is enough to eat up that ground with cattle, to the occupying whereof about husbandry many hands were requisite. And this is also the cause why victuals be now in many places dearer.

13 LATIMER'S FIRST SERMON PREACHED BEFORE EDWARD VI

... My father was a yeoman, and had no lands of his own, only he had a farm of three or four pound by the year at the uttermost, and hereupon he tilled so much as kept half a dozen men. He had walk for a hundred sheep; and my mother milked thirty kine (1). He was able, and did find the king a harness, with himself and his horse, while he came to the place that he should receive the king's wages. I can remember that I buckled his harness when he went unto Blackheath field. He kept me to school, or else I had not been able to have preached before the king's majesty now. He married my sisters with five pound, or twenty nobles apiece; so that he brought them up in godliness and fear of God. He kept hospitality for his poor neighbours, and some alms he gave to the poor. And all this he did of the said farm, where now he that hath it payeth sixteen pound by the year, or more, and is not able to do anything for his prince, for himself, nor for his children, or give a cup of drink to the poor.

1 *kine* cattle.

14 ON ENCLOSURES, 1548

John 'Clubfoot' Hales (d. 1571) headed an enclosure commission at Coventry, 1548. He was a Marian exile who was sent to the Tower by Elizabeth for supporting Katherine Grey both in her claim to the succession and in her clandestine marriage to Somerset's son. This extract shows a set of instructions given by John Hales, a government official, to a royal Commission on enclosures.

At first, to declare unto you what is meant by this word, enclosures. It is not taken where a man encloses and hedges in his own private ground, where no man hath commons. For such enclosures is very beneficial; it is a cause of great increase of wood; but it is meant thereby, when any man takes away and encloses any other men's commons, or has pulled down houses, and conversed the lands from tillage to pasture. This is the meaning of this word, and we pray you to remember it.

15 LANE TO CECIL, 1551

the exchange doth ingendar dere clothe, and dere cloth dothe ingendar dere wolle, and dere wolle doth ingendar many scheppe, and many scheppe doth ingendar myche pastor and dere, and myche pastor ys the dekaye of tyllage, and owte of the dekaye of tyllage spryngethe ij evylls, skarsyte of korne and the pepull unwroghte, and consequently the darthe of all thynges.

16 BARBARO, VENETIAN AMBASSADOR, 1551

'In some places grain abounds, and there would be much more did not the natives shun fatigue; but they satisfy their wants and seek nothing more.'

17 A HUNDRED GOOD POINTS OF HUSBANDRY, 1557

Thomas Tusser (1524?–80) author of this piece, was a farmer-poet educated at Trinity College, Cambridge.

The country enclosed I praise
T'other delighteth not me.
For nothing the wealth it does raise
To such as inferior be.

More plenty of money and beef,
Corn butter and cheese of the best,
More wealth anywhere (to be brief)
More people, more handsome and prest (1),
where find ye (go search any coast)
Than there where enclosures are most.

1 *prest* mentally alert.

18 A POEM FROM 1598

Sheep have eaten up our meadows and our downs,
Our corn, our wood, whole villages and towns,
Yea, they have eaten up many wealthy men,
Besides widows and orphan children:
Besides our statutes and our iron laws
Which they have swallowed down into their maws,
Till now I thought the proverb did but jest,
Which said a black sheep was a biting beast.

Questions

1 What impression of London is given by 8C1 and 3? Is this offset at all by 8C2?
2 What do you think the 'sordid goods' of 8C2 might be?
3 To what extent do 8C4 and 5 agree on the causes of 'evil May day'?
4 Is More's knowledge of farming (8C12) likely to be greater than Latimer's (8C6 and 13)?

104 Social and Economic Issues

5 What arguments against enclosures are used in these materials? Which criticisms seem to you most effective? Do any of the documents lead you to moderate your censure of enclosure?

8D Poverty and the Price Rise

1 LETTER FROM THE DUKE OF NORFOLK TO CROMWELL

2 June 1537. My veray goode Lorde . . . forasmoche as I do nowe wryght to the kinges maiestie I shall not molest you with nothing conteyned in my lettre sent to his highnes. And where I do understand his maiestie hath now sent lettres to thiese parties concernyng vacabonds, your good lordship shall percyve by copies of lettres which I have a good tyme past sent to all the justice of pease and religiouse houses in thies parties, that I haue not neglected that matier; surely I neuer sawe so many as be in thiese cuntrees. And the almes that they haue in religious houses is the great occasion thereof, and also the slackenes of the Justice of pease, for not doying ther dewties. I haue and shall so order thiese cuntrees under my rewle that I thinke ye shall shortely here of no small number of them that shall drawe Southewards.

2 LETTER FROM JOHN BAKER TO HENRY VIII, 1538

Although your most Gracious, noble and excellent Majesty hath set forth many times good laws for the punishment of all vagabonds and beggars, that is to say that none of them shall move from town to town or place to place without lawful licence or cause, or else they shall be taken and punished, yet never the less I still perceive that the number of them doth daily increase more and more.

I am a poor craftsman who has travelled and gone through the most part of your realm to earn my living. I have been in most of the cities and large towns in England. I have also gone through many little towns and villages, but alas it did pity my heart to see in every place so many monuments where houses have been and now there is nothing but bare walls standing. Which I think is very dishonourous unto your highness and causes much inconvenience among your people. It causes men to lie by the highwayside there to rob and it also causes much murder.

Now if it please your grace to hear what is the cause of such decay and ruin within your Realm, it is this. In every place where your majesty has given estates and lordship to any gentleman, if a poor man comes unto one of them asking that he might have a tenement or farm to rent, the lord answers in this way: 'If you want this tenement from me, you must pay me so much money for a fine.' And he raiseth that fine to a great sum of money and the rest to be paid yearly beside. The poor man then seeing there is no remedy but either to have it or to be destitute of any habitation, sells all that he hath to pay the fine.

3 REGULATIONS MADE AT CHESTER, 1539

Because of the great number of idle persons and vagabonds who are strong enough to labour for their livings, and yet daily go on begging within the city, the genuinely poor people, having no other means to get their living except by the charitable alms of good Christian people, are deprived of the same, to the great displeasure of Almighty God and contrary to good conscience and the laws of our Sovereign Lord the King . . .

It is ordained and established that the number and names of all beggars shall be searched and written and divided into fifteen lists. Every list will be assigned to an area of the city, where they shall go and beg, and in no other place. Their names will be written in a bill set up in every man's house within each area for knowledge to whom they shall give their alms and to no other. And if any other persons come to any man or woman's door to beg, not having his name on the bill, then the same man or woman is to give unto the beggar no alms but rather to bring him to the stocks in the same area.

4 'A SUPPLICATION OF THE POORE COMMONS', 1546

Supplications of the poor commons conventionally criticised society and clergy. This one, in addition, shows a hint of disillusionment with the social changes following the dissolution.

For, although the sturdy beggers (the monks) gat all the deuotion of the good charitable people from them, yet had the pore impotent creatures some relefe of theyr scrappes, where nowe they haue nothyng. Then had they hospitals, and alms houses to be lodged in, but nowe they lye and starue in the stretes. Then was ther number great, but nowe much greater.

5 NORWICH CORPORATION COURT BOOKS, 12 SEPTEMBER 1562

How well-off do you think the beggar was? About £44.18 was taken from Mother Arden!

This day was brought into the Courte certeyne money of one Mother Arden who used daly to go a beggyng the strettes, viz., in olde grotes xxix li xiii s iiiid; too olde angelles; in slypper vi li xiiis vid; more in slypper lxliiis; and in new mony lxxiiis viid. And there was taken owte and delyvered to Mother Arden visviiid of the foresayde sume.

6 NORWICH CENSUS, 1570

Robert Rowe of the age of 46 yeres, glasier, in no work, and Elizabeth his wyfe that spinne white warpe and have five children, two sonnes, the eldist of the age of 16 yeres that kepe children, and the other, daughters that spinne, and have dwelt here ever in Thomas Masons house – no alums, indifferent.

John Hubburd, of the age of 38 yeres, butcher, that occupie slaughterie, and Margarit his wyfe of the age of 30 yeres that sell souce, and two young children, and have dwelt here ever – no alums, veri pore.

An Buckle of the age of 46 yeres, wydowe, souster and teaceth children and hath two children, the one of the age of 9 yeres and the other of 5 yeres that worke lace, and have dwelt here ever – no allums but verie poore.

7 INSCRIPTION ON GELL'S BEDEHOUSES, WIRKWORTH, DERBYSHIRE, 1584

Yf thou wilt Our Lord please
Help the pore in ther disease.

8 'DISCOURSE OF THE COMONWEALTH'

The 'Discourse of the Commonwealth' was probably written in 1549. The manuscript was copied by Lambarde in 1565. It was first published in 1581, possibly after revisions. It was by either William Harrison (8B12) or Sir Thomas Smith (6B2); some would consider John Hales to be a possible author. The following extract shows a discourse between a Knight and a Doctor. 'Dearth' is here used to mean high prices.

'I mervayll much, Maister Doctor, what should be the cause of this dearth; seinge all thinges are (thanckes be to Gode) so plentifull. There was never more plentie of cattle then there is nowe, and yet it is scarcitie of things which commonly maketh dearth. This is a mervelous dearthe, that in such plentie cometh, contrary to his kynd . . . how commeth it to passe . . . that the pryces of all things fall not backe to theyr olde rate, whereas now (1570s) long sithence our English coyne (to the great honour of our noble Princesse which now raighneth) hath bene again thoroughly restored to his former purity and perfection?'

Doctor: 'rackynge and hoyssing up of rentes . . . the great store and plenty of treasure, which is walking in these partes of the world, far more in these our dayes, then ever our forefathers have sene in times past. . . . infinite sums of gold and silver, whych are gathered from the Indies and other countries, and so yearely transported unto these costes.'

9 SIR THOMAS GRESHAM TO ELIZABETH I, 1558

Sir Thomas Gresham (1519?–1579), founder of the royal Exchange, dealt with the royal debts from 1540s. He was a friend of William Cecil and, for a time, was the custodian of Lady Mary Grey after her unacceptable marriage to the serjeant-porter in 1565 (see 2B12 and 13).

It may please your majesty to understand that the first occasion of the fall of the exchange did grow by the king's majesty, your late father, in abasing his coin from six ounces fine to three ounces fine. Whereupon the exchange fell from 25.s.8.d. to 13.s.4.d. which was the occasion that all your fine gold was conveyed out of this your realm.

Secondly, by reason of his wars, the king's majesty fell into great debt in Flanders. And for the payment thereof they had no other device but to pay it by exchange, and to carry over his fine gold for the payment of the same.

Thirdly, the great freedom of the Steelyard and granting of licence for the carrying of your wool and other commodities out of your realm . . .

Now, for the redress of these things, in anno 1551 the king's majesty, your late brother, called me to be his agent, and reposed a more trust in me, as well for the payment of his debts beyond the seas, as for the raising of the exchange ... First I practised with the king and my lord of Northumberland to overthrow the Steelyard, or else it could not be brought to pass, for they would keep down the exchange ...

Secondly, I practised with the king's majesty, your brother, to come in credit with his own mere merchants ... I did not only bring the king's majesty ... out of debt.

... it may plainly appear to your highness as the exchange is the thing that eats out all princes, to the whole destruction of their common weal, if it be not substantially looked unto; so likewise the exchange is the chiefest and richest thing only above all other to restore your majesty and your realm to fine gold and silver, and is the means that makes all foreign commodities and your own commodities with all kinds of victuals good cheap, and likewise keeps your fine gold and silver within your realm ...

Finally, and it please your majesty to restore this your realm into such estate as heretofore it hath been; first your highness hath none other ways, but when time and opportunity serveth, to bring your base money into fine of eleven ounces fine, and so gold after the rate.

Secondly, not to restore the Steelyard to their usurped privileges.

Thirdly, to grant as few licences as you can.

Fourthly, to come in as small debt as you can beyond seas.

Fifthly, to keep up your credit, and specially with your own merchants, for it is they must stand by you at all events in your necessity. And thus I shall most humbly beg your majesty to accept this my poor writing in good part; wherein I shall from time to time, as opportunity doth serve, put your highness in remembrance, according to the trust your majesty hath reposed in me; beseeching the Lord to give me the grace and fortune that my service may always be acceptable to your highness; as knoweth our Lord, whom preserve your noble majesty in health, and long to reign over us with increase of honour.

By your majesty's most humble and faithful obedient subject,

Thomas Gresham, Mercer.

Questions

1 What does the Duke of Norfolk allege to be the cause of the number of beggars in the north (8D1)?

2 a What does John Baker believe has caused the increase in the numbers of beggars (8D2)?

  b What does the 'supplication' state to be the cause (8D4)?

  c What was being done about it in 8D3? How does this compare with government action? (See 6C5 and 6.)

3 How are high prices accounted for in 8D8 and 9?

9 Learning and the Arts

The break with Rome cut England off from the European Renaissance. Religious changes caused great losses in the arts, consider the destruction of architecture, stained glass, church ornaments and monastic libraries. But this was also the period of printing and propaganda, of house building, castle building, and of the triumph of English.

9A Education

By the end of the sixteenth century standards of education, at least among the gentry and their superiors, were much improved. An increasing proportion of MPs had spent time at the universities and/or the Inns of Court. One subject for historical debate has been the question of how much damage was done to education by the dissolution of monasteries and chantries. Another question is whether the provision of new schools can be seen as a sign of puritan concern for better education and the diversion of charity from the church to secular institutions of learning.

1 ON STUDYING LAW

Sir John Fortescue (1394?–1476?), chief justice of the King's bench and legal writer, was unpopular with Cade's followers. He was a Lancastrian until 1471. His 'De Laudibus Legum Angliae' (written in about 1468), was first printed in 1537.

... ther is in these greater Innes, yea and in the lesser to, beside the study of the laws as it were in a university or schoole of all commendable qualities requisite for Noblemen. There they learn to sing and to exercise themselves in all kinds of harmony. There also they practise dauncing and other Noblemen's pastimes as they use to doe which are brought up in the king's house. On the working daies most of them apply themselves to the studie of Holy Scripture; and out of the time of Divine Service to the reading of Chronicles. For there indeed are vertues studied and vices exiled.

2 FEES AT IPSWICH GRAMMAR SCHOOL, 1482

And that every burgess, being in the town of Ipswich, shall pay to the grammar school master for his son 8d a quarter and not more; and that the grammar school master shall celebrate for the guild of Corpus Christi for the whole term of his life.

3 LETTERS FROM ERASMUS

Queens' College, Aug 25 1511.
The beer in this place doesn't suit me at all and the wines aren't quite satisfactory either. If you are in a position to arrange for a cask of Greek wine, the best obtainable, to be shipped to me here, you will have done what will make your friend perfectly happy. (But I'd like it to be quite *dry* wine.)

Cambridge, 1514.
In this place are colleges in which there's so much religion and so marked a sobriety in living that you'd despise every form of religious regime in comparison, if you saw it.

4 DEAN COLET'S STATUTES FOR ST. PAUL'S SCHOOL, 1518

Dean Colet (1467?–1519) survived three attacks of 'the sweat'. After studying in Italy he lectured at Oxford on St. Paul. He was a friend of Erasmus and More.

John Colet . . . Dean of Paul's, desiring nothing more than education and bringing up children in good manners and literature in the year of Our Lord one thousand five hundred and twelve built a school in the east end of Paul's Church for 153 to be taught free in the same, and ordained there a Master and a Surmaster and a chaplain with sufficient and perpetual stipends ever to endure, And set patrons and defenders governors and rulers of that same School the most honest and faithful fellowship of the Mercers of London . . .

In the Grammar School founded in the churchyard of Paul's . . . shall be first an high master. This high master in doctrine, learning, and teaching shall direct all the school . . . A man whole in body, honest and virtuous, and learned in the good and clean Latin literature and also in Greek, if such a man may be gotten, a wedded man, a single man, or a priest that hath no benefice with cure nor service that may let his due business in the school . . .

There shall also be a Sur-master, some man virtuous in living and well-lettered, that shall teach under the Master . . .

There shall be also in the school a priest that daily, as he can be disposed, shall sing mass in the chapel of the school, and pray for the children to prosper in good life and in good literature to the honour of God and our lord Christ Jesu. At his mass when the bell in the school shall knell to sacring, then all the children in the school, kneeling in their seats, shall with uplifted hands pray in the time of sacring. After the sacring when the bell knelleth again, they shall sit down again to their learning.

This priest, some honest and virtuous man . . . shall also learn or, if he be learned, help to teach in the school if it shall seem convenient to the high master, or else not.

He shall have no benefice with cure nor service nor no other office nor occupation, but shall attend only upon the school; he shall teach the children the catechism and instruction of the articles of the faith and the ten commandments in English . . .

There shall be taught in the school children of all nations . . . indifferently to the number of 153, according to the number of seats in the school.

The master shall admit these children as they be offered from time to time, but first see that they can the catechism, and also that he can read and write competently, else let him not be admitted in no wise.

A child at the first admission once for ever shall pay 4d for writing of his name. This money of the admissions shall the poor scholar have that sweepeth the school, and keepeth the school clean . . .

The children shall come unto school at seven of the clock, both winter and summer, and tarry there until 11, and return again at one of the clock, and depart at five, and thrice in the day prostrate they shall say the prayers . . .

Also, I will they bring no meat nor drink, nor bottles, nor use in school no breakfasts nor drinkings in the time of learning in no wise; if they need drink let them be provided in some other place.

I will they use no cockfighting, nor riding about of victory, nor disputing at St. Bartholemew's, which is but foolish babbling and loss of time . . .

In general processions . . . they shall go twain and twain together soberly . . .

To their urine they shall go thereby to a place appointed, and a poor child of the school shall see it conveyed away from time to time . . .

I would they were taught always in good literature, both Latin and Greek, and good authors such as have the very Roman eloquence joined with wisdom, especially Christian authors . . . that wrote . . . clean and chaste Latin . . . I will the children learn first the catechism in English . . .

5 A HISTORY OF GREATER BRITAIN AS WELL ENGLAND AS SCOTLAND, 1521

John Major (1470–1550), author of the following extract, was a professor at Glasgow who taught Knox and Buchanan.

There are . . . in England two illustrious universities: of which one – I mean Oxford – is famous even among foreigners . . . Some colleges are of a reputation beyond the others, the new college of the blessed Magdalene, and a college founded by a bishop of Winchester (who was once a fellow of New College) . . .

There is yet another university, that of Cambridge, somewhat inferior to Oxford, both in the number of its scholars and in reputation for letters. It too possesses very fair foundations of kings and queens. One of these, and indeed the chief, is King's college, worthy to be placed along with the New college in Oxford. There to is the Queen's college (that is, founded by a queen), a very fair building, and the King's hall, in revenues and in bursars not inferior to Queen's college. Another college is Christ's . . . A certain convent for women was changed into Jesus college, by the counsel of a most learned and worthy man, Stubbs, a doctor in theology. These women refused to keep their enclosure, and added to their own a society of students of the other sex; and this was a scandal to men of serious mind . . . There are besides many other colleges in which lectures are given daily. The course of study in the arts is in these universities of seven or eight years before the taking of the Master's degree. A Chancellor . . . – a man always of grave repute – is every year elected . . . Two proctors are chosen yearly; in their hands are all the functions of justice – for their authority extends over every layman in the city. And though in number the laymen be equal to or more than the scholars, as a matter of fact they dare not rise against them; for they would be crushed forthwith by the scholars; they are all of them no longer boys; they carry swords and bows, and in large part are of gentle birth.

6 CHRISTOPHER HALES TO HENRY BULLINGER, 10 DECEMBER 1550

Christopher Hales (d. 1541) was an MP, solicitor general and master of the rolls in London.

. . . I have delayed to write to you respecting the study of medicine at Oxford, and the expenses there, until I could give you a correct statement. I have however learned from a friend, who is resident there, that the university of Oxford is not to be compared with that of Paris or the schools of Italy; but still it is one in which a studious youth may be occupied with great advantage. The same is to be said of Cambridge, but I rather recommend Oxford on account of the greater salubrity of the air. Cambridge, by reason of the neighbouring fen, is much exposed to fever, as I have experienced more frequently than I could wish. With respect to expense, my friend informed me, that thirty French crowns would suffice tolerably well for a year; to which if other ten be added, a man might expect to live very comfortably. In my time, ten years ago, twenty crowns were a sufficient allowance; but in these latter days . . . everything has become almost twice as dear as it was.

7 PATENT ROLL, 2 MAY 1554

A patent roll was a roll of parchment containing the letters patent issued in a year. A patent conferred privileges, rights, offices, pieces of land.

As the queen has heard that the academy situated at Oxford, which was once one of the two most celebrated storehouses of learning of her whole realm, is so afflicted by the wrongs of the times that it lies almost uncultivated and in want of the means to sustain its dignity, its public schools, in which on fixed and solemn days there was wont to be crowded concourse of learners, are laid waste and converted into private gardens, its public treasury plundered, its ornaments carried off and its revenues reduced almost to nothing:

And as the queen holds that it pertains to her royal office to raise up the academy, in which the orthodox faith overthrown by heretics cannot enter and be defended, the truth in controversy extracted, nor justice administered, and to cast off its squalor and remove its want by her munificence, so that afterwards it may have the wherewithal to raise up its schools and defend its privileges;

Grant to the chancellor, masters and scholars of the said academy or university of the rectories and churches of Southpetherwyn, co. Cornwall, late belonging to the priory of St. Garmanus, Seyston, co. Leicester, late belonging to Olvescrofte priory, and Holme Coltrame with the chapel of Newton Arloche, co. Cumberland, late belonging to the monastery of Holme Coltram, with the advowsons of the vicarages of the said churches and all lands and privileges in Southpetherwyn, Trenaunte, Seyston, Holme, Coltrame, and Newton Arloche.

Yearlye value £131.19.s. To hold in fee in frankalmooign (1). Issues from Lady day last. Dispensation.

1 *Frankalmooign* tenure by divine service or performance of a religious duty.

8 REGISTER OF CHRIST'S COLLEGE, CAMBRIDGE, 1575

It is agreed betwixte the master and the fellowes that they shall every one of them have ij table napkins bought by the coledge of this condition that every fellowe at his departure shall deliver unto the master ij whole table napkins for the use of his successoure . . . Also it is agreed that if either fellowe or pensioner do wipe his hande or fingers of the table clothe he shall pay for every time 1d to the use of the commins.

9 WILLIAM HARRISON, 'DESCRIPTION OF ENGLAND', 1587

See 8B12.

In my time there are three noble universities in England, to wit, one at Oxford, the second at Cambridge and the third in London, of which the first two are the most famous, I mean Cambridge and Oxford, for that in them the use of tongues, philosophy and the liberal sciences, besides the profound studies of the civil law, physic and theology are daily taught and had: whereas in the latter the laws of the realm are only read and learned by such as give their minds unto the knowledge of the same. In the first also there are not only divers goodly houses builded four square for the most part of hard freestone or brick, with great number of lodgings and chambers in the same for students, after a sumptuous manner, through the exceeding liberality of kings, queens, bishops, noblemen, and ladies of the land; but also large livings and great revenues bestowed on them (the like whereof is not to be seen in any other region, as Peter Martyr did oft affirm) to the maintenance only of such convenient numbers of poor men's sons as the several stipends bestowed upon the said houses are able to support.

... in these our colleges we live in such exact order, and under so precise rules of government, as that the famous learned man Erasmus of Rotterdam, being here among us fifty years past, did not let to compare the trades in living of students in these two places even with the very rules and orders of the ancient monks, affirming moreover ... our orders ... far exceeded all the monastic institutions that ever were devised.

In most of our colleges there are also great numbers of students ... so that at this present ... there are about three thousand scholars nourished in them both ... They were erected by their founders at the first only for poor men's sons ... but now they have the least benefit of them, by reason the rich do so encroach upon them.

Questions

1 What does Colet think his school should teach (9A4)?
2 What precedent for Wolsey (5B) and Henry VIII (7B) is mentioned here in 9A5 in the section on Jesus College?
3 For what different reasons is Oxford preferred to Cambridge in 9A5 and 6?
4 What statement in the second letter of 9A3 is referred to in 9A9?

9B Buildings

With the return of Edward IV in 1471 the period of sterility in the arts was over. Yorkist King and nobility showed a taste for luxury that contrasted with Lancastrian austerity. Building fever began. Brick became a more commonly used material in the late fifteenth century, which simplified and cheapened large scale building. In the 1530s the former monasteries served as quarries for country houses, as well as for the defences of Calais. (See 5A.)

1 MEMORANDUM BY PROVOST WODELARKE ON BUILDING KING'S COLLEGE AFTER MAY 1455

When Henry the Sixth, founder of the college, was taken prisoner by the Earls of Salisbury and Warwick, they pledged their word to him, in order to gain his good-will, that they would hasten the completion of his church and royal building operations in Cambridge; and they ordered me to use all possible despatch in getting together, by the help of royal letters, as many stonemasons and other workmen as I could, with the view of carrying on his buildings at Cambridge, and especially his collegiate church ...

They engaged that one thousand pounds should be paid over to me in each year, without delay or hindrance; that provided the works went on, money should not fail; a compact to which the king very gladly assented. At first these honourable gentlemen fulfilled their promises with much friendship, and with a due regard to their honour and plighted word, aided therein by the receiver general of the Duchy of Lancaster, who had received the king's command to make payments out of the issues and revenues collected by him in virtue of his office, without deception or delay, setting aside all the other claims upon him, and to draw up agreements between himself and the master of the works, so as to carry them forward with the utmost expedition.

By this means money came in occasionally, but to no great amount. Before long, however, fresh disturbances broke out in the kingdom, to put down which ... royal letters were sent under the signet to all the receivers of the duchy, charging them most strictly, under pain of losing their places, to forward all the money they had collected to the king and his council at London. The receiver general was therefore unable to pay the sum stipulated for by his indenture. In consequence the charge for all payments for wages to stonemasons and other workmen, and even to every single carpenter, was thrown upon me, Robert Wodelarke. When it became evident I should be unable to satisfy their claims, I undertook to pay them out of my private means, and from other funds borrowed for the purpose. I succeeded in defraying a considerable portion of their claims out of my own funds, as my actions will shew when investigated one by one, respecting which I shall be ready at all times and on all occasions to answer any questions that may be put to me. When I found that I was never likely to obtain redress, I sent for Thomas Betts, who was auditor both of the college accounts and also of the building accounts, which had always been kept separate from the others; and when the items of expenses and receipts were cast up it was discovered – and so adjudicated by the auditor – that the payments exceeded the receipts by £328 10s. 4d.

2 TOMB OF ALICE, DUCHESS OF SUFFOLK, 1475

Alice, Duchess of Suffolk, was Chaucer's granddaughter and the wife of the Duke of Suffolk (who was murdered in 1450 – see 5C1). She died in 1475. Her son, the Second Duke, erected her tomb entirely of alabaster, at the church at Ewelme. She is shown wearing a ducal coronet and the habit of a vowess.

112 *Learning and the Arts*

3 BOSSES IN THE NAVE VAULT OF SHERBORNE ABBEY COMPLETED BETWEEN 1485 AND 1504

Nave bosses at Sherborne Abbey, Dorset. They include Tudor roses and the rebus of Abbot Peter Ramsam. Note the P (for Peter), the ram (within the loop) and, above, SAM. William Smyth, the architect of the nave vaults, died in about 1490.

4 THE GREAT VAULT OF KING'S COLLEGE, CAMBRIDGE

John Wastell was master mason of King's College Chapel, 1508–15. The stonecarver was Thomas Stockton.

114 *Learning and the Arts*

5 HENRY VII'S CHAPEL, WESTMINSTER

Robert Vertue (d. 1506) was the mason who started Henry VII's chapel at Westminster. His brother, William, continued the work.

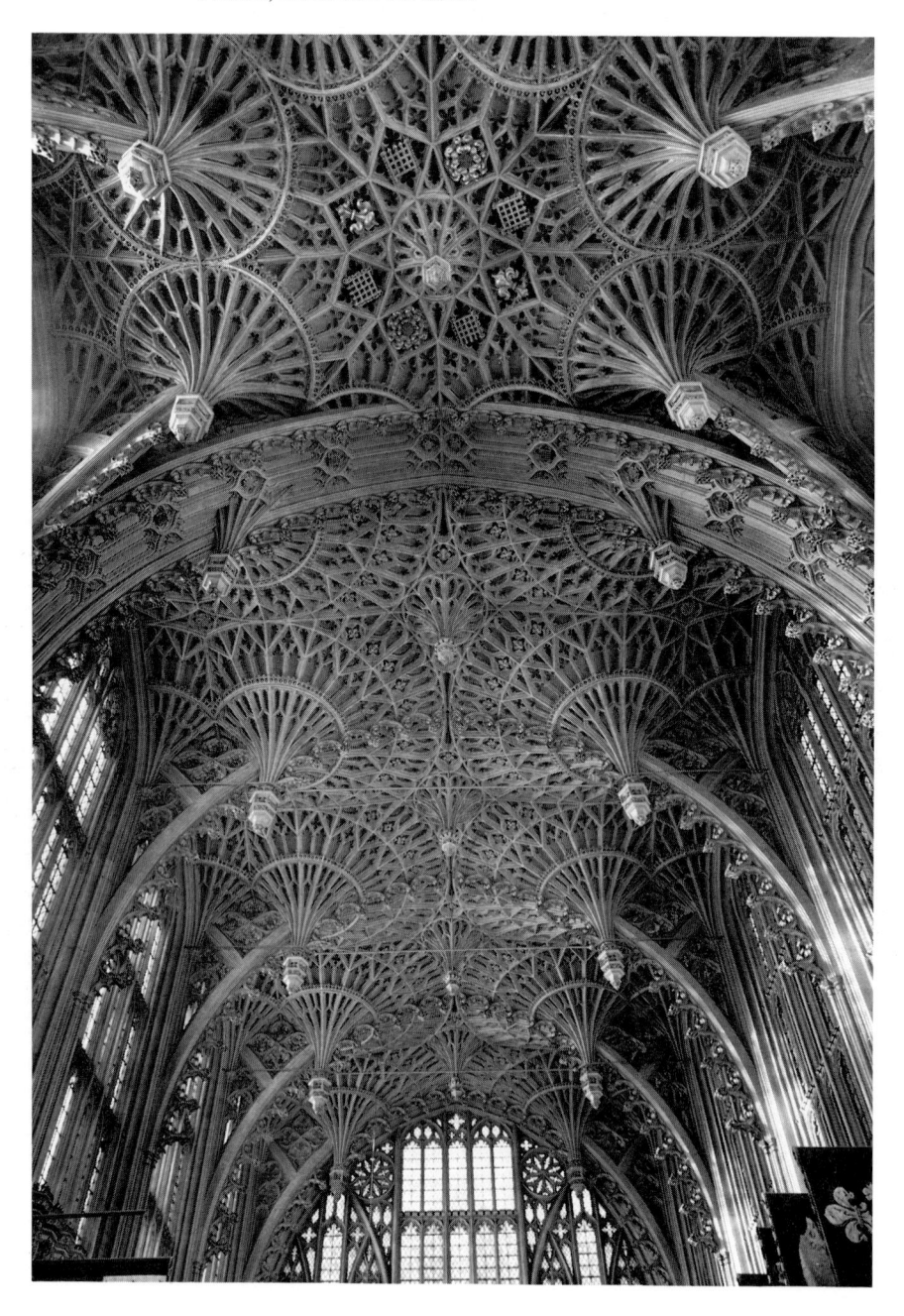

Learning and the Arts 115

6 FROM THE CHAMBER ACCOUNT-BOOKS

26 July 1517: to Walter Forster towards the repairing of the great chamber at Eltham and mending the conduit there and a new chimney in the privy kitchen £100

Feb 1518: to Walter Forster to repair the great chamber at Eltham and other repairs there £200

25 April 1518: to Walter Forster for the making newe of the King's great chamber at Eltham £100

21 April 1519: to Thomas Forster for divers repairs to be done at Eltham & the condute there £200

22 Jan 1520: to Walter Forster for provisions of stone timber lead and other stuff for Greenwich, Eltham and Richmond £300

7 WHITEHALL PALACE: THE 'HOLBEIN GATE'

This gate carried the northern Gallery of Whitehall Palace over the road. It is in the English Gothic tradition, but the busts emphasise the imperial theme that had started with Henry VII, and was to be more fully developed in the 1530s.

A Gate belonging to the Old palace of White Hall.

116 *Learning and the Arts*

8 JESUS COLLEGE, OXFORD

The name of Jesus College – built in the 1570s – was meant to reflect its non-Catholic origins.

9 THE SWAN PLAYHOUSE

De Witt was a Dutchman visiting in 1596. The Swan had been built about a year earlier at Bankside. The stage was a fixed construction. The tiring house, with windows (previously mistaken for supports), was below, surrounded by an alley.

10 CONTRACT FOR BUILDING THE FORTUNE THEATRE AT A COST OF £440, JANUARY 8 1600

... the frame of the said house to be set square and to contain four score foot of lawful assize every way square without, and fifty-five foot of like assize square every way within, with a good, sure and solid foundation of piles, brick, lime and sand both without and within to be wrought one foot of assize at the least above the ground. And the same frame to contain three storeys in height, the first or lower storey to contain twelve foot of lawful assize in height, the second storey eleven foot ... in height, and the third or upper storey to contain nine foot ... in height. All which storeys shall contain twelve foot and a half of lawful assize in breadth throughout, besides a jutty forwards in either of the said two upper storeys of ten inches of lawful assize, with four convenient divisions for gentlemen's rooms and other sufficient and convenient divisions for two-penny rooms, with necessary seats to be placed and set as well in those rooms as throughout all the rest of the galleries of the said house and with such-like stairs, conveyances and divisions without and within as are made and contrived in and to the late erected playhouse on the Bank ... called the Globe; with a stage and tiring-house to be made, erected and set up within the said frame with a ... cover on the said stage ...

And which stage shall contain in length forty and three foot of lawful assize and in breadth to extend to the middle of the yard of the said house. The same stage to be paled in below with good, strong and sufficient new oaken boards, and likewise the lower storey of the said frame withinside; and the same lower storey to be also laid over and fenced with strong iron pikes. And the said stage to be in all other proportions contrived and fashioned like unto the stage of the ... Globe, with convenient windows and lights glazed to the said tiring-house, and the said frame, stage and staircases to be covered with tile ...

Questions

What familiar emblems can you find in 9B3 and 5?

9C The Arts

Your attention is drawn to the examples of architecture, painting and literature elsewhere in the book.

1 ON PRINTING

Caxton (1422–91) was a mercer who, while in Bruges, came to serve Margaret Duchess of Burgundy, his 'redoubtid lady'. He became the first English printer.

... I have practysed and lerned at my grete charge and dispense to ordeyne this said book in prynte after the maner and forme as ye may here see. And it is not wreton with penne and ynke as other bokes ben, to thende that every man may have them attones, for all the bookes of this storye . . . thus emprynted as ye here see were begonne in oon day, and also fynyshid in oon day, whiche book I have presented to my sayd redoubtid lady . . . and she hath well acceptid hit, and largely rewarded me.

2 THE ANATOMIE OF ABUSES, 1583

Philip Stubbs, a puritan pamphleteer, is the author of 'Anatomie of Abuses'. It was so popular that there were four editions between 1583 and 1595.

Do they not maintain bawdry, insinuate foolery, and renew the remembrance of heathen idolatry? Do they not induce whoredom and uncleanliness? Nay, are they not rather plain devourers of maidenly virginity and chastity? For proof whereof but mark the flocking and running to Theaters . . . daily and hourly, night and day, time and tide, to see plays and interludes, where such wanton gestures, such bawdy speeches, such laughing and fleering, such kissing and bussing, such clipping and culling, such winking and glancing of wanton eyes, and the like is used as is wonderful to behold . . . And these be the fruits of plays and interludes, for the most part. And whereas, you say, there are good examples to be learnt in them: so truly there are; if you will learn falsehood; if you will learn cozenage; if you will learn to deceive; if you will learn to play the hypocrite, to cog, to lie and falsify; if you will learn to jest, laugh and fleer, to grin, to nod and mow; if you will learn to play the Vice, to swear, tear and blaspheme both heaven and earth; if you will learn to become a bawd, unclean, and to devirginate maids, to deflower honest wives; if you will learn to murder, flay, kill, pick, steal, rob and rove; if you will learn to rebel against princes, to commit treasons, to consume treasures, to practise idleness, to sing and talk of bawdy love and venery; if you will learn to deride, scoff, mock and flout, to flatter and smooth; if you will learn to play the whore-master, the glutton, drunkard, or incestuous person; if you will learn to become proud, haughty and arrogant; and finally if you will learn to contemn God and all his laws, to care neither for Heaven nor Hell, and to commit all kinds of sin and mischief, you need go to no other school, for all these good examples may you see painted before your eyes in interludes and plays.

3 A LETTER FROM THE LORD MAYOR AND ALDERMEN TO THE PRIVY COUNCIL, JULY 28, 1597

. . . We have signified to your Honours many times heretofore the great inconvenience which we find to grow by the common exercise of stage-plays . . . in respect of the duty which we bear towards her Highness for the good government of this her city, as for conscience sake, being persuaded . . . that neither in polity nor in religion are they to be suffered in a Christian commonwealth, specially being of that frame and matter as usually they are, containing nothing but profane fables, lascivious matters, cozening devices, and scurrilous behaviours, which are so set forth as that they move wholly to imitation and not to the avoiding of those faults and vices which they represent. Among other inconveniences it is not the least that they give opportunity to the refuse sort of evil-disposed and ungodly people that are within and about this city to assemble themselves and to make their matches for all their lewdly and ungodly practices; being as heretofore we have found by the examination of divers apprentices and other servants who have confessed unto us that the said stage-plays were the very places of their rendezvous, appointed by them to meet with such other as were to join with them in their designs and mutinous attempts, being also the ordinary places for masterless men to come together and to recreate themselves. For avoiding whereof we are now again your most humble and earnest suitors to your honours to direct your letter as well to ourselves as to the justices of peace of Surrey and Middlesex for the present stay and final suppressing of the said stage-plays, as well at the Theatre, Curtain and Bankside as in all other places in and about the city; whereby we doubt not but the opportunity and the very cause of many disorders being taken away, we shall be more able to keep the worse sort of such evil and disordered people in better order than heretofore we have been . . .

4 ON DR STILL

Sir John Harington (1561–1612), Elizabeth's godson, wrote the following account of Dr Still, tutor at Christ's College, then Master of St. John's and, finally, Master of Trinity, Cambridge.

His breeding was from his childhood in good literature, and partly in musique, which was counted in those days a preparation for divinitie, neither could any be admitted to 'primam tonsuram', except he could first ... reade well, to conster well, and to sing well; in which last he hath good judgement, and I have heard good music of voyses in his house.

5 EXTRACT FROM CORPUS CHRISTI STATUTES, 1580

All which said schollers shall and must at the time of their election be so entred into the skill of song as that they shall at the first sight solf and sing plainesong.

6 PLAINE AND EASIE INTRODUCTION TO PRACTICAL MUSICKE, 1597

Thomas Morley (1557–1604), author of the following extract, was a gentleman of the Chapel Royal and composer of madrigals.

Supper being ended, and the musicke bookes according to the custome being brought to the table, the mistresse of the house presented mee with a part, earnestly requesting mee to sing. But when, after manie excuses, I protested unfainedly that I could not, everie one began to wonder. Yea, some whispered to others, demanding how I was brought up.

7 ON SINGING

William Byrd (1540–1623) was organist of the chapel royal, a great composer of choral music, and a Catholic.

1 It is a knowledge easily taught and quickly learnt.
2 The exercise of singing is delightful to Nature and good to preserve the health of Man.
3 It doth strengthen all the parts of the chest and doth open the pipes.
4 It is a singular good remedy for stammering.
5 It is the best means to procure a perfect pronunciation.
6 It is the only way to find out where Nature hath bestowed a good voice.
7 There is no music of instruments whatsoever which is as good as that which is made by the voice of men.

8 The better the voice is, the better it is to honour and serve God therewith and the voice of Man is chiefly to be employed to that end ...
Since singing is so good a thing
I wish all men would learn to sing.

Questions

1 **a** How far are the authors of 9C2 and 3 in agreement?
   b What points do they both make to get the decision makers on their side?
2 In what way do 9C4, 5 and 6 echo 9A1?

9D History

As you will see from the materials in this section, there was a great enthusiasm for the study of history in this period. However, in the reign of Elizabeth I Sir Philip Sidney noted: 'The historian ... loaden with old mouse-eaten records, authorising himself ... upon other histories, whose greatest authorities are built upon the notable foundation heresay, having much ado to accord differing writers, and to prick truth out of partiality: better acquaintance with 1,000 years ago than with the present age, and yet better knowing how this world goeth, than how his owne wit runneth; curious for antiquities, ... and a tyrant in table talk.' Perhaps you sympathise more with Sir Philip (named after his god-father, Philip of Spain), than with the following enthusiasts for our subject.

1 CAXTON'S PREFACE TO HIGDEN'S 'POLYCHRONICON', 1482

'Polychronicon' was a universal history written by Ranulf Higden, a monk chronicler who died in 1364; it remained popular for the next two centuries.

Grete thankynges, lawde and honoure we merytoryously ben bounde to yelde and offre unto wryters of hystoryes which gretely have prouffyted our mortal lyf, that shewe unto the reders and herers by the ensamples of thynges passyd what thynge is to be desyred, and what is to be eschewed ... Historyes ought not only to be juged moost proffytable to yonge men, whiche by the lecture, redyng and understandyng made them semblable and equale to men of greter age, and to old men to whome longe lyf hath mynystered experymentes of dyvers thynges, but also thystoryes able and make ryght private men digne and worthy to have the governaunce of Empyres, and noble Royammes, historyes moeve and withdrawe Emperours and Kynges fro vycious tyrannye, fro vecordyous sleuthe unto tryumphe and vyctorye in puyssaunt batayles ... Historye is a perpetual conservatryce of thoos thynges that have be doone before this presente tyme, and also a cotydyan wytnesse of bienfayttes, of malefaytes, grete Actes and trymphal vyctoryes of all maner peple. And also yf the terryble feyned Fables of Poetes have moche styred and moeved men to pyte, and conservynge of Justyce, how much more is to be supposed that Historye, assertryce of veryte, and as moder of alle philosophye, moevynge our maners to vertue, reformeth and reconcyleth ...

2 LORD BERNERS' PREFACE TO HIS TRANSLATION OF 'FROISSART'S CHRONICLE', 1523–5

John Bourchier was second Lord Berners 1467–1523 and Deputy of Calais from 1520. Henry VIII suggested he translate Froissart's 'Chronicle of the Hundred Years' War', and in 1523–5 he did so, dedicating it to Henry.

What ... thanks ought men to give to the writers of histories, who with their great labours have done so much profit to human life. They show, open, manifest and declare to the reader, by example of old antiquity, what we should enquire, desire and follow, and also what we should eschew, avoid, and utterly fly: for when we ... see behold, and read the ancient acts gests and deeds, how and with what labours, dangers and perils they were gested and done, they right greatly admonish, ensign and teach us how we may lead forth our lives ... And albeit that mortal folk are marvellously separated ... yet are they and their acts done peradventure by the space of a thousand year, compact together by the historiographier, as it were the deeds of one self city and in one man's life ... Is it not right noble a thing for us by the faults and errors of others to amend and erect our life into better? We should not seek and acquire that others did, but what thing was most best, laudable and worthily done, we should put before our eyes to follow ...

The most profitable thing in this world for the institution of the human life is history. One, the continual reading thereof maketh young men equal in prudence to old men ... it compelleth the emperors, high rulers and governors to do noble deeds to the end they may obtain immortal glory: it exciteth, moveth and stirreth the strong, hardy warriors for the great laud that they have after they be dead, promptly to go in hand with great and hard perils in defence of their country. And it prohibiteth reprovable persons to do mischievous deeds for fear of infamy and shame.

... only history, truly with words representing the acts, gests and deeds done ... moveth stirreth, and compelleth to honesty ... What knowledge should we have of ancient things past an history were not, which is the testimony thereof ... the president of remembrance and the messenger of antiquity?

3 JOHN BRENDE, 1553

Seeing histories be then so good and necessary, it were muche requisite for mens instruccion, that they were translated into suche tounges as most men myght understand them: and specially the histories of antiquitye, whyche both for the greatness of the actes done in those daies, and for the excellencie of the writers have much majestie and many ensamples of virtue. I therefore havyng always desired that we englishmen might be founde as forwarde in that behalfe as other nations, which have brought all worthie histories into their naturall language, did a fewe yeares paste attempte the translacion of Quintus Curtius, and lately upon an occasion performed and accomplished the same.

4 STOWE, 1580

See 4A4.

Amongst other Bookes which are in this our learned age published in great numbers, there are few eyther for the honestie of the matter, or commoditie which they bring to the common wealth, or for the pleasantnesse of the studie and reading, to be preferred before the Chronicles and Hystories. What examples of men deserving immortalitie, of exploites worthy of great renowne ... is not plentifully in them to be found.

Question

Comment on and summarise the arguments in favour of reading history given in 9D.

10 The Wider World

After 1453, and to an even greater extent after 1553, England's commitment to Europe was gradually reduced. Her rulers became less concerned with claiming lands in France. Her people became both more insular and more interested in the world beyond Europe.

10A France and Scotland: 'The Auld Alliance'

Kings of England claimed to be the true rulers of France. Henry VI was much blamed for the loss of French lands. Edward VI and Henry VII both felt they had to show an interest in fighting the traditional enemies. Henry VIII saw himself as a new Henry V, regaining England's French possessions lost by Henry VI's ineptitude. (It was also a good idea to get warlike nobles out of England, using their energies in France!) The 'auld alliance' of France and Scotland continued to trouble England in Henry VIII's reign, though by the time Elizabeth came to the throne attitudes were changing.

1 ON A MARRIAGE OF CONVENIENCE

The following letter was sent from Sforza de Bettini of Florence, Milanese ambassador in France, to Galeazo Maria Sforza, Duke of Milan, Amboise, June 2nd 1470.

(Louis) is to meet the Earl of Warwick . . . they will arrange a marriage between a daughter of the Earl and the prince of Wales, King Henry's son, and by thus raising up once more the party of the king and earl will return forthwith to England . . . His majesty assists him with money and men.
   The Duke of Burgundy . . . is making preparation of ships and men to go to the assistance of king Edward.

2 SFORZA DE BETTINI TO THE DUKE OF MILAN, JULY 1471

His Majesty approves of your suggestion as to its being desirable to encourage disturbances in England, there yet remaining to him over there the Earl of Pembroke, brother to the late King Henry by the mother's side, who has a good number of towns in Wales; a strong country, with the help of the Scots it holds out constantly against King Edward. To this earl and to the Scots King Lewis has ordered pecuniary assistance, such as is in his power to be given, that they may maintain the war and disturbance, though on this His Majesty does not seem to place any great reliance.

3 EDWARD IV INVADES FRANCE, JULY 1475

This extract is taken from the Mémoires of Comines. (See 2A4.)

We must now speak of the King of England, who was leading his army to Dover to cross to Calais; and this army was the largest that a king of England had ever brought over, and all the men were mounted and were better armed than any that had ever come to France, and nearly all the lords of England were there . . .
   . . . Charles the Bold, Duke of Burgundy, met Edward at Calais, and accompanied him in his advance to Veronne, and then to St. Quentin. There, contrary to his assurances, the Constable of St. Pol. refused to open the gates of the town to the English, and allowed the citizens to fire on them. The Duke of Burgundy on the following day departed from the English army. Louis then made advances to Edward.

4 LETTER TO HENRY VIII, MAY 18 1544

Please it Your Highness to understand that like as we wrote in our last letters to Your Majesty our determination to depart from Leith homewards by land with your army upon Thursday last, and so to devastate the country by the way in our return as we might conveniently, so have we now accomplished the same. And first before our departure from Leith having brent Edinburgh and sundry other towns and villages in those parties as we wrote in our last said letters, we did likewise burn the town of Leith, the same morning that we departed thence, and such ships and boats as we found in the haven, meet to be brought away, we have conveyed thence by sea, and the rest are brent; and have also destroyed and brent the pier and haven. Which damages we think they shall not be able to recover in our time. And in our way homewards we have brent the town of Musselborough, Preston, Seton, with Lord Seton's principal house ... he will see his own house and his own town on fire, also we have brent the touns of Haddington and Dunbar, which we dare assure Your Majesty be well burnt, with as many other piles, gentlemen's and others houses and villages as we might conveniently reach, within the limits or compass of our way homewards. And always had such respect towards the keeping of good order and array in our marching, as notwithstanding the Scots would daily prick about us, and make as many proud shows and braggs, they could not take us at none advantage ...

Finally, we have received letters since our arrival here from the lords of your majesty's council, by which it appeareth that Your Highness' pleasure to have 3,900 soldiers chosen out of this army to be transported hence to Calais to serve Your Highness in France, whereupon I the said Earl have called sundry of the captains afore me, and appointed such as I thought most meet ...

Your Majesty's humble subjects and most bounden servants,
E Hertford, John Lisle, Rafe Sadleye.

5 HOLINSHED'S CHRONICLE, 1545

See 3B2.

... the eighteenth of July the admiral of France ... with his whole navy came forth into the seas, and arrived on the coast of Sussex before Bright Hamsteed (1), and set certain of his soldiers on land to burn and spoil the country: but the beacons were fired and the inhabitants thereabouts came down so thick that the Frenchmen were driven to fly with loss of divers of their numbers; so that they did little hurt there. Immediately thereupon they made to the point of the Isle of Wight, called St. Helen's point, and there in good order upon their arrival they cast anchors, and sent daily sixteen of their gallies to the veryhaven of Portsmouth. The English navy lying there in the same haven, made them ready, and set out toward the enemies, and still the one shot hotly at the other; but the wind was so calm, that the king's ships could bear no sail, which greatly grieved ... the Englishmen, and made the enemies ... bold to approach with their gallies, and to assail the ships with their shot even within the haven.

The twentieth of July, the whole navy of the Englishmen made out, and purposed to set on the Frenchmen, but in setting forward, through too much folly, one of the King's ships called the 'Marie Rose' was drowned in the midst of the haven, by reason that she was overladen with ordinance, and had the ports left open, which was very low, and the great artillerie unbreeched so that when the ship should turn, the water entered, and suddenly she sank. In her was Sir George Carew knight and four hundred soldiers under his guiding. There escaped not past forty persons of all the whole number. On the morrow after about two thousand of the Frenchmen landed at the Isle of Wight, where one of their chief captains ... was slain with many other, and the residue with loss and shame driven back again to their gallies.

The King perceiving the great Armada of the Frenchmen to approach, caused the beacons to be fired, and by letters sent into Hamptonshire, Summerset, Wiltshire, and into divers other countries adjoining, gave knowledge to such as were appointed to be ready for that purpose, to come with all speed to encounter the enemies. Whereupon they repaired to his presence in great numbers well furnished with armour, weapon, vittels, and all other things necessary, so that the Isle was garnished and all the frontiers along the coasts fortified with exceeding great multitudes of men. The French captains having knowledge by certain fishermen, whom they took, that the King was present, and so huge a power ready to resist them, they disanchored and drew along the coast of Sussex, and a small number of them landed again in Sussex, of whom few returned to their ships; for divers gentlemen of the country ... with such power as was raised, upon the sudden, took them up by the way and quickly distressed them.

When they had searched everywhere by the coast, and saw men still ready to receive them with battle, they turned stern, and so got them home again without any act achieved worthy to be mentioned. The number of the Frenchmen was great, so that divers of them that were taken prisoners in the Isle of Wight and in Sussex did report that they were three score thousand.

1 *Bright Hamsteed* Brighton.

6 THE FUGGER NEWSLETTERS, 1581–2

See 3D3.

Antwerp, March 4, 1581.
Letters from London of the twenty-fifth of last month state that the French embassy was very well received by this Queen. It is thought that it only came about the Duke of Alencon or perhaps to form an alliance against Spain.

London, April 29, 1581.
Some distinguished representatives of France, many nobles and some legal experts are here. What they are after is not yet clearly proven. The French give out that they are negotiating the marriage of the Queen with the Duke of Alencon. Others declare that they are here to effect a firm alliance between the French crown and the Low Countries to be under the direction of the Duke of Alencon. This would concern England too, as it could only be accomplished with the previous knowledge, good will and permission of the Queen. She has promised to lend the French £200,000 if they give her the town of Calais so that she may make use of it in the Low Countries War . . .

Antwerp, February 24, 1582.
With an imposing number of smart warships, three of the most distinguished Englishmen and many other persons of high birth the Duke of Alencon arrived here at nine o'clock on the morning of the 19th . . . the entire English Nation had come out to meet him there . . . No doubt France, England and the Low Countries have formed a powerful league, but the King of Spain will do his best too.

Questions

1 What light does 10A2 throw on Louis' motives for his behaviour in 10A1?
2 Who is the Earl of Pembroke in 10A2? (The date of the letter should give you a clue.)
3 What relation was the Duke of Burgundy to Edward (10A1)?
4 What reasons does Holinshed give for the sinking of the 'Mary Rose' (10A5)?

10B Ships and Seamen, Discovery and Exploration

The following material may help explain the changing attitude to Spain during Elizabeth's reign.

1 ON CABOT, 1497

This comes from a letter written by a Venetian merchant, Lorenzo Pascuaglis.

'the king has promised that in the spring he shall have 10 ships, armed according to his own fancy, and at his request he has conceded to him all the prisoners, except such as are confined for high treason, to man them with. Vast honour is paid him, and he dresses in silk. The English run after him like mad people, so that he can enlist as many of them as he pleases, and a number of our own rogues besides.'

2 VITELLIUS A, A LONDON CHRONICLE

'Vitellius A' is a chronicle of London to 1509. It is very like the great 'Chronicle of London'. Both may have been based on the same lost 'Main City Chronicle' that Fabyan used. (See 1C2.)

1498: This year the King at the busy request and supplication of a stranger Venician, which by a chart made himself expert in knowing of the world, caused the king to man a ship with victual and other necessaries for to seek an island, wherein the said stranger surmised to be great commodities; with which ship by the king's grace so rigged went three or four more out of Bristol, the said stranger being conductor of the said fleet, wherein divers merchants, as well of London as of Bristol, adventured goods and slight merchandises; which departed from the West Country in the beginning of summer, but to this present month came never knowledge of their exploit.

1502: This year three men were brought out of an island, found by merchants of Bristol, far beyond Ireland; the which were clothed in beasts' skins, and ate raw flesh, and (were as) rude in their demeanour as beasts.

124 *The Wider World*

3 THE LADIES OF THE QUEEN'S PRIVY CHAMBER TO HENRY VIII, 4 AUGUST 1529

Most gracious and benign sovereign Lord, please it your Highness to understand that we have seen and been in your new Greate Shippe and the rest of your ships at Portsmouth, which are things so goodly to behold that in our lives we have not seen (excepting your royal person and my lord the Prince your son) a more pleasant sight; for which ... we render and send unto the same our most humble and entire thanks, which we beseech your Majesty to accept in good part ...

From your Majesty's haven and town of Portsmouth, the III of August,

Your Highness most bounden and humble servants and bedewomen ...

4 SIR JOHN HAWKINS' VOYAGE TO THE WEST INDIES, 1562

Hakluyt (1551?–1616), author of the following document, was fascinated by geography and the history of discovery. Hawkins (1532–95), whose family already traded with West Africa, was anxious to develop the 'slave triangle'. He was naval commander and treasurer of the navy board. The Spanish behaviour at Vera Cruz (see 10B5) led to Drake's later piratical attacks upon them.

Master John Hawkins having made divers voyages to the isles of the Canaries, and there by his good and upright dealing being grown in love and favour with the people, informed himself amongst them, by diligent inquisition, of the state of the West India, whereof he had received some knowledge by the instructions of his father, but increased the same by the advertisements and reports of that people, and being amongst other particulars assured that Negros were very good merchandise in Hispaniola, and that store of Negros might easily be had upon the coast of Guinea, resolved with himself to make trial thereof, and communicated that device with his worshipful friends of London ... All which persons liked so well of his intention, that they became liberal contributors and adventurers in the action. For which purpose there were three good ships immediately provided ... in which small fleet Master Hawkins took with him not above 100 men, for fear of sickness and other inconveniences, whereunto men in long voyages are commonly subject.

With this company he put off and departed from the coast of England in the month of October, 1562, and in his course touched first at Teneriffe, where he received friendly entertainment. From thence he passed to Sierra Leona, upon the coast of Guinea ... where he stayed some good time, and got into his possession, partly by the sword and partly by other means, to the number of 330 Negros at the least, besides other merchandises which that country yieldeth. With this prey he sailed over the ocean sea unto the island of Hispaniola, and arrived at first at the port of Isabella: and there he had reasonable utterance of his English commodities, as also of some part of his Negros, trusting the Spaniards no further, than that by his own strength he was able still to master them. From the port of Isabella he went to Puerto de Plata, where he made like sales, standing always upon his guard: from thence also he sailed to Monte Christi, another port on the north side of Hispaniola, and the last place of his touching, where he had peaceable traffic, and made vent of the whole number of his Negros: for which he received in those three places by way of exchange, such a quantity of merchandise that he did not only lade his own three ships with hides, ginger, sugars, and some quantity of pearls, but he freighted also two other hulks with hides and other like commodities, which he sent into Spain. And thus, leaving the island, he returned and ... so with this prosperous success and much gain to himself and the aforesaid adventurers, he came home, and arrived in the month of September, 1563.

5 THE FUGGER NEWSLETTERS: SEVILLE, 21ST DAY OF JANUARY 1569

See 3D3.

There have arrived several English letters from Vigo in Galicia, wherein is written as follows: 'In the past year an Englishman with eight well-equipped ships has sailed from England to Guinea into the sea territory of the King of Portugal. After he had exchanged his wares for 1,500 negroes, he has made his way with them to New Spain. In order that he might do this without opposition and in a manner to suit himself, he has occupied a small island called San Juan de Lua near Vera Cruz, where the Spanish fleet was wont to load and unload and by which the Spanish ships must always pass. There he has blocked the water with ships and guns so that the Spanish fleet of 30 ships, which arrived there shortly after him, was unable to get into the harbour of Vera Cruz without his permission. The Spanish General had perforce to make a pact with the said Englishman, that he might sell his negroes freely and take away the money thus gained. A written contract was drawn up as to this, and they delivered unto each other 12 hostages. Several days after the Spanish General had come into the harbour of Vera Cruz, either because he held the contract unfair or out of anger at the overbearing demeanour of the Englishman, he broke the treaty, if not openly and by word of mouth, yet secretly by deed. At his instigation, seven old ships were stealthily set alight and driven from out of the harbour among the English ships. In this manner it was desired to burn all the English ships and that the captain thereof might perish. But when the Englishman espied this and realized the deceit practised upon him, he became wrathful and has, with this other ships, thus pressed the Spanish fleet that four of their ships were sent to the bottom.

But as his own vessels had suffered no little stress, he made his way homewards with the 12 Spanish hostages. But a bad storm scattered his fleet, and he alone reached Vigo with one vessel, badly buffeted and suffering for lack of food. He could not have remained three days longer on the water. There he made provision for all that was needful and set sail for England. It is not known where the other ships have remained or what has befallen them.

6 THE FAMOUS VOYAGE OF SIR FRANCIS DRAKE INTO THE SOUTH SEA, AND ABOUT THE WHOLE GLOBE OF THE EARTH, BEGUN IN THE YEAR OF OUR LORD, 1577

This extract is taken from a narrative by Francis Pretty, one of Drake's Gentlemen at Arms.

The 15 day of November, in the year of our Lord 1577, Master Francis Drake, with a fleet of five ships and barks, and to the number of 164 men, gentlemen and sailors, departed from Plymouth . . .

From the first day of our departure from the islands of Cape Verde, we sailed 54 days without sight of land. And the first land that we fell with was the coast of Brazil, which we saw the fifth of April . . .

. . . the 20 of June we harboured ourselves again in a very good harborough, called by Magellan, Port St. Julian, where we found a gibbet standing . . . which we supposed to be the place where Magellan did execution upon some of his disobedient and rebellious company . . .

In this port our General began to enquire very diligently of the actions of Master Thomas Doughty, and found them to be not such as he looked for, but tending rather of contention or mutiny . . . whereby, without redress, the success of the voyage might greatly have been hazarded. Whereupon the company was called together and made acquainted with the particulars of the cause, which were found, partly by Master Doughty's own confession, and partly by the evidence of the fact, to be true. Which when our General saw . . . the care he had of the state of the voyage, of the expectation of her Majesty, and of the honour of his country did more touch him . . . than the private respect of one man. So that the cause being thoroughly heard, and all things done in good order as near as might be to the course of our laws in England, it was concluded the Master Doughty should receive punishment according to the . . . offence. And he, seeing no remedy but patience for himself, desired before his death to receive the communion, which he did at the hands of Master Fletcher, our minister, and our General himself accompanied him in that holy action. Which being done, and the place of execution made ready, he having embraced our General, and taken his leave of all the company, with prayers for the Queen's Majesty and our realm, in quiet sort laid his head to the block, where he ended his life. This being done, our General made divers speeches to the whole company, persuading us to unity, obedience, love, and regard of our voyage; and for better confirmation thereof, willed every man the next Sunday following to prepare himself to receive the communion, as Christian brethren . . . ought to do . . .

The 17 day of August we departed the port of St. Julian, and the 20 day we fell with the Strait of Magellan, going into the South Sea; at the cape . . . whereof we found the body of a dead man, whose flesh was clean consumed. The 21. day we entered the Strait . . . This Strait is extreme cold, with frost and snow continually . . .

The 24 of August we arrived at an island in the Straits, where we found great store of fowl which could not fly, of the bigness of geese; whereof we killed in less than one day 3,000, and victualled ourselves thoroughly therewith

. . . To Lima we came the 13 of February; and being entered the haven, we found there about twelve sail of ships lying fast moored at an anchor . . . the masters and merchants were here most secure, having never been assaulted by enemies, and at this time feared the approach of none such as we were. Our General rifled these ships, and found in one of them a chest full of reals of plate, and good store of silks and linen cloth; and took the chest into his own ship, and good store of silks and linen. In which ship he had news of another ship called the Cacafuego, which was ... laden with treasure ... and with all speed we followed the Cacafuego ... towards Panama ... And about six of the clock we came to her and boarded her ... and being entered we found in her great riches, as jewels and precious stones, thirteen chests full of reals of plate, fourscore pound weight of gold, and six-and-twenty ton of silver. The place where we took this prize was called Cape de San Francisco, about 150 leagues from Panama ... we went on our course still towards the west; and not long after met with a ship laden with linen cloth and fine China dishes of white earth, and great store of China silks, of all which things we took ...

The fifth of June, being in 43 degrees towards the pole Arctic, we found the air so cold, that our men, being grievously pinched with the same, complained of the extremity thereof ... Whereupon we thought it best ... to seek the land, and did so, finding it not mountainous, but low plain land, till we came within 38 degrees towards the line. In which height it pleased God to send us into a fair and good bay, with a good wind to enter the same. In this bay we anchored; and the people of the country, having their houses close by the water's side, shewed themselves unto us, and sent a present to our General ... Our General called this country Nova Albion ... At our departure hence our General set up a monument of our being there, as also of her Majesty's right and title to the same; namely a plate, nailed upon a fair great post, whereupon was engraved her Majesty's name, the day and year of our arrival there, with the free giving up of province and people into her Majesty's hands, together with her Highness' picture and arms, in a piece of six pence of current English money, under the plate, whereunder was also written the name of our General ...

The 14 of November we fell in with the islands of Maluco.

The 8 of February following, we fell with the fruitful island of Barateve ... At our departure from Barateve, we set our course for Java Major ... From Java Major we sailed for the cape of Good Hope ... We arrived in England, the third of November, 1580, being the third year of our departure.

7 WILLIAM HARRISON, 'THE DESCRIPTION OF ENGLAND', 1587

See 8B12.

The navy of England may be divided into three sorts, of which the one serveth for the wars, the other for burden, and the third for fishermen which get their living by fishing on the sea. How many of the first order are maintained within the realm, it passeth my cunning to express ... Certes there is no prince in Europe that hath a more beautiful or gallant sort of ship than the Queen's majesty of England at this present, and those generally are of such exceeding force that two or three of them being well appointed and furnished as they ought, will not let to encounter with three or four of those of other countries, and either bouge them or put them to flight, if they may not bring them home. Neither are the moulds of any foreign barks so conveniently made, to brook well one sea as another, lying upon the shore of any part of the continent, as those of England. And therefore the common report that strangers make of our ships amongst themselves is daily confirmed to be true, which is that for strength, assurance, nimbleness, and swiftness of sailing, there are no vessels in the world to be compared with ours.

8 SIR WALTER RALEIGH, 'THE DISCOVERIE OF THE LARGE, RICH AND BEWTIFUL EMPIRE OF GUIANA', 1596

Notwithstanding the moistness of the aire in which they live, the hardness of their diet, and the great labours they suffer to hunt, fish and foule for a living, in all my life either in the Indies, or in Europe, did I never behold a more goodlie or better favoured people, or a more manlie ...

The common soldier shall here fight for gold, and pay himselfe in steede of pence, with plates of halfe a foote brode ... Those commanders and Chieftaines, that shoote at honour, and abundance, shal find there more rich and bewtiful cities, more temples adorned with golden Images, more sepulchers filled with treasure, then either Cortez found in Mexico or Pazzarro in Peru; and the shining glorie of this conquest will eclipse all those so farre extended beames of the Spanish nation.

Questions

1 What was the motive for Hawkins voyages described in 10B4 and 5?
2 What motives had Drake for his circumnavigation and his behaviour during its course?
3 What light is thrown on the revolution in foreign policy shown in 10A6 by the material in 10B, C and D?

10C Spain

Relations with Spain deteriorated during the second part of the sixteenth century. Neither Elizabeth nor Philip necessarily wanted war but some of their councillors did. Religious differences supplied one motive, but there were others...

1 TREATY BETWEEN ENGLAND AND SPAIN

Commission of Ferdinand and Isabella to Didacus de Guevara, Doctor de Puebla, and Sepulveda, dated Medina del Campo 26th of March 1489:
Commission of Henry VII to Richard Nanfan and Thomas Salvage, dated Westminster, 11th of December, 4th year of his reign:
1 A true friendship and alliance shall be observed henceforth between Ferdinand and Isabella, their heirs and subjects, on the one part, and Henry, his heirs and subjects, on the other part. They promise to assist one another in defending their present and future dominions against any enemy whatsoever.

The subjects of one of the contracting parties are allowed to travel, stay and carry on commerce in the dominions of the other contracting party, without general or special passport, and will be treated on the same footing as citizens of the country in which they temporarily reside.

The customs are to be reduced to what they were in time of peace thirty years ago.
2 Neither party shall in any way favour the rebels of the other party, nor permit them to be favoured or stay in his dominions.
3 Mutual assistance to be given against all aggressors within three months after the assistance has been requested. The assisted party to pay the expenses, which are fixed by four knights, two from each side.
4 Henry is not permitted to assist Charles, King of France, or any other prince at war with Spain. Ferdinand and Isabella promise the same to Henry.
5 Henry is not to conclude peace, alliance or treaties with France without the sanction of Ferdinand and Isabella, who, on their side, bind themselves to the same effect with respect to Henry.

2 WILLIAM CECIL TO SPANISH AMBASSADOR, 1581

'the pope had no right to partition the world and to give and take kingdoms to whomever he pleased.'

3 MEMOIRS OF SIR JAMES MELVILLE (1535–1617), FIRST PUBLISHED 1683

... there was a great bruit of the Spanish navy bound to land in England, Scotland or Ireland...

What was their intent and purpose was so secret, that the chieftains of the army knew no more, but as they should understand by the opening of their stamped instructions at every appointed landing-place. Many were of opinion, that they were first disappointed by the Duke of Parma Governor of Flanders, who had behaved himself in his charge so circumspectly, in his promises so truly, in enterprises so stoutly, that he won the hearts of the soldiers, and the favour of his enemies, so that he was suspected by the King of Spain to entertain designs of usurping the estate of Flanders: and therefore he was minded to remove him out of that great and rich government. He being hereupon discontent, as was alleged, neither furnished the said army victuals, nor assisted them with ships, nor would he suffer them to land in his bounds. At last they were so jealous of him, that they landed not, but were lying at anchor, where Sir Francis Drake by a strategem subtly devised, of a ship full of powder with a burning link, which kindled up the powder so soon as the English ship was driven by a direct vehement wind within the midst of the Spanish ships, burning thereby several the greatest of them, and causing the rest to cut the cables of their anchors for haste, to eschew the fury of the fire. And in the meantime God sent such a vehement storm of wind, that the whole navy was blown and broken upon divers coasts of our isles, and of Ireland; and their wreck was the greater, that they wanted their anchors.

4 LETTER FROM DRAKE TO WALSINGHAM, 31 JULY 1588

... We have the Armey of Spayne before us, and mynd with the Grace of God to wrestle a poull with them. There was never anything pleased me better than seeing the enemy flying with a Sotherly Wynd to the Northwards. God grant we have a good eye to the Duke of Parma, for with the Grace of God, if we live I doubt it not but ere long, so to handle the matter with the Duke of Sedonya, as he shall wish him at Sainte Marie Port among his orange trees.

God give us Grace to depend on him, so shall we not doubt victory, for our cause is good.

Humbly taking my leave this last July 1588,
    Your Honors faythfully to be commaunded ever,
        FR DRAKE

PS I crave pardon of your Honor for my haste, for that I had to watch this last nyght uppon the ennemy.

5 FROM THE DUKE OF MEDINA SIDONIA'S REPORT TO PHILIP II

At midnight two fires were perceived on the English fleet and these two gradually increased to eight. They were eight vessels with sails set, which were drifting with the current directly towards our flagship and the rest of the Armada, all of them burning with great fury. When the Duke saw them approaching, and that our men had not diverted them, he, fearing that they might contain fire machines or mines, ordered the flagship to let go the cables, the rest of the Armada receiving similar orders, with an intimation that when the fires had passed they were to return to the same positions again. The leading galleass (1) in trying to avoid a ship ran foul of the *San Juan de Sicilia*, and became so crippled that she was obliged to drift ashore. The current was so strong that although the flagship, and some of the vessels near her, came to anchor again and fired off a signal gun, the other ships of the Armada did not perceive it, and were carried by the current towards Dunkirk.

... Ammunition and the best of our vessels were lacking, and we could depend little upon the ships that remained, the Queen's fleet being so superior to ours in this sort of fighting in consequence of the strength of their artillery and the fast sailing of their ships.

1 *galleass* heavily built vessel, powered by sail and oars, used mainly in warfare.

6 PHILIP II TO HIS BISHOPS

In the storms through which the Armada sailed, it might have suffered a worse fate.

7 AN ALLEGORY OF THE DEFEAT OF THE SPANISH ARMADA AS ST GEORGE AND THE DRAGON

Robert Stephenson's allegorical painting, of about 1610, was for a village church. English troops rally under the flag of St. George. In the centre of the dragon's arc lie fireships. Spanish ships are wrecked top left and right, off Ireland and Scotland.

8 THE FUGGER NEWSLETTERS

This document is a translation of a petition addressed by the English ambassador to the Sultan, 8 November 1589. (See 3D3.)

Now from the councillors of Your Magnificence I received four years since a solemn oath that your Magnificence would begin a war with the King of Spain if my Mistress, who hitherto had lived in profound peace with the King of Spain, the chief of all idolaters, should chance to make war with him . . . And now she herself has withal dissolved the ancient alliance with Spain and commenced a most furious struggle by land and by sea, which during the space of three years she has waged with the greatest success. Although the Spaniard has demanded peace of my Mistress on divers untoward conditions, yet has she never granted it to him. I have . . . in my despatches always dissuaded her from peace and incessantly promised her that Your Magnificence, loyal to your early promises, was on the point of preparing a formidable fleet . . . I implore Your Magnificence . . . if you desire not to despatch all your terrible forces against that idolater, then at least to send forth 60 or 80 galleys in his undoing, and moreover into those neighbouring territories from which he has withdrawn all his forces to oppose my Mistress . . . But now it will be the heart's desire of the Spaniard utterly to destroy my Mistress, for she has refused him peace; and he can put complete trust in the help of the Pope, of all the other idolatrous Princes, and of the Emperor. Then he will turn his invincible forces to your overthrow and that of your realm . . . if your Magnificence in concert with my Mistress goes to war at sea wisely . . . then the proud Spaniard and the lying Pope will be cheated of their assured hope of victory and will suffer chastisement for their presumption. God will protect us alone and will punish these idolaters more severely by our means . . . all who live as heretics will return to our faith.

Questions

1 How far does Cecil's statement in 10C2 explain England's attempts to trade with and colonise the New World (10B4, 5, 6 and 8), naval rivalry with Spain (10C3 and 4), and even the troubles in Ireland (10D4–9)?
2 How far does 10C5 bear out 10B7?
3 a Is 10C6 a fair comment given the information in 10C3–5?
   b Which document in 10C reflects 'the ancient alliance' mentioned in 10C8?

10D Ireland: 'England's Broken Arm'

The Tudor drive for centralization and Anglicization spread to Ireland from the time of Thomas Cromwell. Instead of governing through local magnates he introduced direct rule from London. The 'Tudor revolution in government' was possibly even more evident in Ireland than in Wales or England. After Mary's policy of settling English colonists in Ireland, revolt there presented a greater threat to the Crown than rebellion in England. Was nationalism or religion the motive? Is Ireland to be seen as England's first colony? Is Irish policy an aspect of English foreign policy? Consider these questions while reading the documents in this chapter.

1 AN ACT OF THE IRISH PARLIAMENT, 1541

This is 'An Act that the King of England, his Heirs and Successors, be Kings of Ireland'.

'Forasmuch as . . . the Irish men and inhabitants within this Realm of Ireland have not been so obedient to the King's Highness and his most noble progenitors, and to their laws, as they of right and according to their allegiance and bounden duties ought to have been: wherefore at the humble pursuit, petition, and request of the lords spiritual and temporal, and other the King's loving, faithful, and obedient subjects of this his land of Ireland, and by their full assents, be it enacted, ordained and established by authority of this present Parliament, that the King's Highness, his heirs and successors, Kings of England, be always Kings of this land of Ireland . . . to have, hold, and enjoy the said style, title, majesty, and honours of King of Ireland . . . as united and knit to the imperial crown of the Realm of England.'

2 LETTER FROM SIR ANTHONY ST. LEGER, LORD DEPUTY TO HENRY VIII, 26 JUNE 1541

'. . . it was by me, your poor servant, proposed, that forasmuch as your Majesty had always been the only protector and defender, under God, of this realm, that it was most meet that your Majesty, and your heirs, should from thenceforth be named and called King of the same; and caused the Bill devised for the same to be read, and declared to them, in Irish, all the whole House most willingly and joyously consented and agreed to the same. And being three times read, and with one voice agreed, we sent the same to the Lower House, where, in like wise it passed, with no less joy and willing consent.'

3 LETTER FROM THE ANGLICAN BISHOP OF CORK AND ROSS TO LORD HUNSDON, 1596

Our state here is very dangerous ... Here are five justices of peace that sit on the bench every sessions, but they never took the Oath of Supremacy to Her Majesty, nor will ...

Hereby they are generally mightily drawn away from their loyalty to Her Majesty's godly laws now within these two years so far, that where I had a thousand or more in church at a sermon, I now have not five, and whereas I have seen 500 communicants or more, now are there not three ... I have caused churches to be re-edified, and provided books for every church through my diocese, as Bibles, New Testaments, Communion Books, both English and Latin ... but none will come to the church at all, not so much as the country churls; they follow their seducers the priests and their superiors.

4 HUGH O'NEILL REQUESTS HELP FROM KING PHILIP II OF SPAIN, 5 OCTOBER 1596

Hugh O'Neill of Tyrone spent part of his early life at Penshurst Place, Kent. It was there that he learnt modern ideas about warfare.

'The faith might be re-established in Ireland within one year, if the king of Spain would send only 3,000 soldiers. All the heretics would disappear, and no other sovereign would be recognised than the King Catholic. Both I and O'Donnell have besought him to succour the Church. Pray second our petition. If we obtain positive assurance of succour from the King, we will make no peace with the heretics.'

5 KING PHILIP OF SPAIN'S REPLY TO O'NEILL, 22 JUNE 1596

'I have been informed you are defending the Catholic cause against the English. That this is acceptable to God is proved by the signal victories which you have gained. I hope you will continue to prosper: and you need not doubt but I will render you any assistance you may require.'

6 SPANISH COUNCIL OF STATE TO PHILIP II

'Your Majesty would gain enormously in prestige by conquering a kingdom thus unexpectedly.

The bridle which the possession of Ireland by your Majesty would put upon England and the northern powers, would enable you to divert them from all other points of attack, and prevent them from molesting Spain, the Indies, etc. It would enable you to make good terms of peace and recover the Flemish fortresses held by the English for the rebels.

In the event of the Queen's death, your Majesty, as master of Ireland, would be in a greatly improved position to nominate a successor to the English crown.'

7 FROM THE COUNCIL OF IRELAND TO THE PRIVY COUNCIL IN LONDON, 1598

'We have daily advertisements of Tyrone's treacherous practices to extend his rebellion and treason into all parts of the Realm, having his ministers to pass to and fro through every province and other country of the Kingdom, labouring to seduce the people, by many colourable offers and pretences, to right them in their supposed Irish claims and titles to land and countries, long since lawfully evicted from them, and to introduce Papistry, which he beginneth now to make a more firm ground of his rebellion than he did before, insinuating that he is borne up and maintained therein by the Spanish King, by which course he hath wrought dangerous impressions in the hearts of the people ... yet we are of the opinion that it is not religion, nor old beggarly titles, that do carry him, but that it is the alteration of the government and state that he aimeth at, as by his letters, which we have formerly signified to your Lordships, he hath promised to the Spaniards, and is still countenanced and encouraged therein by them.'

8 MATTHEW DE OVIEDO, A SPANISH BISHOP, TO PHILIP OF SPAIN, APRIL 1600

'I came to Ireland by your Majesty's orders to obtain full information from the Catholics, and urge them to continued zeal in the service of the faith of your Majesty . . . I can assert that your Majesty has in this island the most brave and faithful vassals that any king can have, such, indeed, that if they were not already devoted to Spain, it would be necessary to obtain their adhesion . . .

As the oft-promised aid from Spain was hourly expected, when we arrived with empty hands, only again to repeat the old promises, they were overcome with sorrow and dismay, especially as they had news of the enemy in force both by land and sea. Although O'Neill and O'Donnell are full of courage, they cannot prevail over the other chiefs their followers, who fear the long delay in the arrival of succour, and suspect that they are being played with. We have done our best to stiffen them . . . assuring them of your Majesty's desire to help them . . . and promising them that succour shall be sent by your Majesty with all speed. This has tranquillised them somewhat, and they promise to wait five months, as they think they cannot in any case hold out longer than that without help . . . They have done great things this summer, and O'Neill has over-run all Munster and submitted it to your Majesty, whilst O'Donnell has subjected Connacht. That your Majesty may understand what you possess in these Catholics, I may say that O'Neill had almost prevailed upon the Earl of Essex to desert the Queen's cause and join that of your Majesty, and surrender all the Realm to you. O'Neill in the course of the negotiations promised him, Essex, on behalf of your Majesty, that you would show him signal favour, and as Essex was distrustful in consequence of certain injuries he had inflicted on Spain, O'Neill gave him his son as a hostage . . .'

9 FYNES MORYSON'S ITINERARY

Fynes Moryson (1566–1621) toured Europe (Germany, the Low Countries, Switzerland, Italy, Denmark, Poland, Austria) and the Mediterranean, 1591–5. In 1597 he went to Ireland where he was secretary to Lord Mountjoy until 1606. He then wrote a history of the lands he had visited; his 'Itinerary' was published in 1617.

During the . . . civill warre betweene Yorke and Lancaster . . . the English Irish . . . began to repair into England . . . And the meere Irish boldly rushed into the possessions . . . And from that time, under the governement of English Liefetenants and Deputies, seditions and murthers grew more frequent, the authority of the English Kings became lesse esteemed of the Irish . . .

After the appeasing of the said bloody warre I finde some 1000 men sent over by Henry the seventh to suppresse Perkin Warbeck, an English Rebell, and 500 men sent by Henry the eight to suppresse the Geraldines of English race, rebelling against him. Otherwise . . . no great or generall rebellion in Ireland . . . till the happy raigne of Queene Elizabeth. For in this onely age, Religion rather than Liberty first began to be made the cloake of ambition, and the Roman Locusts, to maintaine the Popes usurped power, breathed every where fire and sword, and not onely made strong combinations against those of the reformed religion in all Kingdomes, but were not ashamed to proclaime and promise Heaven for a reward, to such cut-throates as should lay violent hands on the sacred persons of such Princes, as opposed their tyranny. Amongst which, this famous Queene being of greatest power . . . they not only left nothing unattempted against her sacred person, and her Crowne of England, but wither encouraged by the blind zeale of the ignorant Irish to Popery, or animated by an old Prophesie: 'He that will England winne Must with Ireland first beginne,' did also raise two strong and dangerous rebellions in Ireland, the one of the Earle of Desmond, and the other of the Earle of Tyrone (not to speake of the troubles made by Shane Oneale . . .) Howbeit the wonted generall peace seemes to have continued till after the 19 yeere of the Queenes raigne, being 1577 . . .

The Spanish (forsooth) invincible Navy, sent to invade England, in the yeere 1588, being dispersed, and proving nothing lesse than invincible, many of them were wrecked on the Coasts of Ireland, whereof some were harboured by the Earle of Tyrone, with whom since he was thought to have plotted the following mischiefs . . .

1594 . . . the fier of this dangerous Rebellion is now kindled, by . . . the hatred of the conquered against the Conquerors, the difference of Religione, the love of the Irish to Spaine (whence some of them are descended) . . . Besides that, the Army . . . instead of hurting the enemy, oppressed the subject, thereby daily drivng many into Rebellion . . .

Tyrone hearing that . . . the old soldiers of Britany, were comming for Ireland, and that garrisons of English were to be planted . . . about this time of this yeere ending, or the first entrance of the yeere of 1595, he drew his forces together, and in open hostilitie, suddenly assaulted the Fort of Black-water . . .

The Lords . . . sent over Sir John Norreys . . . famous in the warres of the Low countries and France . . .

1598 . . . Ireland being in this turbulent state, many thought it could not bee restored but by the powerfull hand of Robert Earle of Essex, this noble Lord had from his youth put himselfe into military actions of greatest moment, so farre as the place he held in Court would permit, and had of late yeeres wonne much honour in some services by Sea and Land . . . and for his noble worth was generally loved, and followed by the Nobilitie and Gentrie. In which respects the Queene knew him fit for this service. He had long been a deare favourite to the Queene, but had of late lien so open to his enemies, as he had given them power to make his imbracing of military courses, and his popular estimation so much suspected of his Soveraigne, as his greatnesse was now judged to depend as much on her Majesties feare of him, as her love to him . . . his enemies gladly put foward his designe, that they might have him at more advantage by his absence from Court . . . the vulgar gave ominous acclamations to his enterprise . . .

The Earle of Essex had in special charge from the Queene, to bend all his forces against the chiefe Traitor Tyrone, (and the Ulster rebels his confederates) . . . 1599 . . . The five and twenty of June . . . the Lord Liefetenant wrote unto the Queene this Letter . . .

'. . . The people in generall have able bodies by nature, and have gotten by custome ready use of armes, and by their late successes boldnes to fight with your Majesties troopes . . . in their rebellion they have no other end, but to shake off the yoke of obedience to your Majesty, and to root out all remembrance of the English nation in this Kingdome . . . The Irish Nobility and Lords of countreys . . . are divided from us in religion, but have an especiall quarrell to the English governement, because it limitteth . . . them who ever have beene, and ever would be as absolute Tyrants, as any are under the Sunne. The Townes, being inhabited by men of the same religion and birth as the rest, are so carried away with the love of gaine, that for it, they will furnish the rebels with all things that may arme them, or inable them against the State, or against themselves . . . The expectation of all these Rebels is very present, and very confident, that Spaine will either so invade your Majesty, that you will have no leisure to prosecute them here, or so succour them, that they will get most of the Townes into their hands, ere your Majesty shall relieve and reinforce your Army . . .'

. . . Her majestie being highly offended, that so royall an Army, maintained with her excesive charge, had in six moneths effected nothing, and now gave no hope of any important service to be done against the rebels, wrote a sharpe letter to the Lord Lieutenant, and the Counsell of Ireland . . .

The Lord Lieutenant being nettled . . . with this letter, resolved to leave . . . and presently sayling into England, posted to the court, where altogether unlooked for, he arrived the eight and twentie of September, and presented himselfe on his knees to the Queene, early in the morning, being in her private chamber, who received him not with that chearefull countenance, which she was wont to shew him, but after a brief conference, commanded him to retire to his chamber, and there to stay, until hee knew her further pleasure; from whence his Lordships next remove, was to the Lord Keepers house, in state of a prisoner . . .

Now her Majestie . . . understanding that the rebels daily increased in number and courage, that the meere Irish aspired to liberty, and that the English Irish . . . were daunted by the ill success of the Queens affaires (whose great expences, and Royall Army they had seene vanish into smoke) and were besides exasperated . . . to be excluded themselves from Government . . . And having intelligence, that Tyrone . . . did every where bost himselfe as Champion of the Irish Libery and Romish Religion . . . and that he was growne confident to roote out the English Governement, as well by former successes, as by the succour of the King of Spaine, (who already had sent him some munition and a little mony, with bragging promises of greater supplies), and by the faire promises . . . sent from the Pope . . .

Her Majestie . . . having these advertisements . . . made choice of Charles Blount, Lord Mountjoy to be Deputy of Ireland . . .

1601 . . . his Lordship was by letters advertised, that a Frier in a Souldiers habit, was dispatched from Kinsale the foure and twenty of September . . . That he had Buls from the Pope, with large indulgences to those who should aid the Spaniards (sent by the Catholike King to give Irish liberty from English tyranny, and the exercise of the true olde Apostolike Roman Religion) and had authority to excommunicate those that should by letters, by plots, or in person jouyne with her majesty . . . That he gave out, the Spaniards at Kinsale were 1000, besides 2000 dispersed by tempest, which were landed at Baltimore, having treasure, munition, and victuals for two years . . .

The last of December Don Jean Generall of the Spaniards, offered a Parley . . .

His first conference . . . tended to this. That having found the Lord Deputy . . . though a sharpe and powerfull, yet an honourable enemy; and the Irish not onely weake and barbarous, but (as hee feared) perifidious friends, hee was so farre in his affection reconciled to the one, and distasted with the other, as he was thereby induced to make an overture of such a composition as might be safe and profitable for the state of England, with least prejudice to the Crown of Spaine, by delivering . . . the towne of Kinsale, with all the other places held by the Spaniards in Ireland, so they might depart upon honourable tearmes, fitting men of war not forced by necessity to receive conditions, but willingly induced for just respects to relinquish a people by whom their King and Master had ben notoriously abused, if not betrayed . . .

1603 . . . the Arch-Traitor Tyrone . . . humbly submitted himselfe to Queen Elizabeth, finding mercy at her royall feet, whom he hath proudly offended, and whose sole power (in despite of his domesticall and forraigne support), hath brought him on his knees . . . the victory was fully atchieved by the sole Sword of the English Nation and well affected English-Irish . . .

Questions

1 How far do 10D1–8 justify Fynes Moryson's statement that in Elizabeth's reign, 'Religion rather than Liberty first began to be made the cloake of ambition'?
2 How far is his explanation of the causes of trouble in 1594 (in the fourth paragraph of 10D9) warranted by the other evidence?
3 How accurate do you think is Essex's analysis of the situation in the paragraph beginning '. . . The people in generall . . .'?